DEDICATION

Dedicated to the New Organizational Superheroes

This book is dedicated to all those who are leading, sponsoring and contributing to super ambitious projects, programs and initiatives. Whether it is the launch of a new product or platform, an op-ex initiative, an organizational restructuring or a transformation initiative, you are the unsung heroes at the forefront of change. You are shaping your organizations, industries and even societies.

So, to those who make super projects happen, telling your story is our privilege.

APPRECIATION

A big thank you to all our peers who fueled and inspired our work. Obviously, we cannot name everybody, but here are just a few:

A.G. Lafley	Mark Johnson
Roger L. Martin	Josh Suskewicz
Antonio Nieto-Rodriguez	Patrick Lencioni
Brent Flyvbjerg	Patrick Viguerie
Chris Zook & James Allen	Peter Senge
Chris Ertel & Lisa K. Solomon	Phil Fernandez
Dan Gardner	Richard Rumelt
Don A. Moore	Rita Gunther McGrath
Donald Sull	Robert Kegan
Frank Cespedes	Lisa Laskow Lahey
Gary Hammel	Scott D. Anthony
Gary Klein	Scott Keller
Henry Mintzberg	Shane Parish
Jeroen De Flander	Colin Price
J.P. Kotter	Simon Sinek
Margaret Heffernan	Steve Woods
Margaret J. Wheatley	Alex Shootman

We are very proud of this 'Super Projects' research and have always sought to 'break new ground.' This, however, would not have been possible without the insight and inspiration gained from so many others.

SUPER PROJECTS

Making Extraordinary Things Happen

Ray Collis & John O'Gorman

© **Growth Pitstop, 2025**

Dublin – Oslo – London

www.super-projects.co

ISBN: 978-1-78119-673-1

Published by Oak Tree Press, Cork T12 XY2N

www.oaktreepress.com / www.SuccessStore.com

Cover design: Kieran O'Connor Design, Cork

corporate group

© EDI PRO JΣB ◆ © LBRP

CONTENTS

PREFACE

Is your organization ready to profit from accelerating change and uncertainty? **Will it be a winner or a loser** in the adoption of Ai, or in responding to increased competition, new regulations and geo-political uncertainty? The answer to these questions is at the center of this book. So much so, that we even considered putting this message on the front cover. The visual shows what it might have looked like.

For every trend – from Ai to Chinese competition – there will be winners as well as losers. This book is a **surprising insight to the reasons why**.

Spoiler alert: It is not just a matter of strategy or vision, as we were once led to believe. These, of course, are important, but they are not enough.

AI, COMPETITION, REGULATION. ETC.
WILL YOUR ORGANIZATION BE

Alternative Book Cover

A **WINNER** OR A **LOSER?**

RAY COLLIS & JOHN O GORMAN

'Your strategy won't save you!'
That is another title that we considered for this book about responding to accelerating change and uncertainty (shown overleaf). The subtext would have said: 'Well, at least not by itself!' It is an arresting title and an important warning.

For decades leaders have been warned about accelerating change and the risk of falling behind. The prescription has always

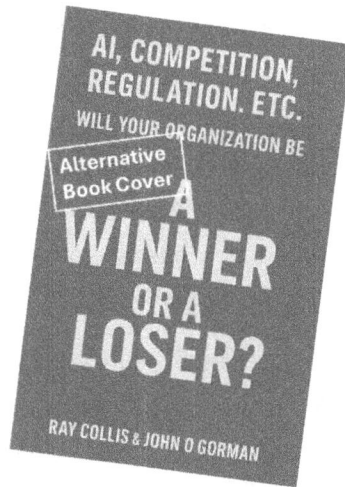

been more ambitious strategies for growth, efficiency and innovation. But meeting **change requires more than ambitious strategy**.

The reason 'your strategy won't save you' is that lots of organizations have ambitious strategies, inspirational missions and visions too. However, that these will be successfully brought to life is far from certain.

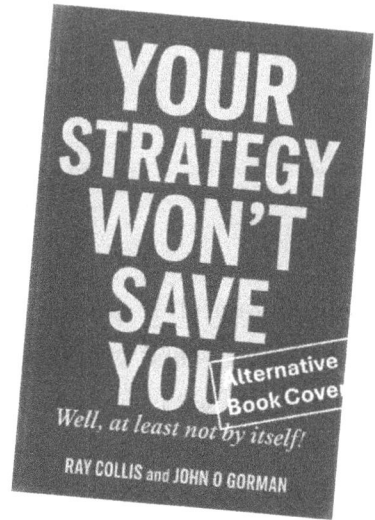

YOUR STRATEGY WON'T SAVE YOU

Alternative Book Cover

Well, at least not by itself!

RAY COLLIS and JOHN O GORMAN

Every ambitious strategy holds out so much promise. The promise of growth, innovation and transformation, as well as new products, technologies and markets. But, how much of that potential will be realized? In the case of most strategies, the answer is 'Not enough.' That is because the success rate of the big projects, change and transformation initiatives that must deliver on the strategy is not high enough.

In an increasingly complex and fast-changing world, the ultimate source of competitive advantage rests not just in the strategy, but in **the ability to bring it to life**. That is the ability to successfully deliver on the organization's biggest projects and initiatives – its Super Projects. That is how we arrived here – with a book of that name. It is perhaps a surprising choice for **a book on strategy, leadership and change**. It is also a courageous choice for the title – let's explain why.

Here is a quick recap: This is an extraordinary time to be in business – a time of accelerating change and uncertainty. How organizations respond is key. Yet there is growing fatigue and frustration around change and transformation. Thus, while the need for innovation has never been greater, **our organizations and societies have never been more 'down' on change and transformation**. Just listen to how people talk about big projects from digital transformation to organizational restructuring and the latest efficiency drive.

Read any of the analysts' reports and you will come away thinking that most change and transformation initiatives are doomed to fail. Let's not be fatalistic, however.

Our message is '**Don't Give Up on Change & Transformation**' – which coincidentally is another book title we considered.

Super Projects is a book for **CEOs, CFOs, COOs and others** to reignite their enthusiasm and passion regarding strategy, change and innovation. It is to help them to double down the level of confidence and ambition regarding their most ambitious strategies. Especially at a time of scarce resources, accelerating change and uncertainty. Paradoxically, that starts with changing how leaders talk about their big projects and initiatives.

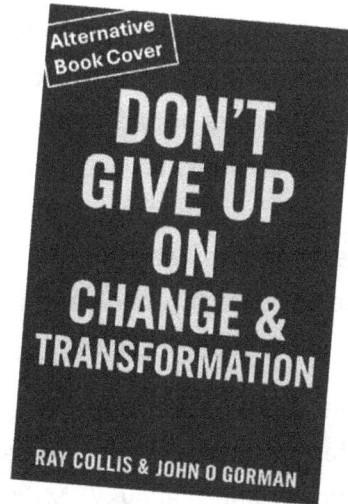

Alternative Book Cover

DON'T GIVE UP ON CHANGE & TRANSFORMATION

RAY COLLIS & JOHN O GORMAN

The concept of **strategic conversations** has become popular in recent years. It is a retake on the traditional notion of strategy being written by one or a few and then disseminated 'Moses-like' to the rest of the organization. The contemporary view is of strategy being dynamically co-created and adapted through a process of strategic conversations across the organization. The irony is what when we talk about big projects, change and transformation, the quality of the conversation no longer seems to matter. With this in mind, spot the odd word out in the table below.

Spot the odd word out:

Change	Transformation	Project
Restructure	Initiative	Execution
Strategy	Super	Program

Super Projects has a simple goal – **to put the 'super' back in conversations about strategy, change and transformation**. In so doing, we are not advocating denial or self-deception, but rather greater ownership and responsibility in respect of our biggest projects and initiatives. Hence, we ended up with the title on the cover of this book and the focus on Super Projects.

This book takes up where strategy geniuses like Porter, Rumelt and Lafley / Martin finish off. You could say that this is a book about execution, but we prefer to think about it as about **bringing ambitious strategies to life**. That is because, at a time of accelerating change and uncertainty, strategy and execution are not separate, but a dynamic and two-way loop. It is about how

organizations can go from '**good to great,**[1] by becoming super at big projects and transformation.

The goal is to re-ignite greater leadership **pride and excitement in the organization's biggest projects and initiatives**. As leaders, we can no longer accept that most big projects will be a source of failure and frustration, and that they are someone or something else's fault. Rather, the fate of our organization's big projects is in our hands. We own it!

Big projects and transformation initiatives are essential to progress, not just in our organizations, but industries and societies too. So, let's switch the narrative, celebrating all that is *super* about big projects and the heroes who are making them happen.

And, critically, given the times we live in, we have included a **bonus chapter** on tackling **Ai: The Ultimate Super Project**. Enjoy your reading!

INTRODUCTION
TO SUPER PROJECTS

INTRODUCTION

GETTING STARTED

SCENE SETTING

INTRODUCTION

The world is waiting for the next iPhone, Tesla or Ervebo (Ebola vaccine).[2] These could just be one super project away! Also, the success of your organization's ambitious strategy for growth, innovation or transformation lies no more than a super project (or two!) away.

Super projects are about **making extraordinary things happen**, at a time of extraordinary change and uncertainty. They are the catalysts for strategy, growth and innovation. As a leader, super projects are critical to your personal and professional success, as well as to that of your organization.

A SUPER QUESTION

How ambitious is your strategy? Is it a moonshot with big hairy audacious goals? Will it transform your organization, perhaps even its industry?

If the answer is yes, then another question immediately arises: What is it going to take to deliver on your ambitious strategy? Answering that question is the focus of our research and of this book.

What is it going to take to bring your ambitious strategy to life? Whether it is a strategy for digital transformation, or organizational restructuring or taking a new product to market, **what will be required to make it happen**?

You may be thinking it will take a long list of things, including talented people, organizational commitment, resources, and so on. Of course, these things are among the essential ingredients of success. But, how to bring it all together? What is the overall framework for making it happen?

Given the level of ambition, an ordinary or everyday project is unlikely to be enough. A piecemeal, *ad hoc* or lack-luster approach won't work either. It is going to take a massive, sustained and coordinated effort, together with careful planning and intelligent / adaptive execution.

In short, your ambitious strategy **will require a super project to make it happen**. But have you got one? Is yours a super project? Could, or should, it become one?

WHAT ARE 'SUPER PROJECTS'?

The aim of this research and this book is to put the 'super' back in big projects, ambitious strategies and transformation initiatives.

When people hear the words 'super project,' they typically think of super *big* projects. However, while most super projects are big projects, not all big projects are super projects. Five criteria are needed to qualify as a super project

'Super Projects' – 5 Criteria

STRATEGIC LEADERSHIP
S**U**CCESS
S**P**ANS ORGANIZATION
EXTRA-ORDINARY
T**R**ANSFORMS

Strategic Leadership

Super projects are the top-tier or first division of transformation initiatives, big projects and ambitious strategies. They exist in the realm of leadership and strategy, rather than in the domain of projects and project management.

Super projects are about **strategic leadership, change and innovation**. They deliver on the strategy; they bring the vision to life at a time of accelerating change and uncertainty. Super projects are the vehicle for change and innovation – they promise to shape the future. In short, every super CEO needs super projects; every super strategy needs them too.

> Blurring industry boundaries, increased regulation, changing customer needs and rapid shifts in technology: these are just some of the disruptive changes across many industries. For each of these challenges, there is a project, often a big project. Sometimes, even a super project!

Business Success

It is hard for any big project to be 'super' without being successful. However, the bar for success in respect of super projects is higher than delivering on time, to budget and to scope. While those are very important, they are not enough.

Ultimately, super project success is measured in terms of **business impact and organizational success**. The link to the success of the organization and its strategy is why CEOs, C-suite executives and board members care about super projects.

There is a simple equation behind any super project: **Business Success = Project Success**. In other words, there is a clear link between the success of the project and the success of the organization. Super projects must be among the top 3-5 priorities of a senior leader or leadership team.

The Super Project Equation:

$$\underset{\textbf{SUCCESS}}{\text{BUSINESS}} \quad = \quad \underset{\textbf{SUCCESS}}{\text{BIG PROJECT}}$$

As we will explore later, super projects have a clear and compelling 'why.' We call this a **'super why'** and it is one of the most universal aspects of any super project (underpinning super ambition, super alignment, super collaboration and so on). Importantly, it is not just about spreadsheets and business targets (as explored in **Chapter 2: Super Ambition**). A Super Why connects to **a vision of success for all project stakeholders** – in particular, customers and staff.

> 'If this initiative succeeds, we succeed' said the unit head with conviction. After a brief pause, she continued: 'If it fails then, as a leadership team, we fail.' Looking around the room, the leader continued in a steely tone: 'This initiative cannot and will not fail!' Clearly, the initiative in question was a Super Project.

Spanning Organizational Boundaries

Super projects cannot be delivered by one department or team working in isolation – silos and solo-runs are not enough.

Super projects are **an all-of-organization responsibility (AOR)**. They require effective cross-functional collaboration, spanning departments, functions and teams. They challenge traditional ways of working, even the shape of the organization (e.g., functional hierarchy *versus* network of cross-functional teams).

Regardless of what a big project is called or what department it originates from, it **has a shot at being a super project**. It could be a growth, compliance or efficiency initiative – or it could be a change and re-structuring initiative. If there is a clear link to business success, any big initiative can potentially lay claim to the super projects title.

Is it a **SUPER** Or just a **BIG PROJECT?**

PERFORMANCE
G**R**OWTH
C**O**MPLIANCE
JECT?
EFFICIENCY
CHANGE
TRANSFORMATION
RE**S**UCTURING

Extraordinary

Ordinary strategies are delivered by ordinary projects, but ambitious strategies need more. They require super projects.

Super projects **aim to achieve extraordinary things**. Moreover, they aim to do so in extraordinary ways – often with levels of speed, agility, collaboration and innovation that were previously unimaginable. For example, taking a new product to market in 10 months rather than 24 months. Here new ways of working will be required; sequential handovers between departments and functions won't be enough. How super projects make this possible is explored in **Chapter 5: Super Collaboration**.

'Extraordinary - that is the word that I would use to describe this project' said the senior leadership stakeholder. 'It is setting the new standard in terms of pace of progress, level of agility and the effectiveness of collaboration' he added. Heaping praise on the project team he concluded: 'While some would say that (as an organization) we are too big and too slow, you have demonstrated what is possible and what is necessary in today's market.'

Super Projects are **pockets of the extraordinary**. Relative to the rest of the organization they are capable of extraordinary speed, agility, collaboration and innovation. With a clear purpose and a compelling business imperative, they reveal what the organization is truly capable of. Super projects connect some organizations to the excitement of their founding years, for others they connect to a more agile future.

Super projects stretch organizations and showcase their leaders. They build confidence, competency and capacity, thereby contributing to further success in the future.

'On paper this strategic initiative aims to deliver an additional $40 million over the first 5 years, based on a total investment of $6.5 million' explained the sponsor. 'If we deliver that return, we will be entitled to call this a super project' she added. Clearly the level of investment and payback are factors that determine how 'super' a project really is.

Transform

CEOs love super projects. Wall Street loves them too! Whether it's an internal re-organization or the launch of a new product platform, super projects have **the potential to transform organizations, even industries and societies**. This is a key part of what it means to be Super Ambitious (explored in **Chapter 1**).

Super projects are the answer to accelerating change and innovation. They are a departure from business as usual, challenging traditional ways of planning, managing, budgeting, resourcing, and even working. For organizations spanning decades, even centuries, super projects present the greatest opportunities as well as challenges. But they can also challenge industry upstarts too.

Super projects face challenges like any other big project when it comes to change and innovation. What is different is how they derive **strength from engaging with the real-world complexity** of delivering ambitious strategies. In **Chapter 3**, we will see what it means to be super at engaging with complexity.

'Yes, you are working in a big organization, but don't let that restrict your creativity or innovation' said the division head. 'In leading these ambitious projects don't rely on corporate management or come unstuck with bureaucracy.' With a definitive tone she concluded: 'Take ownership and make it happen! You are the Corporate Entrepreneurs that this organization needs!'

WHAT'S IN A NAME?

The term 'super project' has a specific meaning in relation to our research. It defines a particular type of big project, based on the 5 criteria we have just examined. However, the term 'super projects' has **symbolic or metaphorical value** too.

5 Reasons for using the term 'Super Projects'

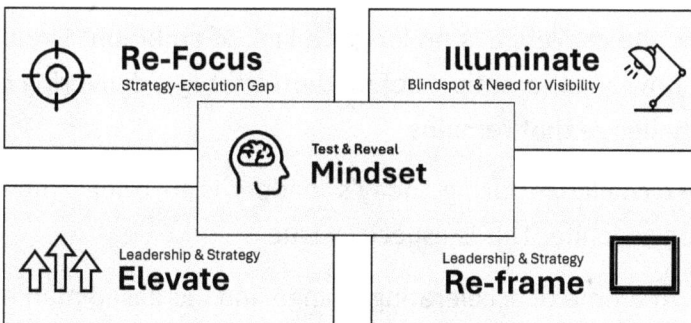

Re-Focus Strategy-Execution Gap	**Illuminate** Blindspot & Need for Visibility
Test & Reveal **Mindset**	
Leadership & Strategy **Elevate**	Leadership & Strategy **Re-frame**

If this was yet another book on projects, even big projects, it would probably struggle to grab your attention. By focusing on 'super projects' we hope to inject the topic of big projects, transformation and change with new importance – and some excitement too. Our purpose in doing this is to:

1. **Re-focus** attention on the role of big projects in bridging the gap between strategy and execution, or success.

2. **Illuminate** the need for greater visibility of big projects and portfolios among senior leaders.

3. **Elevate** big projects to the realm of leadership and strategy.

4. **Reframe** – With so much talk of struggling or failed projects and initiatives, we want to focus on what makes some big projects 'super.'

5. **Mindset** – Asking if a project is 'super' provides an insight to the narrative or sentiment around a project.

Let's explore these in a little more detail next.

Re-Focus

For decades, a lack of ambition and innovation was held to be **the principal problem in respect of strategy**. Countless articles and books warned leaders of the need for moonshots, blue ocean strategies[3] and big hairy audacious goals.[4]

Today, the challenge is no longer a lack of ambition! Dreaming big is now an inherent part of modern strategy; **delivering big is the challenge that remains**.

The #1 challenge facing today's leaders is to bring ambitious strategies to life. This is especially true:

- At a time of accelerating change and increased market uncertainty.
- Where there are more priorities and projects than available resources, with cutbacks and efficiency being the order of the day.
- Where there is increased pressure on short-term performance, as well as long-term transformation.

- Where risk, governance and compliance are key issues.

The challenge for leaders is to **bridge the gap between strategy and execution**, or more fundamentally, success. This is where our research on super projects comes into play.

Super projects aim to leap the gap between strategy and success or **today's performance and tomorrow's transformation**. They connect:

- Big project success to business success.
- Project goals to business needs and priorities.
- The project plan to the business strategy.
- The project team to the C-suite (e.g., CFO and CEO).

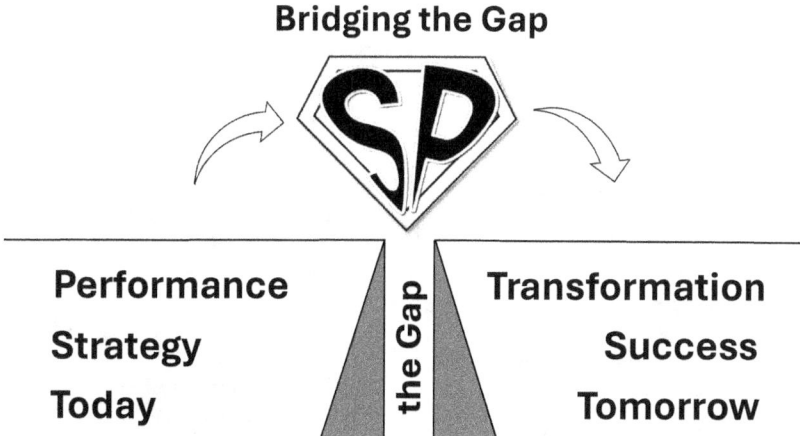

Bridging the Gap

Performance		Transformation
Strategy	the Gap	Success
Today		Tomorrow

Illuminate

Another reason for the title 'super projects' is to illuminate a **traditional blind spot** in respect of leadership and strategy. That is where leaders had only limited engagement with and visibility of the big projects upon which the success of their ambitious strategies depend.

Many senior leaders have a strangely **hands-off approach to big projects**. But a 'don't ask, don't tell' approach leaves leaders vulnerable to hidden risks and surprise setbacks.[5] Moreover, it denies big projects, and those leading them, access to one of the most precious organizational resources – the knowledge and experience of senior leaders.

Super projects present the case for senior leaders to **stay closer to their big projects.**

Is it a super project? Well, ask the CEO. That is the real test of how important or super any big project or initiative really is: (a) Does the CEO **know** about it? (b) Does the CEO **care** about it? (c) Does the CEO **brag** about it? Pause for a moment to answer these questions.

If the answer isn't 'yes' to at least 2 of the 3 questions, then your big project may not be as 'super' as you think.

This CEO test illuminates the link from your big project to the strategic business agenda, and ultimately to business success.

CEO TEST: SUPER

PROJE**C**T
PROJ**E**CT
PR**O**JECT

CHIEF EXECUTIVE
KNOWS ABOUT IT
CARES ABOUT IT
BRAGS ABOUT IT

Elevate

In all the talk of strategy, or even execution, big projects feature little. Super projects don't feature at all. Why is this? Isn't it interesting or relevant enough to talk about big projects and their role in bringing ambitious strategies to life? We believe the answer is yes, but the old way of strategy was different.

Traditionally, there was a demarcation between strategy and implementation. Leaders were content to focus on setting the vision and outlining strategy, while making it happen was left to others.

Putting 'super projects' in the title is a deliberate, if high-risk, strategy, aimed at engaging those at the top of the organization with something they often adopt a hands-off approach to. However, while projects and project management typically struggle to get a foot inside the C-suite, **super projects are the essence of leadership and strategy**.

The message is: **super projects need super leaders**; just as super leaders need super projects. After all, super projects are where strategy, innovation and change happen. Super projects are key drivers of long-term business success.

It's about:

Business
SUCCESS

$UPER PROFIT RESULTS RESOURCES BUDGET PAYBACK RETURN $AVINGS

Super projects are **the stage for today's leaders – tomorrow's leaders too**. Nowhere is leadership more needed, nowhere can leadership have a greater impact and nowhere is it more demanding! Super projects are where great leaders learn, develop and grow. This is where they shine!

> 'Something does not add up' said the experienced coach as she tried to reconcile the apparent contradictions in what the CEO had just said. In particular, two statements:
>
> - "There is very little innovation happening in this organization."
> - "There are over 200 projects running at this time, with many more in the pipeline."
>
> 'Surely, many of those projects involve innovation of some kind?' she mused. 'What are all those projects and initiatives doing if they are not finding better solutions, improving business processes, exploring new technologies, and so on?'[6]

Reframe

'Super projects' aim to reframe the conversation around change, transformation and executing on ambitious strategies. This is important because **the word 'project' isn't always helpful**.[7] Indeed, it can alienate many senior leaders. And words such as 'transformation' and 'change' have as much, if not more, negative baggage.

Many articles and books on big projects, transformation and even strategy get off on the wrong foot. Somewhere in the opening pages or paragraphs, you will find the usual statistics regarding the level of failure involved. Typically, the numbers suggested range from 70% to 85%, or even higher.[8] Even if we really believed the figures (or believed that they were helpful), that's not a mistake we're going to make with this research. **We are not going to start by telling you that you're probably going to fail**. We would rather focus on illuminating the key success factors and risks, rather than talk up the likelihood of failure. Moreover, we want to shine a light on what is super about big projects.

Ambitious leaders are confident that their initiatives will succeed, yet they know that the path from strategy to success is not a straight line. Super Projects is a way of thinking and talking about big projects. It is also a set of tools that **enables leaders to double-down on the level of confidence and ambition** regarding their big projects and initiatives.

> Talk of transformation is replete with the F Word. That is: Fatigue, Frustration and Failure! Yet, **our research shows there is much room for optimism**. Transformation may not always be happening in giant leaps, and there may be setbacks and missteps along the way. However, the picture emerges of leaders who are steadfast in their determination to meet the commercial opportunities and challenges their organizations are facing at a time of unparalleled change and uncertainty.

Our goal is to channel some of the fatigue around transformation and disillusionment regarding change into **curiosity and excitement around super projects**.[9] That doesn't mean we will shy away from the risks and obstacles. Rather, like those who are leading super projects, we will lean into complexity, embracing the real-world challenges of making ambitious things happen within large organizations and fast-moving markets.

Mindset

Let's be completely transparent, the use of **the phrase super projects is also a test**. Not a pass / fail test, but a means of revealing project sentiment or narrative. When we ask: 'Is your project a super project?' the responses are fascinating and can take many forms:

- Some say 'Yes' or 'It has the potential to be a super project.' Others may say it is 'super' in some ways and not in others. Here we find ourselves excited to learn more.

- Others will frown, roll their eyes or even grimace. There may be a cautious silence, a deflective laugh or quip, or people may start to vent their frustrations. All this makes us even more curious still: Has this project the potential to be super? What is required to move in that direction?

- Then there is a third group. These are the 'thinkers' that will ask what is a 'super project.' For some, this is a necessary clarification, for others it is a perfect stalling technique.

So here is the question: 'Have you got a super project?' or 'How super is your project?' Regardless of the specific answer, the point is that mindset matters. For a big project, narrative or sentiment can be as important as reality. Asking if a project is 'super' provides a window into **how people are really thinking –**

to their hopes and fears, as well as their level of energy and engagement. It is also a test of the ability to talk openly and honestly, and to acknowledge and take ownership of any challenges or setbacks facing a project.

A SUPER CHALLENGE

We like to say: 'the organization's moonshot or most ambitious strategy is **only a super project away from success**.' But that is not a flippant remark. Bridging any perceived or real gap between strategy and super project execution is not easy.

Super projects cost millions and promise many more in terms of payback. But they are a Herculean task, a monumental effort and a colossal undertaking. Indeed, successfully delivering super projects is one of the **most challenging, riskiest and costliest** things that organizations do.

Super projects are complex, with many moving parts (e.g., budgets, priorities and stakeholders), but that is not all. To add to the complexity, they are happening within large organizations at a time of accelerating market change and uncertainty. Indeed, if the widely reported rates of failure and frustration regarding transformation and change (typically put at 70% plus) have a value, it is to highlight just **how complex and demanding super projects really are**.

Typically, there is much hype around super projects. After all, 'bigging-up' projects is essential to securing resources. But super projects must **balance 'selling the dream' with 'keeping it real,'** especially in environments where resources are scarce, but projects and politics are plentiful.

Projects and initiatives are the building blocks of an organization's strategy. They are its DNA. To really understand the performance and potential of any strategy, you need to explore this **DNA – the portfolio of strategic projects and initiatives.**[10] Strategy is aspirational until the organization commits manpower and resources to those specific projects and initiatives that will bring it to life. A telling indicator of the likely success of any ambitious strategy is just how close its biggest and most important projects are to being super projects.

SUPER REAL

You might be thinking that everything about super projects is 'super,' but that's not exactly true. **Super projects have a messy side too!**

Away from the public gaze, even super projects have moments where their teams are overburdened, and their plans are called into doubt. They must wrestle with a long list of challenges – internal bureaucracy, scarce resources, changing business needs and priorities and possibly even misaligned stakeholders.

In reality, it is difficult for any project or initiative to be 'super' all the time – to be super ambitious, super confident and super aligned. It is also difficult to ensure super teamwork and collaboration – regardless of how much those leading wish it was so. To pretend otherwise flies in the face of the reality of working in a large organization. Also, in the face of everything that is written about transformation and change.

Paradoxically, 'super projects' are not super because they don't have flaws, or don't face obstacles, but rather because they do. They are 'super' because, **despite everything that is thrown at them, they keep on going**. Being undaunted by challenges and setbacks is what really makes projects and the teams running them 'super.'

'You would want to be crazy to lead one of these transformation projects' said the consultant. 'The rates of failure are so high and the risks so great' he added. 'The technology is, of course, complex. But that is only part of the challenge' he continued. 'Accessing resources, aligning stakeholders, managing vendors and navigating internal bureaucracy – those can be even greater challenges. It takes a special type of person to be able to manage (much less master) all of these things' he concluded.

SUPERHEROES

Behind every super project, there are superheroes, indeed **teams of superheroes**. They are at the forefront of change and transformation – shaping the future of their organizations, industries and even societies. Importantly, they shape it not just through strategy and vision, but through action too. This book is a celebration of the organization's new action heroes, their passion, dedication and skill (see **Chapter 6**).

However, being at the forefront of change – at the 'coal face' or cutting edge of strategy and ambition – isn't easy. Our heroes can find themselves pulling and pushing for change, while their organizations, or parts thereof, seem reluctant or are easily distracted. Thus, **it can be a lonely and stressful journey**, often requiring tremendous personal sacrifice.

Although they are no strangers to setbacks or disappointments, our super project leading heroes refuse to listen to those who say that it cannot be done. Despite everything that is thrown at them – internal bureaucracy, scarce resources, misaligned stakeholders, etc. – they keep on going. They are the new organizational super-heroes.

This book is a good news story. It is about how leaders navigate change and complexity to bring ambitious projects and initiatives to life. It is a homage to those who are making it happen, despite constraints, obstacles and setbacks. It draws inspiration from those ambitious leaders who are going to extraordinary lengths to shape their organizations, their industries, too.

> Embracing a **project-centric view of talent** is the next big step for HR. Super Projects, in particular, attract ambitious talent, develop cohesive and resilient teams, showcase leaders and build talent pipelines.
>
> Moreover, projects are re-shaping how we think about work and careers. For example, traditional CVs offer a limited, often dull, view of an executive's true experience, whereas detailing projects, including their highs and lows, can provide a much richer narrative.

PUTTING IT TO WORK

Super Projects is aimed at getting you to think, perhaps even re-think success and what it requires. You will find lots of questions asked throughout the book, the first of these is below:

Q: How super is your big project or ambitious strategy?

The extent to which your big project is a super project depends on the extent to which you agree or disagree with the statements in the table.

My big project ...	Your Score
Is about Strategic Leadership Change and Innovation.	
Is clearly connected to organizational or business success.	
Spans the organization (i.e., cross-functional).	
Aims to achieve the extraordinary in a way that is extraordinary too.	
Has the potential to transform the organization, its industry or even society.	

Write your score in the right column (where 5 = 'Absolutely Agree' and 1 = 'Absolutely Disagree'). Then reflect on what the completed table is saying about your big project and how super it is.

Next, let's jump into the research – exploring the factors that make some big projects super projects.

INTRODUCTION TO THE RESEARCH FRAMEWORK

WHAT IS SUPER?

WHERE TO FIND IT?

HOW

QSTE

INTRODUCTION

In the previous section, we explored what super projects are and why they matter (there is a reminder in the panel on the next page). Now, let's jump straight in, by asking: **Is your big project or ambitious strategy a super project?** This question is intended as a primer for action, as follows:

- If you answer 'No,' then: How can your big project **become** a super project?

- If 'Yes,' then: How to ensure your big project will **stay** super (regardless of the inevitable setbacks and surprises)?

- If you answered 'maybe' or 'not sure' then what information do you need to be able to confidently arrive at an **answer**?

This book has been written to answer these questions. The result is **an actionable framework** – one that you can put to work for your big project or ambitious strategy.

The SEARCH FOR SUPER

There is plenty written elsewhere about project flaws and failures. By contrast, super projects (as the name suggests) focuses on **successful rather than struggling projects** – it highlights and celebrates what makes some big projects, ambitious strategies and transformation initiatives super.

Telling stories of greatness is not the primary goal, however. Rather, the ultimate purpose of super projects is to help more projects (including yours) to be super. Specifically, to provide an **actionable framework or blueprint for big project success** – one that can be applied by all ambitious leaders. In developing this framework, we set the following as our scope of work:

- Scientific – Based on evidence and research.
- Accessible – Easy to use regardless of functional background.
- Re-frames – Helps people to apply creative problem-solving to the opportunities and challenges being faced.
- Affirmative – Focuses on the positive, while at the same time engaging with the full complexity involved.
- Tools based – Provides a set of tools and frameworks that can be applied by leaders, their stakeholders and teams.

For us, the last criterion is perhaps the most important of all. We didn't want to write an interesting book, but rather guide people through **a structured process of analysis and reflection** on their most important projects.

Super Projects: Quick Recap

What are they? Super projects are about strategic leadership, change and innovation and are linked to business success. They span the organization, aim to achieve extraordinary things, often in extraordinary ways. Also, they have the potential to transform organizations, industries or even societies.

Why do they matter? Big projects address the key opportunities or challenges facing an organization. Those big projects that are super projects bridge the gap between strategy and execution. They matter to the CEO because they are linked to business and organizational success.

The aim of our work on Super Projects is to help leaders and their teams unlock the super potential of their projects, strategies and initiatives. This often means a list of actions, but even more important still is a **shift in mindset and awareness** (for leaders, their organizations and teams). This is why the super projects model or framework looks different, as you will see next.

Putting it to work: Think of your biggest and most important project: What is super about it? Answer this question by writing **2 or 3 things that are good or great** about the project. Maybe that includes something that is exciting or innovative about it. You can use the spaces below:

1. _____

2. _____

3. _____

This question aims to tap into your energy and excitement. If it helps you to do that, super projects is for you. The question reveals our mindset and intent in writing this book. It is to be helpful – positive, supportive and challenging too. From the very start, this book is about amplifying what is (and can be) super about your big project. So, consider: Does everybody know what is super about your project?

THE SUPER FRAMEWORK

The results of our research into what makes big projects and ambitious projects super can be summarized in the following visual framework.

Let's take a moment to get familiar with this framework:

The labels: The labels on the diagram reflect the 5 factors that make some big projects super projects. We call these superpowers, and they are as follows:

1. **Super Ambition** propels projects further and faster. It is a type of ambition that goes deeper and connects more widely. At its core is a 'super why.'

2. **Super Confidence** – a type of confidence that balances the need to 'sell the dream' with the need to 'keep it real.' it is a surprising test of leadership at a time of change and uncertainty.

3. **Super Alignment** – the alignment of big projects with business strategy and success. Nowhere is this more

important than in respect of projects driven by one department or function (e.g., IT).

4. **Super Complexity** occurs where engaging with complexity galvanizes, rather than paralyzes, a project or team. Thus, projects and their teams can profit from change and uncertainty.

5. **Super Collaboration** – transforms teamwork and collaboration from a drain on time and resources to a force-multiplier in term of productivity and innovation.

Most big projects and ambitious strategies face challenges in some or all these areas. Not necessarily because they're doing something wrong, but because of the complexity involved in delivering big projects within large organizations at a time of accelerating change and uncertainty. This is especially true where leaders are relying on traditional tools, mindsets or methodologies. Hence, the reason for the creation of this framework: **To equip leaders with the tools required to make extraordinary things happen** in extraordinary times.

The shape: The 5 'superpowers' are shown around the instantly recognizable 'super' pentagon as the cover art for this book and its box of tools. The rigor of the science behind super projects is matched by the sophistication of the approach to its communication. This is important because while there are many models for strategy, there are few for execution. Moreover, those related to traditional project management or execution struggle to get inside the door of the C-suite. As one of our colleagues puts it: 'This (the super projects framework) is what the project triangle looks like when it comes out of the C-suite.'

The big letters: The 'SP' in the middle most obviously stand for Super Projects, but the initials could also stand for Super Powers (i.e., the 5 labels in the diagram) or Sophisticated Process too (referring to the process behind the model).

You may be surprised to learn that there is a lot of science behind the **use of models** and their effectiveness. The good news is that you do not need to know any of this to benefit. If you are interested, however, here are some of the key principles incorporated into the design of the super projects framework:

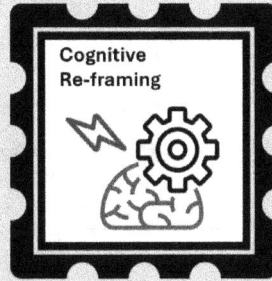

Cognitive Re-framing

- **Cognitive Reframing** – Looking at things from a different angle, or through a different lens, to alter emotional responses and behaviors, thereby leading to more positive or constructive outcomes.

- **Mental Models** are how we see or make sense of the world. But how accurate or helpful are they? Models can help to reveal or even challenge how we think.

- **Metaphors** convey complex ideas, emotions, or concepts in a simple, relatable, and vivid way. They are 'weapons of mass understanding.'[11]

You could think of the Super Projects framework as 'a brain hack.' By interrupting traditional patterns of thinking, the model and related tools have the power to accelerate the process of insight, prevent analysis paralysis and reduce the risk of bias or error.

THE 5 SUPERPOWERS

A superpower is an **extraordinary ability, capacity or strength.** But these superpowers are not about leaping tall buildings, flying through the sky or x-ray vision. They are more down to earth, yet super at the same time. They help make extraordinary things happen, bringing ambitious strategies to life. In short, superpowers make super projects.

There is a chapter for each of the superpowers, aimed at helping you **leverage the 5 powers for your project** and providing you with checklists and tools along the way.

Before jumping into specific superpowers, let's talk more generally about the superpowers.

- **They are powerful.** They are linked not just to project success, but business or organizational success more widely. It will be difficult to succeed without them.

- **They are rare.** After all, while most super projects are big projects, only a minority of big projects are super projects. Indeed, depending on how strictly you apply the criterion, super projects could be as rare as 1 in 10 or even 1 in 20 big projects.

- **They are situational**, reflecting what is happening in a project, and its environment. They are not fixed but will go up and down over time (e.g., from phase to phase).

- **They must be cultivated and continuously nurtured.** No matter how great or successful a project is, it can probably optimize at least one of these 5 factors.

- **They are about mindset** as well as techniques, tools or skills. Indeed, the 5 superpowers are a new definition of strategic leadership.

Talking about superpowers keeps the focus on what is super, it keeps the metaphor going too. In the tales of superheroes, superpowers can derive from many sources, including radioactive accidents, magical forces or even outer space. Other heroes leverage technology to give them superpowers, while more still develop their powers through training and discipline. **Superpowers are not magically bestowed on projects**, nor are they naturally occurring. Wishing them won't make them so. Moreover, there is little that technology alone can do. What is required is super leaders and teams – what we call action heroes (**Chapter 6**).

Having explored the concept of superpowers (SPs), let's look behind the labels to understand each power in a little more detail.

SP#1: SUPER AMBITIOUS

Most big projects are big on ambition. However, higher targets or loftier goals don't necessarily **propel projects further or faster**. That requires a form of ambition that connects more deeply and widely – we call this super ambition.

As you will see in **Chapter 1**, there are **8 ways to power your project with super ambition**. These are summarized in the mnemonic: 'Why smart+ bold conviction can transform visions of meaningful value for many.' Let's take the first of these – it relates to the 'why.'

Super Projects derive their power from a clear and compelling why – that is, a **super why**. This goes beyond the project mission statement or spreadsheet. Importantly, clarifying the 'why' is one of the most powerful ways to energize a project, engage a project team and align its stakeholders. Indeed, 'the why' is 3 to 5 times more powerful than 'the how.' This is just one of the ideas presented in this chapter to challenge traditional thinking about ambition and the power of motivation.

SP#2: SUPER CONFIDENT

Naturally, you would expect super projects to enjoy super levels of confidence. However, when you look at the data, confidence is a conundrum. While the research reveals high levels of confidence as the default for most big projects and strategies, it fails to demonstrate a clear link between confidence and success.

Confidence is essential in protecting leaders and projects from doubt, uncertainty and criticism. Also in safeguarding resources, reputations, and power. However, confidence can be dangerous when it shields a project from reality or inhibits open communication (especially about risks and obstacles).

This chapter provides a practical tool to explore project confidence, deconstructing it into six key areas:

1. Confidence in **Project Success** (overall).
2. Confidence in the project driving **Business Success**.
3. Confidence in the **Project Plan**.
4. Confidence in **Project Execution**.
5. Confidence in the **Project Team**.
6. Confidence in **Organizational Support** for the project.

Those leading and sponsoring big projects must balance the need to 'sell the dream' with the necessity of 'keeping it real.' This requires 4Cs – curiosity, candor, courage, and clarity. Plus, a fifth C which calibrates confidence with compliance.

SP#3: SUPER ALIGNED

When everyone pulls together, amazing things can happen. However, with competing projects and priorities, people often find themselves being pulled in different directions. They can even lose sight of the business needs that their big project aims to address. This is especially important when an initiative is being driven by a particular business function, such as IT.

In this section, we argue that there are no more 'technology initiatives,' only 'business initiatives led, driven or enabled by IT.' The same applies to HR, Compliance or any other initiatives. This change highlights the role of technology as a strategic business enabler, also the importance of business – IT alignment.

In this chapter, we share a tool for super alignment and Business Efficiency & Success *via* Technology (BEST). Inspired by the technical stack as used by IT leaders to manage technical complexity, the business stack, helps manage the non-technical or business-related aspects of a big project. The different layers of the business stack are:

1. **Business Fundamentals:** Aligning the project with business needs and strategy.
2. **Execution:** Proactively identifying success factors and risks.
3. **Stakeholder Engagement:** Ensuring shared ownership and clear expectations.
4. **Collaboration:** Optimizing the effectiveness of teamwork and internal collaboration.
5. **Reality Check:** Creating an environment where people can 'call it' when required.
6. **Portfolio Linkages:** Leveraging linkages, synergies and dependencies with other projects and initiatives.

The twin stack approach (business stack and technical stack) presents opportunities as well as challenges for IT leaders. Done right, it can significantly boost the business impact of IT, as well as the success of all those initiatives that have a significant technological component.

SP#4: SUPER COMPLEX

If projects were less complex, they would be easier to manage and control. However, that is wishful thinking, and it flies in the face of reality. Big projects are complex, so too are the organizations running them and the environments in which they are operating.

Super projects are not necessarily any more complex than other big projects, but they are super at engaging with complexity. They embrace key vulnerabilities, including:

1. **Business Myopia:** Losing sight of evolving business needs and market realities.

2. **The First Mile:** Neglecting critical groundwork and fundamental issues in the rush to launch a project.

3. **Stakeholder Aversion:** Failing to secure active engagement as well as shared responsibility from key stakeholders.

4. **Pollyanna:** Fostering a culture of excessive optimism that silences concern and hinders risk mitigation and effective governance / compliance.

Use the powerful framework in the chapter to engage with hidden complexity, strengthening your project in the process.

SP#5: SUPER COLLAB.

Teamwork and collaboration are the bane of many big projects, particularly those that involve cross-functional teams. This is evident from the amount of time spent on internal meetings and the volume of internal email or IM.

Imagine transforming teamwork and collaboration from a drain on productivity to a force multiplier in terms of performance and innovation. That is what Super Collaboration can help your big project achieve. The way of the super collaborator has 4 parts; here are 2 of them:

- **The Way We Work** – How your project team organizes its work (ensuring that the right people are in the right roles, doing the right work, etc.).
- **The Way we Interact** – The quality of interactions within your project team, also called team dynamics.

Collaboration is multi-directional – up, down and across the project. Optimizing it has the potential to be 3 to 5 times more powerful than an organizational restructuring or cultural change initiative.[12] However, it requires a shift from traditional top-down hierarchical control to empowering networks of cross-functional teams.

'SUPER' REQUIRES A RE-THINK!

Like any powerful framework, the Super Projects model is simple and clear. At the same time, it is also robust and challenging. On the surface, the five labels or superpowers are self-obvious. They are super ambitious, super confident, super aligned, super complex and super collaboration. Look more closely, however and each one requires a re-think of the requirements of leadership, change and innovation. This is a good thing, as it reveals new insights and strategies.

Re-thinking Super Ambition

You may be thinking that **super ambition** simply means more ambition in the form of higher targets or bigger goals. However, propelling a project or strategy further and faster requires more. It requires a form of ambition that connects more deeply and more widely than traditional spreadsheets or mission statements.

At the core of super ambition is a clear and compelling why, called a 'super why.' But Super project leaders and sponsors don't just tell people 'why.' As we will see, there is a more powerful way.

Re-thinking Super Confidence

What does it mean to be Super Confident about a big project or ambitious strategy? Well, you may be thinking that **super confidence** is an unshakeable confidence that shuns doubt or uncertainty. Paradoxically, however, super projects are galvanized rather than paralyzed by engaging with risks, obstacles and uncertainty. As we will see, super confidence enables leaders to balance the requirements of 'selling the dream' (required to access funding and support), with the necessity of 'keeping it real' (required to make things happen).

Re-thinking
The Requirements of Big Project Success

Re-thinking Super Alignment

Super alignment means there are no more IT, HR or Compliance projects! Only 'business initiative led or sponsored by IT, HR or compliance.'

Super Alignment requires putting business needs and priorities, ahead of departmental, project and team goals. It requires a **'business first' approach** to big projects and project portfolios.

However, such alignment can never be taken for granted. Keeping pace with changing business needs and priorities requires **dynamic alignment**.

Re-thinking Super Complexity

You may be thinking that **super complexity** (or being super at complexity) requires holding tighter to the reins and adhering more rigidly to plans. However, embracing complexity requires organizations to do what is counterintuitive. To become more agile when the temptation is to become more rigid.

Complexity is an important source of project risk. However, it is often hidden. The result of this hidden complexity is misplaced certainty and rigid adherence to overly simplistic plans.

Most hidden of all, is **internal complexity** – yet it is a key factor in the ability of an organization to adapt to change and uncertainty. Super Projects reveals 8 ways to transform internal complexity into a source of big project resilience and strength.

Re-thinking Super Collaboration

Super collaboration doesn't mean more collaboration, especially given that people are already spending so much time on internal meetings. The goal is to transform teamwork from a drain on time and energy to a force multiplier in terms of performance, productivity and innovation. However, new platforms or technologies are not the answer. Nor are 'meeting-free Fridays.' Super collaboration goes deeper. It requires **empowering**

project teams to take control over the way they work. The steps to achieving super collaboration are set out in the chapter.

THE 'SUPER' MINDSET

The above are examples of how the super projects framework will challenge some of the ways in which we traditionally think about big projects and ambitious strategies. This is important as the framework is **adaptive, as much as technical**. That is to say, mindset matters. It is not just about new techniques or skills in these areas; some change of attitude is likely to be required too.

Being super isn't just about more ambition, more confidence or more collaboration. More isn't always the answer, but better too. Most important of all, it's about a project being the best that it can be.

Every project is different, and so too is the situation or environment in which it is operating. Thus, what is super for one project may not be super for another. In this respect, 'super' is not an absolute standard.

The goal of super projects is to help leaders to **unlock the full potential** of their own big project, its stakeholders and teams. However, keep in mind that not every project can be or even needs to be a super project.

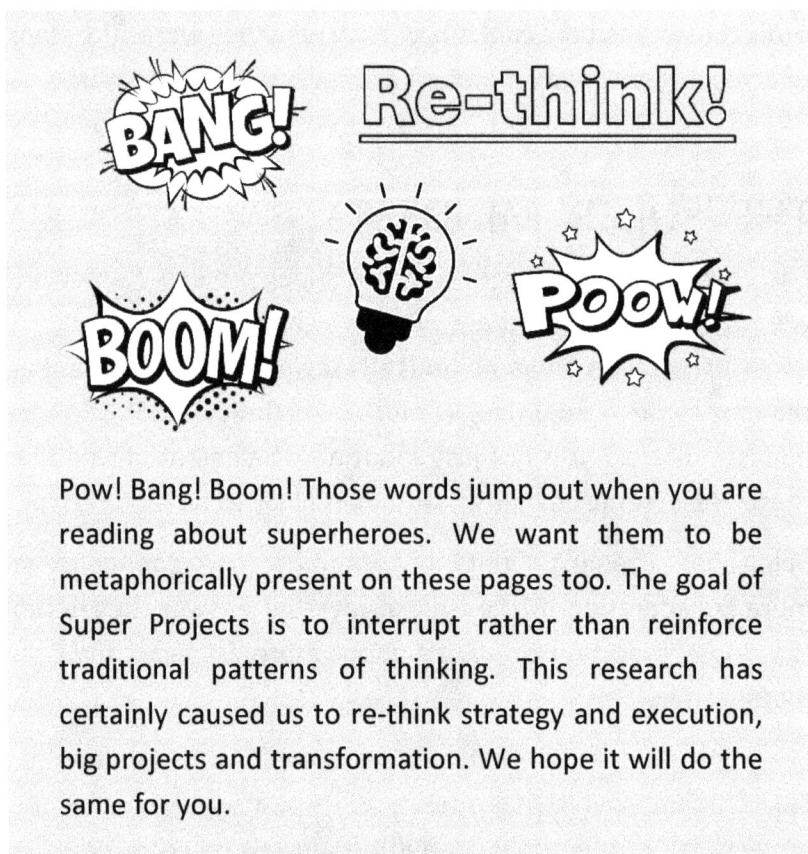

Pow! Bang! Boom! Those words jump out when you are reading about superheroes. We want them to be metaphorically present on these pages too. The goal of Super Projects is to interrupt rather than reinforce traditional patterns of thinking. This research has certainly caused us to re-think strategy and execution, big projects and transformation. We hope it will do the same for you.

SUPER REAL TOO!

You might be thinking that everything about super projects is 'super,' but that's not exactly true. **Super projects have a messy side too!**

Away from the public gaze, even super projects have moments where their teams are overburdened, and their plans are called into doubt. They must wrestle with a long list of challenges – internal bureaucracy, scarce resources, changing business needs or priorities and misaligned stakeholders.

In reality, it is difficult for any project or initiative to be 'super' all the time – to be super ambitious, super confident and super aligned. It is also difficult to ensure super teamwork and collaboration – regardless of how much those leading wish it was so. To pretend otherwise flies in the face of the reality of working in a large organization. Also, in the face of everything that is written and known about transformation and change.

Paradoxically, 'super projects' are not super because they don't have flaws, or don't face obstacles, but rather because they do. They are 'super' because, **despite everything that is thrown at them, they keep on going**. Being undaunted by challenges and setbacks is what really makes projects and the teams running them 'super.'

READY TO GET STARTED?

Having read an overview of each of the 5 superpowers, pause for a moment to reflect on your project. Specifically, what is super about your big project or ambitious strategy?

Super Projects is a framework for putting the super in big projects (and keeping it there). A great way to get started is to use the page overleaf to describe and rate your project using the framework.

Completing the tool on page 43 will:

- Generate some **new insights**, perhaps even getting you to think about your project in a new way. Think of this a form of 'appreciative inquiry' that seeks to recognize progress and build on strengths.

- Provide you with a baseline or **reference point** – you can compare what you write against the new standard for super ambition, super confidence, and so on (as shared in subsequent chapters).

- Help you to determine: **Where to go next?** For example, which superpower(s) interests you most? If you were to power up your project, where might you start?

Where to next? Each superpower has its own chapter (starting with Super Ambition next). You can navigate to find the superpower you want, or work through them in order.

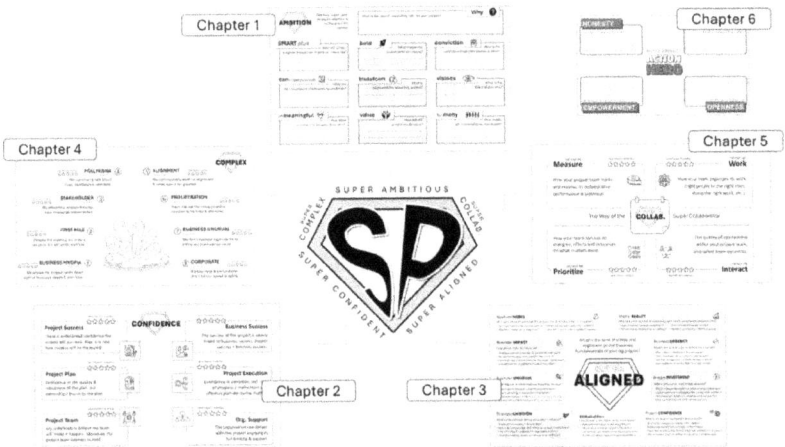

One-page tools or frameworks are very popular – take the business canvas or the beermat business case as examples. But should there be a one-page tool for big projects and important initiatives? We believe the answer is 'yes,' so we created one (as overleaf). Well, we actually created a series of them – one for each of the 5 superpowers (shown throughout this book).

What is super about your big project or ambitious strategy?

Use the panels to describe your project.

AMBITION

What is the ambition driving your big project? How does it propel the project forward?

YOUR PROJECT'S RATING: ☆☆☆☆☆

COMPLEXITY

What aspects of your project are difficult to control or predict? How is this managed?

YOUR PROJECT'S RATING: ☆☆☆☆☆

CONFIDENCE

How confident are people in your project? How does this show up?

YOUR PROJECT'S RATING: ☆☆☆☆☆

COLLABORATION

What words would you use to describe teamwork & collaboration on your big project?

YOUR PROJECT'S RATING: ☆☆☆☆☆

ALIGNMENT

Are there any signs of cross -functional misalignment? Where?

YOUR PROJECT'S RATING: ☆☆☆☆☆

SUPER COLLAB.

SUPER AMBITIOUS

SUPER ALIGNED

SUPER COMPLEX

SUPER CONFIDENT

CHAPTER 1:

SUPER AMBITION

INTRODUCTION

Naturally, big projects tend to be highly ambitious. But super projects are fueled by something more powerful still. That is super ambition.

Super Ambition doesn't just mean higher targets or bigger goals. It is the type of ambition that **connects more deeply and more widely** than any mission statement, business case or spreadsheet.

Here, our research reveals what it takes for a big project to be powered by super ambition. Moreover, it provides a framework to help leaders cultivate the level of ambition necessary to drive extraordinary outcomes in their big projects.

THE MOST AMBITIOUS EVER

For decades, leaders were told they **needed to be more ambitious**. Rather than ordinary goals, they needed 'big hairy and audacious goals' (BHAG). Moreover, an ordinary strategy was no longer enough – leaders needed blue ocean strategies, moon shots too!

Leaders have listened to these demands, taking business ambition to a whole new level. Indeed, our data suggests that this is probably the most ambitious generation of leaders yet.[13]

Just how ambitious are today's leaders? Well, the answer is to be found in the number 7. That is the average number of transformation initiatives planned or underway.[14] However, the number of projects could be up to 10 times that figure. More and bigger projects are a natural product of ambitious strategy.

It is not just that organizations and their leaders want to achieve more; they need to achieve more. It is expected of them, and it must be achieved in better and faster ways too. Otherwise, they risk being overtaken by change.

This may be the **golden age of corporate ambition**, but it is also a time of unparalleled change and disruption. Increased globalization, ever-shorter product life cycles, blurring industry boundaries, and of course, technological revolution (e.g., Ai, digitization and automation). These are just some of the factors that put pressure on short-term performance, as well as longer-term transformation.

One of the defining books of the 1990s was titled *Only the Paranoid Survive*. That title today might read **'Only the Ambitious Survive.'** At a time of accelerating change and uncertainty, ambition is not a nice-to-have. Rather, it is a necessity and the more, the better! Across the corporate landscape, it is no longer 'survival of the fittest,' but 'survival of the most ambitious.'

EXPLORING AMBITION

The most important thing to know about any project is why it exists, what it aims to achieve, and why that matters. Thus, ambition is **the first of the 5 superpowers** or characteristics of a super project that we will explore.

Our research is probably one of the deepest explorations of big project ambition ever.[15] It aims to understand **the nature of the ambition driving today's leaders and their big projects:**

- Are there different forms of ambition?
- Is some ambition more potent than others?
- If all big projects are ambitious, then what is it that makes some big projects super ambitious?

- What are the implications for the scale of ambition in terms of how big projects are planned and resourced, as well as implemented, led and even reviewed?

Super ambition is what you might expect to find in Venture Capital-backed startups in tech or bio. Surprisingly, however, we also found it in large established organizations, often in complex and highly regulated industries. That is what makes it so interesting. As one of our coaches says, '**It is like moving Wall Street to Silicon Valley!**' This gives rise to a serious question, however: How can leaders in big corporations deliver start-up levels of ambition and change?

WHAT IS 'SUPER AMBITION'?

One of **the most powerful big project conversations** you can have is about the ambition driving it. This is a truly strategic conversation – a conversation about what matters most.

What immediately becomes clear is that **ambition comes in many shapes and sizes**. Obviously, there are project goals and deliverables. Then there is the business impact of the project and how it drives business performance and success. These factors are important in defining the ambition behind a big project. However, as our research points out, there is more.

Naturally, big projects tend to be highly ambitious – they **set out to achieve something extraordinary**. However, super projects are not just highly ambitious, they are what we call 'super ambitious.'

What is super ambitious? Is it 10%, 20% or 50% more ambitious than a typical big project? Well, our data suggests that the number is not the critical factor that distinguishes super ambition.

Super Ambition doesn't just mean more ambition in the form of higher targets or bigger goals. Often, that is true, but it is not the defining factor. Rather, super ambition is **a type of ambition that connects more deeply and more widely** than any business case or even mission statement. Thus, it has the power to propel projects farther and faster – that is what defines super ambition.

SUPER AMBITION REVEALED

Ambition propels big projects. How far and how fast the ambition can propel a project depends on as many as 10 factors. These are the characteristics that define super ambition.

Super Ambition Has 10 Parts:

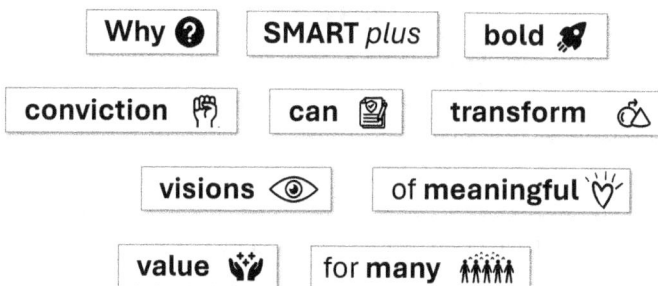

Why ❓ | SMART *plus* | bold 🚀

conviction ✊ | can 📖 | transform 🐲

visions 👁 | of meaningful 🔆

value 🌱 | for many 👪

Together, the words create a mnemonic or memory device: 'Why SMART plus bold conviction can transform visions of meaningful value for many.' That's a mouthful and a tongue twister. But don't worry, it'll make sense in just a moment:

Factor	Description
Why	There is a clear and compelling 'why,' understood and embraced by all key stakeholders.
SMART *plus*	Success is clearly defined, with a robust framework for tracking progress, evaluating performance and ultimately success.
Bold	The goals are bold and daring, pushing boundaries, entailing risk and challenging the *status quo*.
Conviction	The big project is powered by conviction, not just aspiration, backed up by actions and resources.
Can	Ambition is calibrated with compliance.
Transform	The project has the potential to transform the organization, perhaps its industry.
Meaningful	The big project connects to purpose and passion.
Visions	It is connected to a shared vision of success.
Of Value	It is value-creating, generating not just financial returns, but also customer value, employee value and societal impact.
For Many	The ambition is shared by many, not just by a few senior leaders or investors.

The 10 factors (from our mnemonic) listed in the table collectively define what makes Super Ambition 'super.' Here is what makes this research important: **How far and how fast your project can go** depends on how it connects with these factors.

You can use the table (on the previous page) to **explore the nature of the ambition driving your project**. If you like, you can rate your big project against each of these factors – for each of the factors and the descriptions provided, rate your project on a scale of 1 to 5, where 1 = 'absolutely disagree' and 5 = 'absolutely agree.' The maximum score is 50, and we define super ambition as being in the range of 45 to 50.

Note: It is not latent ambition that fuels a project, but the process of talking about, discovering and giving ambition expression. So, putting a score on the level of super ambition behind your project is only a secondary factor. This is **a framework to help leaders cultivate the level of ambition** necessary to drive extraordinary outcomes in their big projects.

Let's explore the 10 dimensions of super ambition, starting with what most would argue is the most important. That is the 'why' of a big project.

> Books about big projects rarely become popular, so when one does it is worth paying attention. In *'How Big Things Get Done'* by Brent Flyvberg and Dan Gardner, one of the key pieces of advice is to: 'Start with the most basic question of all: Why?'[16]

SUPER AMBITION = 'WHY?'

Super Ambition derives from **a clear and compelling 'why.'** This is the ultimate source of power for any big project. Yet, as our research highlights, it often goes untapped.

Naturally, much of the **focus for any big project is on 'the how,'** including the project plan and Gantt chart. But, as important as it is, 'the how' may have little to do with what is really driving a project. By contrast, super projects look beyond project logistics and execution, to connect with the 'why' — that is **the fundamental reason why** a big project exists and why it matters.

Many big projects are **heavy on 'the how,' but light on 'the why.'** You need both; however, a deficit in terms of the 'why' is likely to penalize your big project most. After all, if the 'why' is compelling enough, people will find a 'how.' Similarly, if the 'why' is not clear, you can spend all the time and money you want on the 'how' and still come up short.

Without a clear and compelling 'why,' a big project will likely **struggle to get approved**, access sufficient resources, or secure effective cross-functional collaboration. The 'why' is one of the simplest and yet, the most powerful tools in leadership and strategy, yet it is typically missing from the big project planning toolkit.

Where leaders are clear on the 'why' of their big project, they tend to assume that others are clear too. That is **a dangerous assumption**, however. For example, you may be thinking that the 'why' of your project is clear but think again. Our research points to as many as 10 different reasons the 'why' of a big project gets neglected. That is a long list, but most leaders can relate to at least 2 or 3 of the factors listed here:

1. **'Surely, they must know!'** Those leading and sponsoring the project typically set their minds on the

'why.' As they know the 'why,' they assume that others must know it too.

2. **'It should be obvious!'** Yet, with so many projects happening, it can be difficult for those who are not directly involved to keep track of every project and its 'why.' This is particularly true for projects with fancy titles, such as Project Jupiter or Horizon 2026.[17]

3. **'Why are we even talking about this?'** As important and fundamental as the 'why' is, it often gets neglected. Indeed, it is **a major project blind spot** for many big project leaders and sponsors.

4. **'We have told them often enough!'** However, while people may have been told the 'why' of the project, they may not have engaged in the process of clarifying objectives or defining success.

How many other projects have the people working on your project got? For one big organization, people had 6.3 other projects underway. Some on the project leadership team wondered what those other projects might be and why there were so many. For the project sponsor, however, the question was: How to ensure that her project was #1 rather than #6 on the list? How to ensure that people would put her project at the top of their list of priorities? There needed to be a clear and compelling why, she thought.

5. **'Enough talk, let's get going!'** In the rush to get started, there may be little consultation or debate regarding the 'why.' You may hear sponsors saying:

"The time for talking about the why has passed. Now, we need action."

6.   **'It is in the project plan!'** A big project's clear and compelling why (its 'super why') is **unlikely to be found in a business case or project plan**, but rather in talking and listening to key stakeholders.

7.   **'It is in the spreadsheet!'** Leaders often assume that the business case and a set of targets represents a compelling 'why.' However, for most people the numbers are only a part, perhaps even a small part, of the 'why.'

8.   **'It depends on who you ask!'** There may not just be one single 'why,' with the answers varying across stakeholders and by role or function.

9.   **'I'm afraid to ask!'** Some leaders may be afraid to ask the 'why' question. The lack of a clear and compelling 'why' could reflect badly on them, perhaps even undermining the project itself.

10.   **'We defined it at the outset!'** Typically, the 'why' gets set at the start of a project, with the assumption that it will remain valid throughout. Yet, the 'why' behind a big project can – and must – evolve in response to the changing needs and priorities of the organization (and its key stakeholders).

Super Ambitious means people are fired up by a clear and compelling 'why?' We call this a **'super why.'** It gets people going and keeps them going despite obstacles and setbacks. But, how do you know **if your big project has a 'super why?'** Well, ask people 'why?' and then reflect on the answers:

1.   What is the level of clarity about the 'why' – can people articulate it in a clear and consistent manner?

2.   What is the level of energy, engagement and
        exploration as they talk about it?[18]

> Of all the skills required by big project leaders and
> sponsors, the most unexpected is storytelling. Yet too
> many leaders **struggle to tell a convincing, even engaging
> story** regarding their big projects. The result is that when
> they talk about their big project people yawn, rather than
> get excited. Much of this stems from the lack of a
> compelling 'why,' or shared vision of success. Without
> these, project leaders talk about the more mundane,
> including operational details, obstacles and the need for
> more resources. The result is project conversations and
> reviews that struggle to engage, or perhaps even
> frustrate, senior leaders impatient for success.

Your project may have a clear and compelling 'why.' The problem
is that others may not know or fully appreciate what it is. Thus, the
real issue is the level of **clarity and alignment** on the 'why.' It is not
enough that leaders know and are fired up by the 'why.' If it is to
be a 'super why' other key stakeholders must be fired up by it too.

Q: Has your big project got a 'super why?'

Don't worry if your project doesn't yet have a 'super why.' That is
actually **good news and a great opportunity.** Clarifying the 'why' is
one of the most powerful ways to re-ignite a project – re-energize
the project team, re-engage key stakeholders and ensure the
organization doubles-down on its commitment of resources.

The most powerful way to engage and align people, especially
busy senior leaders, is around the 'why.' Indeed, our research

suggests that it is 3 to 5 times more powerful than talking about the 'how.' Yet, the 'how' is where most project leaders focus in project conversations, presentations and reviews.

> Brad, a seasoned project leader at a global corporation, led a transformation initiative poised to revolutionize the organization's digital infrastructure. Despite its importance, senior leadership, especially the CEO, seemed reluctant to ask about or discuss the project. That left Brad feeling frustrated and isolated. The lack of an evident commitment to the project by senior leadership was damaging the project team's morale and hampering cross-functional collaboration. Determined, Brad requested a private meeting with the CEO, **reconnecting with 'the why' of the project** and its importance. As Brad discovered, the lack of engagement wasn't due to a lack of interest, but rather the level of busyness of the CEO. Indeed, the chief believed in the vision and was determined that the initiative would succeed. With renewed senior engagement, the project regained its momentum, ultimately becoming a major success and a testament to the power of C-suite involvement.

As the leader or sponsor of a big project, **think of yourself as 'the why guy.'** Your job is to ensure your big project has a clear and compelling 'why,' not just on paper, but in the hearts and minds of all those involved. This is the most effective way to ensure your big project matters to the organization and its stakeholders.

Getting clarity on the 'why' is particularly exciting for big technology projects. A digital transformation initiative, for example, has both **a technical 'why' and a commercial 'why.'** Addressing both is key to enabling IT to talk to Commercial and most importantly, to connect the technology to business strategy and success. There may be a compliance and finance department and other 'whys' too.

> Efficiency and cost reduction are today's #1 business obsession. Indeed, they could even account for up to 80% of projects and initiatives in some organizations.[19] But what does this trend really mean? Are the words 'project' or 'initiative' becoming shorthand for cost-cutting and productivity? Does the 'why' behind 4 out of 5 projects live only in a spreadsheet? On the surface, that might seem to be the case. But stopping there would be a missed opportunity.
>
> Invite people to explore why these 'efficiency projects' matter and you could be in for a surprise. Given the space, they often connect the dots – seeing what might look like a narrow efficiency drive as part of a broader and more meaningful story. That includes eliminating friction points that frustrate employees and customers, building resilience for the future, and making smarter, more sustainable use of resources. The lesson? Even a cost-cutting initiative can have a super why – one that earns its place on the business fundamentals one-pager (**Chapter 3**).

SUPER AMBITION IS SMART+

Management by objectives has been around for a long time, yet many big projects struggle with it. For example, what is **the**

difference between a goal, an objective and a result? It can get confusing, leaving the ambition behind a big project vague and unmeasurable. However, for super projects, **success is clearly defined**. So too is how progress and ultimately success will be measured. That requires goals that are not just SMART, but more.

Super Ambition is built on SMART goals (specific, measurable, actionable, realistic / relevant and time-bound). But that is not all. Super projects strive to ensure that objectives are clearly linked to tangible results (OKRs), with **a range of metrics for progress, performance and ultimately success** – as shown in the table.[20]

Super Projects: 5 Types of Results

Project Inputs	The things we need to deliver the project (e.g., money, people and any other resources).
Project Activities	The things we do in delivering the project (e.g., steps, processes, work streams, etc.).
Project Outputs	What the project delivers / produces (e.g., new system or process).
Business Outcomes	The knock-on business benefits (e.g., what the system or process enables the business to achieve over the short to medium term).
Business Impact	The longer-term impact on business performance and success (as seen by stakeholders).

Being more than SMART about objectives and results requires working in both directions in the table:

- From top to bottom – encouraging those who are tied up in delivery to look beyond inputs and activities to outputs, outcomes and impact.

- From bottom to top – encouraging those who are focused on business results to link them back to inputs (resources) and activities, thereby injecting new transparency and realism.

Pause for a moment to reflect:

Q: Has your big project got results or targets in all the categories shown in the table?

The ultimate success of a big project may be a long way off into the future. However, **super ambition leverages the power of progress** when the end goal may seem far off. Longer-term goals or results are broken down into stages, or chunks, enabling progress to be tracked along the way.

SUPER AMBITION IS BOLD

Super projects dream big. They are **bold, daring and imaginative**:

- They are often moonshots, blue ocean strategies and big hairy audacious goals.

- Typically, super projects aim for massive, rather than marginal gains.

- Typically, super projects are playing to win, rather than playing not to lose.[21]

- The ambition is to grow and innovate, rather than simply to protect or sustain.

- The aim is to profit from change and disruption, with innovation being central. The *status quo* is no longer acceptable.

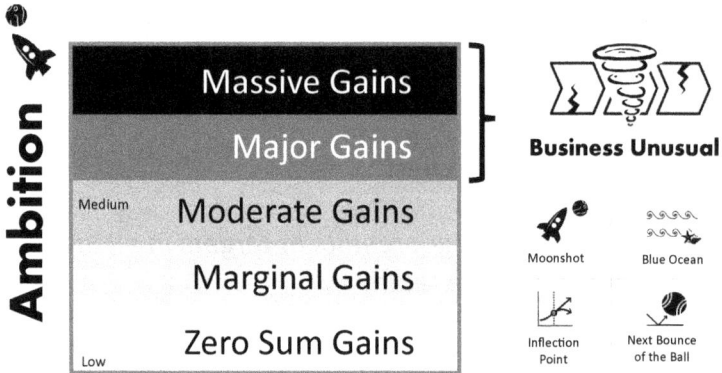

When ambition is bold, there will likely be people who say that it cannot be done. After all, others are likely to have failed in their attempts. **Conviction in the face of cynics and skeptics** is important, as much as leadership and vision.[22]

A big project can be **bold in its approach, as well as its aims**. For example, taking a product to market in 12 rather than 24 or 32 months and thus challenging traditional ways of working. Typically, bold moves require greater speed, agility, collaboration and innovation.[23]

Q: How bold is your big project?

Where is your big project on the scale from risk-averse (1) to daring (10)? When you have given your project a number, pause for a moment to consider:

- What would be required to move your project higher up the scale?

- What are the implications for how the project is being led, reviewed or resourced?

'I cannot square that circle' said the commercial leader in a perplexed tone. 'The growth targets are bold and ambitious, yet the stance regarding risk has not changed. In particular, the approach adopted by compliance, legal and credit control is risk-averse' he continued. 'On the one hand the organization's leadership is saying "grow, grow, grow" while on the other hand its administrative functions are saying "slow, slow, slow!" After a brief pause, he concluded: 'The problem is, I don't see how we can do both!' The CEO listened intensively and after a brief pause responded: 'Thanks for bringing this issue to me, it is something that we must address as the leadership team.'

SUPER AMBITION HAS CONVICTION

The word **strategic intent** is often used in strategy. But super projects need more than intent; they require conviction.

Some project goals feel like aspirations, hopes or dreams. The project mission statement can **read more like a PR statement** rather than a rallying call. However, super ambition is characterized by strength of conviction, determination and belief. Phrases like 'burn your boats or bridges' apply, as organizations and their people commit themselves to an irreversible course. The goals set are neither optional nor merely a nice-to-have.

The project's leadership team came from different departments and backgrounds. Yet, they shared one vital thing in common – a determination that **'failure is not an option.'** The deadlines were ridiculously tight and the compliance burden enormous, but the leaders were determined. This was clear in the extraordinary efforts made from the very start and a pace of progress the organization had never seen before. Regardless of what was thrown at them, the team was determined to pull it off, even if they had to burn themselves out in the process.

Fine words are not enough to demonstrate conviction – leaders need to 'walk the walk,' as well as 'talk the talk.' Moreover, they must 'put their money (and their time) where their mouth is.' As the research highlights, real conviction is demonstrated on 3 levels.

1. **Words** – Where strategies are set out in PowerPoint presentations and people 'talk the talk.'

2. **Deeds** – Where words are matched with deeds, with commitments being put into behaviors and actions.

3. **Resources** – Where the organization's commitment is reflected in the allocation of resources and the commitment of its people is reflected in how they spend their time.

Conviction entails making some choices, often difficult choices regarding which projects to support and which ones not to support. As strategy guru Richard Rumelt puts it, most people and organizations have *a bundle of ambitions* – multiple intentions, visions of the future, and things they would like to see or achieve.'[24] In this context, true conviction starts with the decision to fund one project or initiative ahead of another.[25]

For leaders of big projects, it is important not to **mistake compliance, for commitment**[26] **or even engagement**. A test of conviction is the extent to which people will fight for something and how far they are prepared to go to make it happen.

Q: Is your big project driven by aspiration or conviction?

Highlighted by the CEO as tangible evidence of the organization's brave first steps in a new direction, the strategic initiative had its own stylized logo and slick slide template. This packaging would be important in presenting the right image to stakeholders anxiously awaiting progress.

A minority of stakeholders were skeptical and weary of press releases, fancy slides and 'marketing speak.' They feared that when the gloss was stripped from such high-profile initiatives, there was often little underneath. Such initiatives *'talked the walk but did not walk the talk,* with little in terms of tangible details or specifics.' The project sponsors' willingness to engage with skeptics would be an important test of conviction.

Some element of hype is essential in getting big projects approved. But executives have learned to be wary of the fanfare around new initiatives. Thus, big projects must walk a fine line between 'selling the dream' and 'keeping it real.' However, leaders must **signal commitment in tangible ways**.

Q: How does your organization and its leadership signal its conviction/commitment for your big project?

'Yes, there is alignment and conviction regarding the key strategic bets we are placing as an organization' said the Head of Strategy. 'All of the Senior Leadership Team is bought in' she added. 'Now, when it comes to the point of execution that is another question' he added. 'On paper everyone agrees, but when it comes to the difficult choices about resources, competing priorities and projects, that is where agreement gets tested, and the real level of commitment becomes clear' continued the leader. 'My goal is to test that commitment early and often, and never to assume anything' she concluded.

SUPER AMBITION CAN

While most organizations face an increasing regulatory burden, some industries, such as pharma or finance, have more regulations than others. Interestingly, even for organizations in the same industry (and thus with the same regulations) the approach varies greatly. Specifically, how leaders engage with the compliance obligations of their ambitious projects and strategies varies depends on two factors – attitude and ownership, as shown in the diagram.

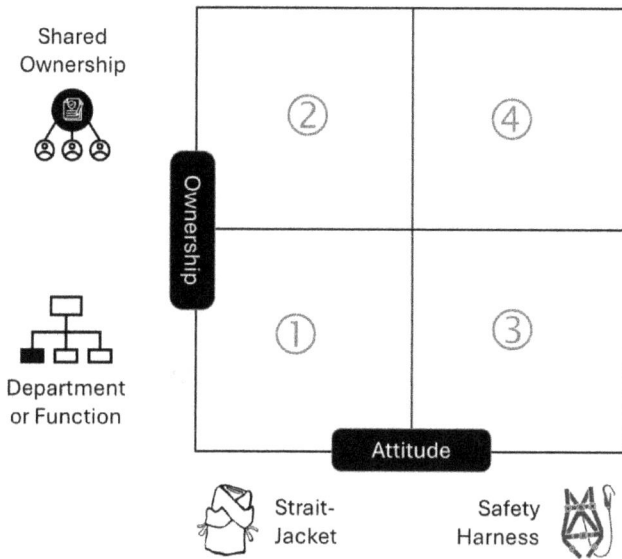

October 2022 and investors were bracing themselves for 'the possibility that Citibank would have to prioritize compliance over growth, potentially for years.'[27] This was the result of a $400 million fine for the bank's 'long-standing failure to establish effective risk management and data governance programs and internal controls.'[28]

Fast-forward two years and the bank had since spent more than $7.4 billion to overhaul its technology and fix its data integrity problems. But it was not enough, with an additional $136 million levied in fines for not fixing its problems quickly enough.[29] Some US senators were even calling for restrictions on the bank's growth claiming it had become too big to manage.[30]

The matrix on the previous page helps in understanding the various relationships between big projects (or more specifically the leaders of big projects) and compliance. It shows that how different projects and their leaders balance ambition with compliance is a matter of ownership and attitude. Let's explore these next.

Attitude

Attitudes vary greatly, and this has an important bearing on how different projects and their leaders engage with compliance and risk. For some leaders, compliance is a 'strait-jacket' (as in the 'slow-grow' example earlier), while for others it is a 'safety-harness' (as in the example that follows).

> 'You have an important role to play on this leadership team' said the director to the newly appointed Head of Compliance. 'Your job is to keep the rest of us out of the courts!' he added with a smile. While the comment was made in a light-hearted manner, it was further evidence of a growing awareness among senior leaders that they could be held personally responsible.

Q: Has there been a compliance impact assessment for your big project?

There are two contrasting attitudes to compliance:

Strait-jacket	Safety Harness
Compliance is seen as a bureaucratic 'blocker' to innovation competitiveness and productivity. Leaders complain that: • Compliance always says 'no,' before you even tell them what the plan is. • They don't realize or appreciate commercial reality / necessity. • Other competitors can do things that we cannot, because of their approach to compliance and risk.	Compliance is necessary to protect the organization, its shareholders and customers. Also, to protect senior leaders who are increasingly in the firing line when things go wrong. Compliance are important partners, helping us to deliver the project / strategy. Regulations are necessary for the public good, they are in the long-term best interests of everybody and create a level and fair playing field in the industry.

Reflecting on the table, which of the two attitudes best reflects your big project(s)? Please use the scale below.

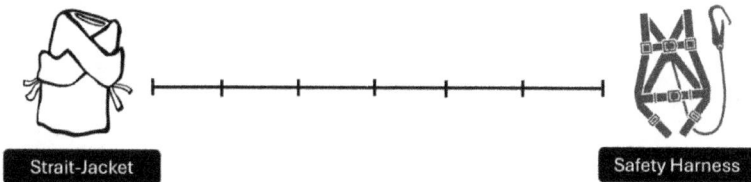

Strait-Jacket

Safety Harness

Attitude is more important than you might think, after all it shapes behavior and everything else. If compliance is seen as an impediment to getting things done, then it will naturally face resistance from leaders. Moreover, attitudes towards compliance tend to be self-perpetuating – we tend to get what we expect.

Importantly, when we start to expect more (greater engagement by compliance with the business or project challenges being faced), we tend to get more.

Ownership

Closely related to attitudes regarding compliance is the issue of ownership. Specifically, who owns or is responsible for compliance? In some organizations compliance is seen as a function; for others it is a shared organization-wide responsibility. These two contrasting styles are explored in the table overleaf.

Use the table to position your organization or project on the ownership continuum, as follows:

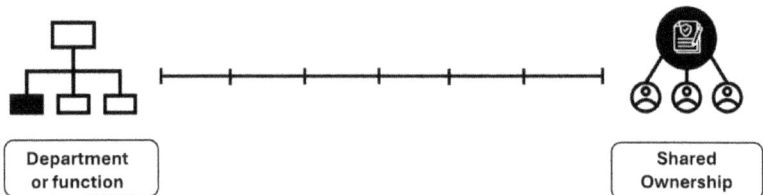

Department
or function

Shared
Ownership

Department or Function	Shared Ownership
Compliance is a department or function, rather than a shared responsibility.	Shared ownership (knowledge and understanding) of compliance and governance obligations.
Tension / tug-of-war between compliance and other business / project objectives.	Proactive approach, where compliance is involved early and throughout.
There may be an unequal relationship, with compliance playing 'bad cop' or seen as a 'blocker.'	Parity of esteem and effective collaboration and joint problem-solving between compliance and project teams.
Siloed approach. A 'them versus us' attitude and reluctance to involve compliance. When involved, it may be too late.	Strategic alignment and unified business goals. Operational resilience and risk management are seen as integral compliance requirements.
Leaders may 'talk the talk' but not 'walk the walk' when it comes to compliance. A culture of accountability may be lacking.	Compliance shares responsibility for project and strategy success.

Importantly, in the context of super projects, all functions and stakeholders must be aligned around business strategy and success. Regardless of functional targets or goals, they put the business first. Thus, shared ownership doesn't just mean that business or project leaders co-own compliance, but that compliance owns its share of business strategy too.

Without alignment in respect of business strategy, there is a risk of business leaders being set up for a futile tug-of-war between the commercial and the compliance agenda. For example, trying to pursue high-growth or high-risk strategies as mandated by the board, but coming up against a stone wall in terms of compliance.

This requires that compliance has a seat at the table when it comes to strategy – that it is represented at the very top of the organization. Compliance doesn't just get to say 'no' and not contribute to finding a better way. They share responsibility for making the project or strategy happen.

There has been a lot of talk about DORA. For those in (or supplying) the EU's financial service sector, DORA stands for the Digital Operational Resilience Act. For everyone else, DORA means something different: **Distributed Ownership of Risk and Accountability**. It reflects a general trend towards increased leadership accountability in respect of corporate governance, resilience and risk.

Regardless of what DORA means to you; the implication is the same. In the coming years we are likely to see more leaders being personally held to account by their organizations, shareholders and, of course, regulators too. As a leader, how you engage with risk, governance and compliance matters more than ever. Adopting a new, more proactive approach is key.

Your Project's Compliance-Ambition Dynamic

Having reflected on what happens, when ambitious projects and strategies meet with compliance, pause to consider:

Q: What steps can your project take to build a collaborative culture around compliance?

The issues of ownership and alignment reflect how leaders of big projects engage with their internal compliance functions but also mirrors how organizations engage with their regulators.

It is important to note that while regulatory complexity is growing, new technologies (incl. Ai) and approaches (e.g., sandboxing) can make it more efficient. These can also play a role in shifting ownership and attitudes towards compliance.

SUPER AMBITION TRANSFORMS

Big projects that are super ambitious have the **potential to transform** organizations, industries and even societies.

If a big project is simply a continuation of what has gone before, then it is probably not ambitious or innovative enough. This is especially true **at a time of accelerating change**. With super projects, the ambition is to transform, **not just to tweak, optimize or improve**. That is to say, super projects are high on the 'business unusual' scale,[31] involving new processes, systems, products, markets and technologies. They tend to be high-risk and high reward.

Q: To what extent is your big project BAU or BU?

To determine the level of business unusual for your big project study the table on the next page. As you will see, business unusual (BU) and business as usual (BAU) differ in terms of ambition, focus, risk/reward and timeframe.

Business Unusual is exactly what it says on the tin: Unusual. It will likely challenge existing ways of working, organizing and managing existing mindsets and behaviors (culture). Indeed, many innovative big projects are **a standoff between business unusual and business as usual**.

Business As Usual	Business Unusual
Modest Ambition	Highly Ambitious
Builds on the Past	Shapes the Future
Focuses on Core Business	New Products, Bus. Models, etc
Marginal / Modest Gains	Major or Massive Gains
Efficiency & Profitability	Transformation
Low Risk / Uncertainty	High Risk / Uncertainty
Short & Medium Term	Long Term

'We are at a crossroads' said the CEO in a matter-of-fact tone of voice. 'I have no doubt that our business in 3 to 5 years will be dramatically different from what it is today' he added. 'It will have to be...' he continued, 'because our market will be very different – some aspects of our customers, channels and competitors will be unrecognizable.' He concluded by saying 'business as usual is not an option.'

Big project leaders often find themselves battling bureaucracy, hierarchy, silos and traditional ways of working. This adds to project complexity (as explored in **Chapter 4**) and can represent a major drain on productivity and energy.[32] To minimize this conflict, big projects may seek to adhere to business as usual, as much as is possible. However, **managing BU projects using BAU methods generally results in under performance**.

Q: Is your business unusual project being managed using traditional methods?

Delivering on BU (business unusual) big projects requires levels of speed, agility, collaboration and innovation that cannot be achieved using BAU (business as usual) methods and processes.

Let's pause there for a moment to check our progress. We have covered the first 6 parts of Super Ambition.

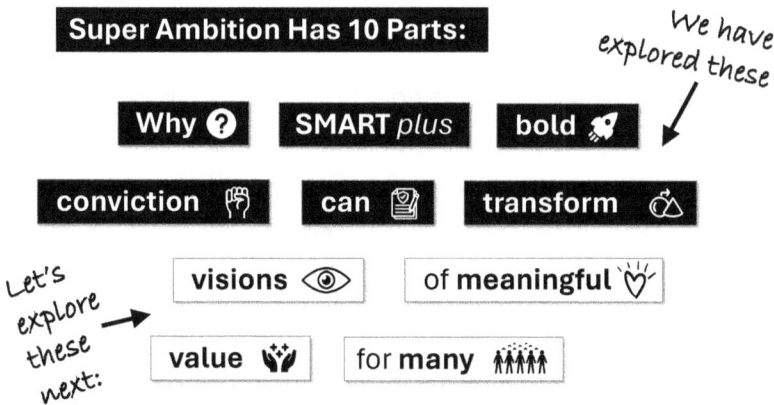

Super Ambition Has 10 Parts:

We have explored these

Why ❓   **SMART** *plus*   **bold** 🚀

conviction 👊   **can** 📝   **transform** ⛰

Let's explore these next:

visions 👁   **of meaningful** 🕯

value 💐   **for many** 🚶

We have passed the half-way mark, so let's finish out the last 4 characteristics of Super Ambition.

SUPER AMBITION = VISION

Ambition is 'super' when it connects to a shared vision of success. That is a vision of success for the project, the organization and all the key stakeholders involved.

Q: Is your big project powered by a shared vision of success?

You may be thinking that success has already been defined in the project plan. However, reading that probably won't get people excited. It may not generate the required shared ownership, engagement, or buy-in either.

A written definition of success can be a powerful part of the planning process. However, **visualizing success** takes goal-setting to another level. It is more powerful because it connects to imagination and emotion.

Asking people to share (in their own words) their vision of success is one of **the most powerful ways to energize** and engage key internal stakeholders. It connects to something much more powerful than the project mission statement or list of deliverables.

Visualizing success means **beginning with the end in mind**. It is essential to **ensure resilience and discipline** in the face of inevitable setbacks and disappointments. Moreover, a vision of success entails **imagining or re-imagining the future**. That may be a future that others probably cannot see, so it requires leadership belief and conviction.

As one of the most popular strategy books of the past decade puts it: 'Winning should be at the heart of any strategy.'[33] Every big project or initiative should be based on a **shared vision of success** and the benefits that it will bring for all those involved. However, that does not mean that everybody's vision is the same. The vision for compliance or for credit control may be different from that for marketing or HR, for example.[34] That is not a problem when they get shared and if they complement rather than conflict with each other.

In a day of back-to-back presentations, one presentation stood out. It made a bold promise – in the form of a simple visual that caught the attention of the board:

Product X: What success looks like...

2024
35m

2027*
95m

*Net of growth through acquisitions.

Most of the other presentations were full of detail on the 'what' and the 'how,' yet vague on the 'why.' Few had **reliable information about the price tag or the payback**. This was a proposal that sold the sizzle. The goal was both ambitious and clear.

The vision of a brighter future is an important element of strategy, so too is **confronting challenges and problems** head on.[35] Often this can be the greatest spur to innovation and change.

SUPER AMBITION IS MEANINGFUL

Super Ambition goes beyond targets and numbers to **connect with passion and purpose** for those involved. In other words, it is meaningful. This is the 8th factor tied to super ambition in our research.

'There are only two ways to influence human behavior' writes the bestselling author Simon Sinek.[36] That is '...you can manipulate it, or you can inspire it.' Taking this advice, big project leaders need to **discover the passion** that ignites their key stakeholders and teams. Very often that is not what they assume it to be.

The real motivations of stakeholders and teams are often a 'black box.' However, a leader cannot tap into motivations and passions if they don't know what they are. People themselves decide what is meaningful to them. So, **telling them what matters, or why, is not enough.** Leaders must ask them, too.

There is a lot of talk about burning platforms – an existential crisis that compels action. But which is the more powerful motivator – pressure or passion? Well, **a burning passion could be up to 3 times more powerful than a burning platform** in terms of its intrinsic motivational power. That is because it connects to purpose and passion, not just to spreadsheets and shareholder values.[37]

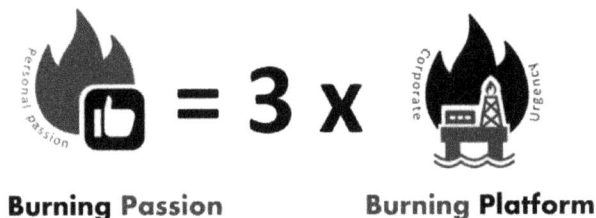

Burning Passion   **Burning Platform**

It is unlikely that **a description of what your project does**, or will do, is enough to give it meaning or define its purpose. Finding meaning requires asking more fundamental questions, such as:

- Why does this project exist?
- Why does it matter?
- What gives its work meaning?

Here are some other questions to give your big project meaning:

- Why does the project team exist?
- What makes us special? What sets us apart?
- Who do we serve? Why? How?
- What value do we create? What good do we do?
- Why do we want to belong to this team?
- What are we most proud of?
- What does the team want to be known for / as?

Use these questions to connect to the passion and purpose for your project team. Integrate these questions into regular project reviews and presentations to continuously **connect to meaning and purpose**.

'The strategy is to double revenue within 5 years' proclaimed the CEO brimming with confidence. If only everyone shared the same enthusiasm. 'How was that goal set?' many wondered. 'Does this not jar with last year's decision to cut the field engineering team by 20%?' they wondered. 'Here we go again' others thought, recalling how rushing previous product extensions had resulted in returns and lawsuits.

The above is not an unusual story, with more strategies being dictated by a spreadsheet in response to the need to deliver a particular number to meet shareholder and ROI expectations. However, it can be a crude exercise, leading to short-term financially expedient decisions, with long-term consequences. A more wholesome agenda, fueled by sustainable growth, value creation and innovation, is central to super ambition.

SUPER AMBITION IS VALUE CREATING

In times of market uncertainty and slowing growth, the focus turns to cost-cutting, consolidation and efficiency. However, super projects must also focus on **value creation, innovation and growth**.[38]

Naturally, business performance and maximizing shareholder returns are the central goal. But cuts alone won't deliver long-term performance. Customer focused **value creation is the primary source of sustained performance and growth in organizations**, industries and even societies. It is the ultimate driver of profitability and the root source of competitive advantage.[39]

Super projects create value or enhance the organization's capacity for value creation. That is not just financial value, but customer value, brand value, employee value, etc.

Super projects contribute to a better future and **strive to make the world a better place**. They resist the temptation to sacrifice long-term value for short-term results.[40] Labels such as customer-centric, people-positive, ethical, socially responsible and sustainable apply.

'You cannot serve two masters' thought the product team leader. Speaking out loud, he was trying to make sense of the data. 'Our stakeholders say we are very committed and indeed important to the organization – rating these at 90% plus. But, in terms of importance and commitment to them, they rated our team at just 60%. It is fascinating! Are their needs different from those of the business?' he asked rhetorically. 'They must be!' he answered after a pause.

However, the clarity the leader sought came on the next page, where stakeholders rated the team's understanding of their needs in the early 50s and of their roles and responsibilities in the early 60s. For the leader, the conclusion was clear: 'Our stakeholders feel we don't know or understand them.' After a short pause, he said with determination: 'This is something that we need to change immediately.'

Here are all the things that value creation could mean – use this list to create your own definition:[41]

- Unlocking Potential: Creating an environment where your people can realize more and more of their full potential.[42]
- Job Creation: Providing employment opportunities and skills training.
- Inclusivity: Equality and diversity – ensuring that benefits reach marginalized or underrepresented groups.
- Social Impact: Addressing societal issues such as poverty, healthcare, and education.

- Environmental Sustainability: Initiatives to combat climate change and protect natural resources.

- Ethical Conduct: Promoting fairness, equality, and justice.

- Cultural Development: Arts, heritage, and community.

- Innovation: New technologies, products, or processes that improve the quality of work / life.

- Public Welfare: Creating public goods and services that benefit a broad section of the community.

- Civic Engagement: Encouraging participation in governance and community decisions.

- Education: Access to quality education and information.

Pause to reflect.

Q: How will your big project create or add value for your organization and its stakeholders?

The CEO's statement was carried widely in the media. It promised major investment in strategies for growth and value creation, with particular emphasis on new products and technologies that would ensure the organization's 'continued success in the digital future.' For the middle managers, the message would have been welcomed if it had been believed. However, it jarred with the reality of an organization whose internal focus was almost exclusively on cost reduction and efficiency, including the closure of offices and head count reduction. Meanwhile, those leading the organization's biggest projects knew that they must stay focused on what was in front of them.

SHARED BY MANY

The question arises: **'Whose ambition is it?'** Often the answer is: 'It is the ambition of senior management' or 'these are the demands of investors and shareholders.' But super projects are not just the ambition of a few, but of many.

Leaders are ambitious, often envisioned as visionary figures charging ahead, pursuing a vision unseen or misunderstood by others. However, the real challenge for those leading super ambitious projects is not to race ahead alone, but to empower others to lead the charge alongside them. That **model of shared ambition is at the core of super ambition**.

Super ambitious big projects appeal to a wider stakeholder audience. That includes the project team, customers, suppliers and others too. Super ambition to **generate a win-win for all their key stakeholders**, not just shareholders or those at the top of the organization.

Surprised at the data that suggested a lack of clarity and alignment around the project, the pharma leader began to restate the project goals, deliverables and deadlines. Adding, 'surely this is stuff that everybody knows.' 'Interesting' replied the coach after a short pause. 'Is there another aspect to "the why" of the project?' she asked. 'For example, what about the patients' lives that will be improved with this drug?' 'Oh, of course," said the leader, adding: 'We always forget that, yet it is the real reason why we do this work.'

For every initiative, there will **be winners and losers**. Then there will be those for whom the impact will be neutral. So, break your audience into these 3 groups and adapt your approach accordingly. You will be hoping that some of the people who think that they are in the loser group can be moved to some of the other groups.

Q: How widely shared is your big project's ambition?

ANALYSIS & REFLECTION

Super projects are powered by a special type of ambition that propels projects further and faster. Use the panel on the next page to explore your big project's super ambition.

There is a sure way to boost project success and reduce the risk of failure or frustration. However, although very effective, it is neither an attractive nor a desirable solution. That is to curtail the level of ambition – setting more modest goals and playing it safe.

When we dream big, when we strive for innovation and creativity, we inevitably risk disappointment and perhaps even failure. We open ourselves up to criticism, cynicism and doubt. But that is what those leading and sponsoring super projects do daily. What is fascinating is when super ambition meets with super confidence, as we will see in the next chapter.

Why ❓

What is the clear & compelling why for your project?

_____
_____
_____

See how 'super' your project's ambition is by filing out the panels:

SUPER AMBITION

conviction ✊

How is the conviction driving the project evident?

_____
_____
_____

bold 🚀

What makes this project bold and daring?

_____
_____
_____

visions 👁

What is the vision of success?

_____
_____
_____

transform 🐦

What is transformative about this project?

_____
_____
_____

for many 👥

How wide will the benefits be distributed?

_____
_____
_____

value 🌿

How will this project create value?

_____
_____
_____

SMART _plus_

How will project progress & business impact be measured?

_____
_____
_____

can (compliance) 📋

What are the compliance constraints on ambition?

_____
_____
_____

of **meaningful** 💓

How does it connect to purpose & passion?

_____
_____
_____

CHAPTER 2:

SUPER CONFIDENCE

INTRODUCTION

It takes confidence to deliver a big project. Indeed, the bigger the project, the more confidence is needed. So, **super projects must need super confidence**, right? Well, that was one of the central hypotheses behind our research, and we were confident that it would be readily validated. However, we were in for a surprise. The result is a re-think of super confidence and the means of connecting it not just to success, but to reality too.

WHAT IS SUPER CONFIDENCE?

Super Confidence is **an unshakable belief**, among senior leaders, in the success of their big projects and ambitious strategies. We were certain that the data would highlight this super confidence as a key differentiator among big projects, their leaders, and sponsors. **To our surprise, it didn't!**

Mapping levels of confidence to big project success resulted in more questions than answers. Especially, when we tried to map high levels of confidence (such as 90%, 95% and 100%) against project outputs and business outcomes. **The data failed to show a clear link** between super confidence and big project success.

Could the numbers be wrong, or were we missing something? For some time, we were left scratching our heads, looking for an answer. Finally, after plenty of conversations, data and analysis, **the conundrum that is big project super confidence** became clearer.

WHO IS SUPER CONFIDENT?

At a time of accelerating change and uncertainty, when there are so many projects competing for scarce resources, **the demand for confidence is up. But so too is the supply!**

At senior leadership levels, **super confidence is a given**. It is now the norm, or the default state, regarding big projects and ambitious strategies. As one of our colleagues often jokes: 'leaders who express doubt or uncertainty about a big project are almost as rare as unicorns and mermaids.'

Little wonder that it is difficult to distinguish between big projects and super projects based on the level of confidence in success. That is because **almost everybody in senior leadership is confident** of big project success. Indeed, most are super confident.

WHY SO CONFIDENT?

Big projects must compete for scarce resources against other departmental and organizational priorities and agendas. Moreover, big projects have the power to **make or break reputations** and even careers. These are the realities of big projects within large organizations.

For any ambitious project, there will be people who say that it cannot be done, that the plan has holes, or the execution is flawed. Some will even doubt the capability and commitment of the leader and the team. **In the face of uncertainty, cynicism and doubt**, project leaders and sponsors must demonstrate super confidence.

Q: What is the level of confidence around your big project?

Fact, feeling or fiction: confidence is all these things and more besides. Most important of all, confidence is a critical strategy for (a) promoting or selling new projects and (b) protecting and sustaining existing ones.

Key to understanding the importance, as well as the prevalence, of super confidence is the realization that big project **confidence is a political and social construct**, not just a logical or analytical one. There can be times when it is influenced more by power, position and even ego, than the quality of the strategy, the probability of success or even the nature of reality.

> 'Some call it the shark pool' said the ambitious sponsor. 'You have 90 minutes in front of the 15 senior executives that form the investment committee' she explained. 'The focus is on selling the project, with no room for doubt or uncertainty. To demonstrate total confidence in the required outcome you drop words such as *may*, *could* or *should*' she added. It was the opposite to the type of project conversations she hoped to have with her own team.

AN ORGANIZATIONAL DEFAULT

Here are some of the reasons why super confidence has become **an organizational default** when it comes to big projects:

1. Super confidence is key to **selling a project**, enlisting support and accessing scarce resources (ahead of competing projects and priorities).

2. There can be a lot of **hype** around big projects; living up to the hype requires super confidence.

3. Failure is not an option. Increased **pressure to perform, and** business urgency make visible confidence essential.

4. It is **not safe** to talk about risks, obstacles and setbacks. People often stay silent or simply nod in agreement.[43]

5. Confidence has long been held as an essential **leadership trait**, especially required in inspiring others.[44] Moreover, there is a **general belief** that confident people and teams are likely to be more successful.[45]

6. There is a long-standing, yet **mistaken, belief** that talking about risks, obstacles and setbacks is negative and demotivating.[46]

7. There has long been a gap between strategy and execution. Those at the top may be **divorced from reality on the ground,** with many senior leaders adopting a 'don't ask, don't tell' approach to big projects.[47]

Added to the above, there are the everyday **biases that shape our thinking**. Written about by Nobel Prize-winning economists and bestselling authors, heuristics such as the optimism bias, the planning fallacy and groupthink help to put the 'super' in super confidence.[48] The warning is stark:

> *"Perhaps the most robust finding in the psychology of judgment is that people are overconfident."*
> Werner De Bondt & Richard Thaler[49]

Rather than a steady upward progress curve, **complex 'business unusual' projects have ups and downs**. Like the classic hero's journey, the story of a big project starts with great hope and promise. Inevitably, that does not last, with obstacles and setbacks testing our project leading organizational heroes.

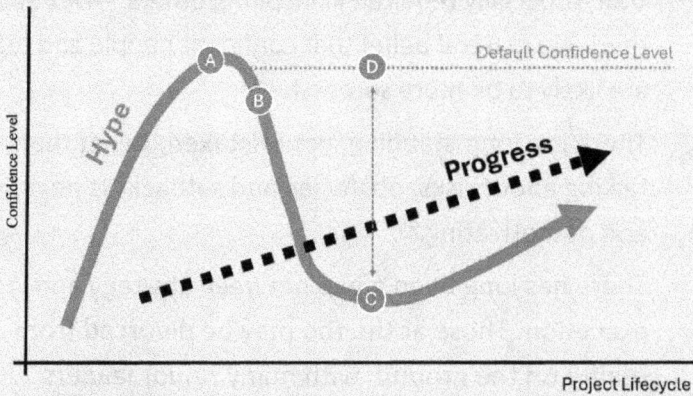

For every project, two curves intersect. First, the roller-coaster shaped hype curve reflects the requirements of enlisting support and accessing resources. Second, the progress curve, as a project starts to gain momentum and demonstrate progress. Key points on the journey include:

A = Max. Confidence – the goal is to 'sell' the project.
B = Reality starts to kick-in and challenges become clear.
C = Crisis of Confidence – a project's wobbly moment.[50]
D = Default Confidence – leaders can't go below this!

Pause for a moment to reflect on where your big project is on the diagram above.

A LINK TO SUCCESS?

The prevalence of super confidence helps explain why confidence is **not enough to predict success**. After all, if something so widespread was the vital ingredient, then big project success would be universal. Clearly, however, it is not.

Based on our research, super confidence is everywhere except in the data on big project success. The reason is obvious and does not require any more statistical analysis. It is because, no matter how confident big project leaders may be, **super confidence is not certainty!**

Super
Confidence  Absolute
Certainty

There is a **gap between super confidence and certainty** regarding success. The gap is greatest for business unusual projects and initiatives that involve a leap into the unknown and unfamiliar (e.g., new products, processes, technologies and so on).[51]

Change, innovation and disruption stretch the super confidence / certainty gap. This is most evident when business unusual big projects are run using business as usual methods.[52]

Those leading ambitious big projects must **walk a tightrope** between 'selling the dream' (required to access resources and gain support) and 'keeping it real' (required for effective execution). That is another way of looking at the gap between super confidence and success.

Selling The DREAM!

Keeping It REAL!

To ensure access to funding and support, 'selling the dream' is essential. But dreamland is not the home of effective planning and execution. 'Keeping it real' is essential to bring ambitious plans to life.

Pause to reflect: On a scale where 1 is 'keeping it real' and 10 is 'selling the dream,' where is your project today? Moreover, how effectively is your project walking the tightrope between the two?

LOOKING INTO THE GAP

We started this 'super projects research' expecting to find a link between super confidence and big project success. Instead, we found a gap to explain **why project performance and project success often diverge**.

The gap is the reason super confidence alone is not enough. Filling the gap requires something in addition to super confidence. But what might that be?

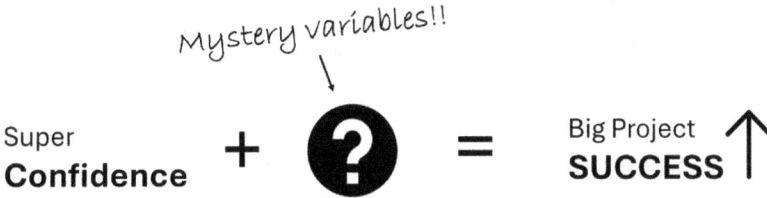

Mystery variables!!

Super **Confidence** **+** **?** **=** Big Project **SUCCESS** ↑

We peered into the gap between super confidence and certainty of success through our datasets. Before long, **a few surprise variables caught our attention**. When combined with super confidence, these mystery or rogue variables seemed to narrow the gap. They had the power to shift patterns of behavior, conversation and even analysis regarding big project success.

WHAT ARE THE MYSTERY VARIABLES?

Let's reveal the mystery variables with reference to **two archetypical super confident leaders**:

- The first leader instructs his team to **hide the slides on risks and dependencies** ahead of a big project update to the senior leadership team. For this super confident leader, talk of risks and obstacles is dangerous and could signal a lack of commitment or determination.

- The second leader asks her big project team to **keep risks and obstacles in the spotlight**, believing that talking about these would galvanize, rather than paralyze, the project team or its key internal stakeholders. Also, that it is essential to the management of project risk.

Have these two real-world scenarios helped you to figure out what **the mystery or rogue variables** might be? They are the variables which, when added to super confidence:

- Bridge the gap between confidence and certainty.
- Strengthen the link between confidence and success.

Based on the stories of the two leaders, we asked executives **what the mystery variables might be**. The answers included: 'talking about risks,' 'obstacles and dependencies,' 'engaging with uncertainty,' 'embracing complexity,' 'entertaining doubt' or even 'keeping it real.' These are all good answers. However, the 6 mystery or rogue variables identified from our research are **strategic curiosity, candor, courage, clarity, credit and compliance**. We call these the 6Cs of Super Confidence.

THE MYSTERY VARIABLES REVEALED

Big projects and their leaders already have super confidence, so what else do they need? The answer is:

1. **Strategic Curiosity**[53] – Ask bold questions to unlock new possibilities. The ability to keep an open mind, engage with and be curious about alternative options and scenarios, perspectives and information or data. Other words for curiosity include openness, searching, learning, exploring, experimenting and reflecting.

2. **Strategic Clarity** – Know what matters and make it unmistakably clear. Ensuring greater clarity regarding key aspects of the strategy, with ongoing communication that avoids assuming people already know.

3. **Credit** - Recognize progress and give credit to yourself and others. Recognizing progress is a powerful, low-cost way to fuel confidence and maintain momentum in big projects.

4. **Strategic Candor** – Speak the truth with respect and precision. The ability to 'call it' and to listen to (and even encourage) others to do the same. Another term for this is 'respectful challenge.'[54]

5. **Strategic Courage** – Act decisively, especially when the outcome is uncertain. The ability to be curious and candid (as above) when the temptation is to be neither.[55] Being curious and candid often requires courage.

6. **Compliance** – The compliance regime now mandates operational resilience and risk management in respect of projects that impact on core systems and services.

These 6Cs are an expanded definition of Super Confidence. They calibrate confidence, narrowing the gap between super confidence and the certainty of success by enabling a new engagement with potential risks and dependencies, alternative data, perspectives and scenarios.

Bridging the Gap: 6Cs

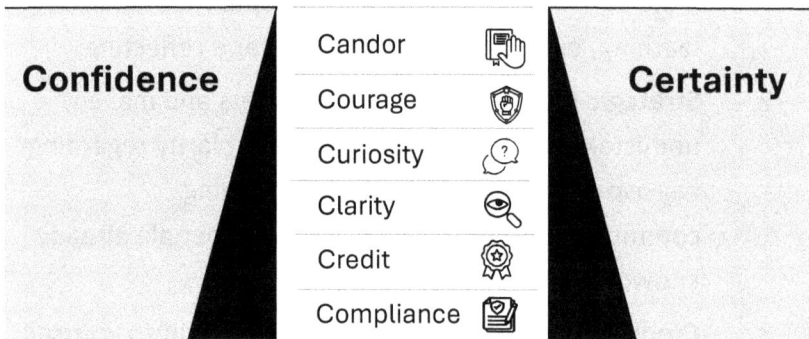

Confidence	Candor	Certainty
	Courage	
	Curiosity	
	Clarity	
	Credit	
	Compliance	

The 6Cs play an important role in calibrating confidence. Senior leaders can easily find themselves in a 'high confidence / good news only' bubble, impervious to talk of setbacks or obstacles. That is because, as a **'high status individual'** people are likely to tell you what you want to hear, rather than telling you the truth, especially if it is bad news. Moreover, the fact that you are busy and under pressure means that you have little time or patience to be involved in mundane project conversations, especially those where people seem to be focused on problems (such as a lack of resources) rather than solutions. Escaping the 'high confidence / good news bubble' requires the 6Cs. That is leaders being more curious, while encouraging others to be more candid and courageous in speaking up. Also, leaders being increasingly aware of the requirements of compliance.

The first phase of our research highlighted the importance of doubt (or what we called 'niggling doubt') in bringing ambitious strategies to life.[56] Full of conviction, we started encouraging leaders to embrace doubt and uncertainty. In hindsight, that was a mistake!

Today, we ask leaders **what they need in order to double-down on the level of confidence and ambition behind their big project(s)**. Moreover, we share the 6Cs as ways to double-down. The first is to be a little more curious. For example, 3%, 5% or 10% more curious about alternative scenarios, divergent perspectives and project risks, obstacles or setbacks. The other related strategies are to encourage others to be more candid and courageous in project conversations, presentations and reviews. Also to strive for greater clarity.

SUPER CONFIDENCE: An Expanded Definition

Apply the 6Cs to illuminate:

- Potential risks, obstacles, dependencies & setbacks.
- Alternative perspectives, scenarios or outcomes
- Conversations that need to be had.
- Progress being made.

strategic Curiosity
strategic Clarity
Credit For Progress
strategic Candor
SUPER CONFIDENCE
strategic Courage
Compliance
Resilience & Risk Management

LET'S NOT GET PERSONAL!

The temptation when it comes to variables such as curiosity, candor or courage is to get personal. To point to a particular big project leader or sponsor and their personality or character as either being curious or not, candid or not, and so on.

However, this is not a character debate. These factors say as much about the organization, as it does about any specific leader or their big project. Curiosity, candor or courage are not just a personality trait, but **an organizational necessity**.

The **challenge for organizations is to inject greater curiosity, candor and courage** into big projects and ambitious strategies at all stages. That includes project plans, project reviews, updates and presentations. Furthermore, into the various aspects of strategic planning and resource allocation.

> **Candor became a popular leadership concept** in recent years. It argued that leaders had been avoiding difficult conversations, to not 'rock the boat' and 'spare people's blushes.' But, if leaders have been more inclined to 'tell it like it is,' have they also been more prepared to listen to others do the same?
>
> Well, a decade of research into psychological safety tells us that many executives (even senior executives) are likely to stay silent or nod in agreement, rather than speak truth to power, or even to the spreadsheet, the project plan and the project review.[57] Yet, the leaders of super projects see safety in talking about risks, obstacles and setbacks. They see it as too dangerous not to do so.

An Expanded Definition of SUPER CONFIDENCE

Where are the 6Cs Needed?

- Project Planning
- Project Reviews
- Project Conversations
- Project Presentations
- Forecasting & Budgeting
- Risk Management

STRATEGIC CLARITY

Curiosity, candor and courage may require some work on the part of leaders and their teams. A more direct and straightforward means to underpin confidence is to **improve clarity around strategy**. That means including transparency around decisions, choices and tradeoffs, as well as how they are made.

Naturally, people will struggle to be confident in the strategy if they are not fully clear on what it is, why it matters or how it will be implemented. This doesn't mean that those running or sponsoring projects have not set out clear strategies or plans, but rather that this information may not have reached all those who need to know. Some may have been given the information, but have failed to read it, others will have read it but may have forgotten. Hence the importance of ongoing communication regarding a project even when you think that 'everybody already knows.'

Taking a drug to market can be a high stakes gamble.[58] In particular, costs quickly escalate as an asset moves through the different stages of development. Paradoxically, therefore, companies with higher early-stage attrition enjoy greater overall success in commercializing their R&D. However, this is an area where over-confidence can be very costly. Analysts in pharma warning is that: 'Imprudent progression decisions are pervasive in the industry.'[59] Hence the importance of greater curiosity, courage and candor in enabling project leaders to 'call it early.'

CONFIDENCE THROUGH CREDIT

Many leaders and teams underestimate the value of recognizing progress. Yet giving credit – both to others and to oneself – is one of the simplest, most effective ways to build confidence. It reinforces the sense that the goal is achievable and energizes people to keep going.

Recognizing what's been accomplished so far, even in small steps, helps people feel that their work matters and is making a difference. This isn't about celebration for its own sake. Rather, it's about fueling belief, creating momentum, and building the emotional reserves needed when things get tough. Recognition is powerful, free, and too often overlooked. In the rush to deliver, organizations frequently forget to mark progress, missing an easy opportunity to boost motivation and resilience.

QUICK RECAP

Now that we have explored the first five of the 6Cs at a high level, pause for a moment to reflect on **how they apply to your big project**. Using the page overleaf, rate the factors using the stars provided. Next, you can use the panels to:

- Explore areas where any of the 5Cs (clarity, courage, etc.) may be required

- Note times when you or your team displayed the 5Cs.

Four of the five Cs (as on the page overleaf) could be considered 'soft,' as they deal with attitudes and behavior. However, the 5th C is the opposite as it relates to regulatory compliance. Let's explore how considerations of compliance calibrate confidence next.

COMPLIANT CONFIDENCE

Super confident leaders abound, except in one part of the business. Yes, you guessed it – the compliance function. As one leader put it, 'to be working in compliance is to be constantly concerned about what could go wrong.' Increasingly, however, that effect is **spreading beyond the compliance function**.

Leaders have been progressively spending more time on issues related to governance and compliance. Like it or not, that is going to continue, with increased leadership accountability for, as well as an expanding definition of, governance and compliance. This is a shift in the regulatory environment as well as in organizational culture. This is having an important mediating effect on high levels of confidence.

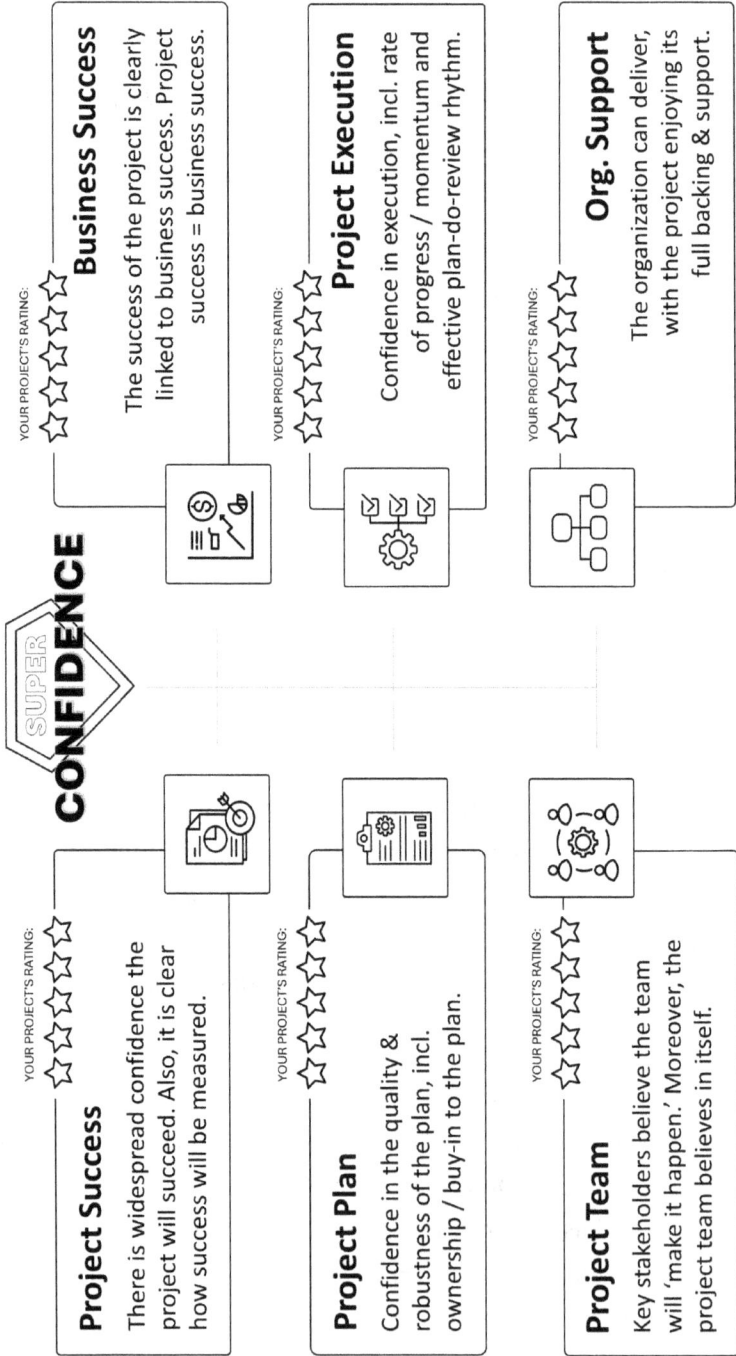

CONFIDENCE

SUPER

Business Success

YOUR PROJECT'S RATING:
☆☆☆☆☆

The success of the project is clearly linked to business success. Project success = business success.

Project Execution

YOUR PROJECT'S RATING:
☆☆☆☆☆

Confidence in execution, incl. rate of progress / momentum and effective plan-do-review rhythm.

Org. Support

YOUR PROJECT'S RATING:
☆☆☆☆☆

The organization can deliver, with the project enjoying its full backing & support.

Project Success

YOUR PROJECT'S RATING:
☆☆☆☆☆

There is widespread confidence the project will succeed. Also, it is clear how success will be measured.

Project Plan

YOUR PROJECT'S RATING:
☆☆☆☆☆

Confidence in the quality & robustness of the plan, incl. ownership / buy-in to the plan.

Project Team

YOUR PROJECT'S RATING:
☆☆☆☆☆

Key stakeholders believe the team will 'make it happen.' Moreover, the project team believes in itself.

In times gone by, the term CYA ('Cover Your Ass') was seen as a selfish and underhand behavior that put personal and political interests ahead of organizational goals. However, the changing regulatory environment means that **CYA has a new meaning** – 'Cause You're Accountable.' This is our clear warning to leaders with big projects and big portfolios.

Things will go wrong – even if DORA[60] or similar regulations don't affect you, Murphy's Law certainly does! As business leaders we need to be able to show that we have taken all reasonable precautions to prevent disaster and disruption, also to mitigate the effects when it does happen. The first step here is the ability to engage openly with obstacles, dependencies and setbacks – talking about them, documenting them, planning for them and so on.[61]

As leaders we can be prone to optimism bias, which can be costly, especially in a regulated sector such as financial services. There management and mitigation of risk demands more than *'forward-looking Statements of Good Intention or Expectation.'*[62] So said the UK regulator in fining one banking CIO approx. $100,000 following a failed systems migration within the TSB bank (estimated to have cost the bank over $400 million).[63] It was a watershed moment, with an executive being fined, not just their organization. So, beware of SOGIE (Statements of Good Intention or Expectation) – it is a false and a dangerous form of super confidence.

Increasingly, the 'manager in charge' is on the firing line if a big project goes wrong with both regulators and boards. So, let's look at ways of calibrating ambition with compliance, as well as the 6Cs more generally.

> While DORA has stolen the headlines, there are a total of 18 critical sectors (pharmaceutical manufacturing facilities, government administrative agencies, etc.) affected by a lesser-known EU **network and information systems** (NIS) **cybersecurity directive.** This is further evidence of the increasing role of compliance. As a rule, medium-sized and large entities in these critical sectors,[64] must take appropriate cybersecurity risk-management measures and notify relevant national authorities of incidents that could cause significant disruption or damage.

CONFIDENCE AS A SHIELD

Let's take a different tack on super confidence and the traditional warnings against both over-confidence and under-confidence. In particular, leveraging the knowledge that big project super confidence is largely a political and social concept.

Super Confidence is an essential part of the leadership armory:

- **It shields leaders and their projects** from the potentially paralyzing effects of doubt and uncertainty.
- It protects against attack from **skeptics and cynics**, from competing projects and priorities, too.

- It **shields reputations and protects** the leader's power and position.
- It safeguards strategies, **budgets and resources**.

While confidence is essential, it **should <u>not</u> be used to**:

- Shield a project from reality.
- Block new ideas and information.
- Deflect all doubt and uncertainty.
- Prevent the questioning of assumptions or exploration of alternative scenarios.
- Block constructive feedback.
- Inhibit strategic conversations.
- Stop people talking about risk, obstacles or setbacks (and thereby neglecting their compliance responsibilities in respect of operational resilience and risk management).

With so much ambition driving strategy, calibrating super confidence with reality is key. Greater curiosity can prevent super confidence turning into **systematic organizational overconfidence** or hubris.

The project coach was baffled. After 2 hours talking about the practical challenges and obstacles being faced, the project leadership still rated confidence as 'high' or 'very high.' **Confidence is surely a conundrum,** mused the coach. Did the team really believe success was inevitable, or were the stubbornly high ratings:

- A sign of overconfidence?
- A reflection of the determination of the team, or the reality that failure was not an option?
- An indication that it was not safe to talk of risk?
- A blind spot re risk management and compliance?

Using the diagram, how can your project shield against the factors on the left, while engaging with the factors on the right?

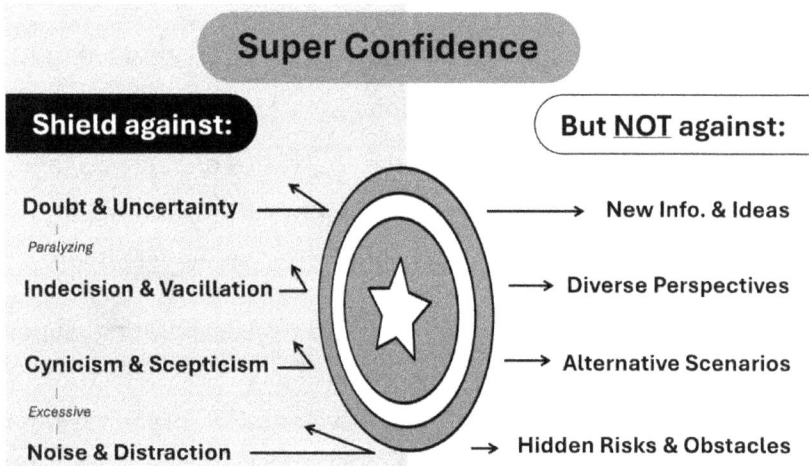

READY TO DROP THE SHIELD?

Given the pressure to sell new projects and to deliver in respect of existing projects, many leaders feel that they can never drop their shield of super confidence. For example, they 'only do good news' and cannot talk (or allow others to talk about) risk, obstacles or setbacks.

Yet, big project leaders and sponsors **cannot always be on the defensive** – seeing threats everywhere – in stakeholder interactions, project reviews, board meetings and so on. When this happens, a project's primary concern becomes promoting and protecting itself. The power, budget and reputation of the project and its leaders come first, and stakeholders and the organization come second.[65] People's focus turns to playing it safe, making themselves look good and covering their backs.

Even the most confident big project leader must occasionally lower the shield (of super confidence) to let in new ideas and information.

Fatigue had set in. The strategy committee had been sitting for 3 hours, with just one short break. The projects discussed in the first hour had received ample time for questions and debate. However, the pace had accelerated steadily with each successive presentation. Now, the last projects would have just 15 minutes! Stay high and keep it positive, thought the project sponsor as she started her presentation. There would be **no time for curiosity, candor or even conversation.** For the plain-speaking project leader, ditching her factual style for a more 'salesy' approach would be a challenge.

ANALYSIS & REFLECTION

Are you ready to drop the shield and add curiosity, candor, courage and clarity to your super confidence? If yes, here is a tool to help you. It deconstructs project confidence into 6 parts, as shown overleaf.

First, take a moment to check the meaning of the different headings (e.g., Overall Project Success). There is an overview of each of these over the coming pages.

Next, rate your big project on each of the factors using the 5 star scale. When you are finished you can add up the total number of stars. The max. score is 30, with Super Confidence being a score of 25 or above. As a second step, reflect on any of the headings that are rated 3 or below. How might confidence in these areas be increased?

Note: The objective is not to boost confidence, or even to go beyond super confidence. It is to leverage curiosity, candor, courage and clarity in exploring the gap between super confidence and certainty of success. This analysis is part of our suite of analytical tools. In the following pages you will find details for each of the 6 dimensions of confidence.

'Cultivate a culture that is open to dissent' is the advice of Prof. Adam Waytz, Kellogg School of Management[66] in a review of the Citibank Mortgage Fraud settlement of $158 million in 2012. Rather than being seen as an act of disloyalty, calling-it should be seen as *'an act of larger loyalty – loyalty to the community in which you operate, loyalty to society, and ultimately loyalty to the long-term success of your company.'*

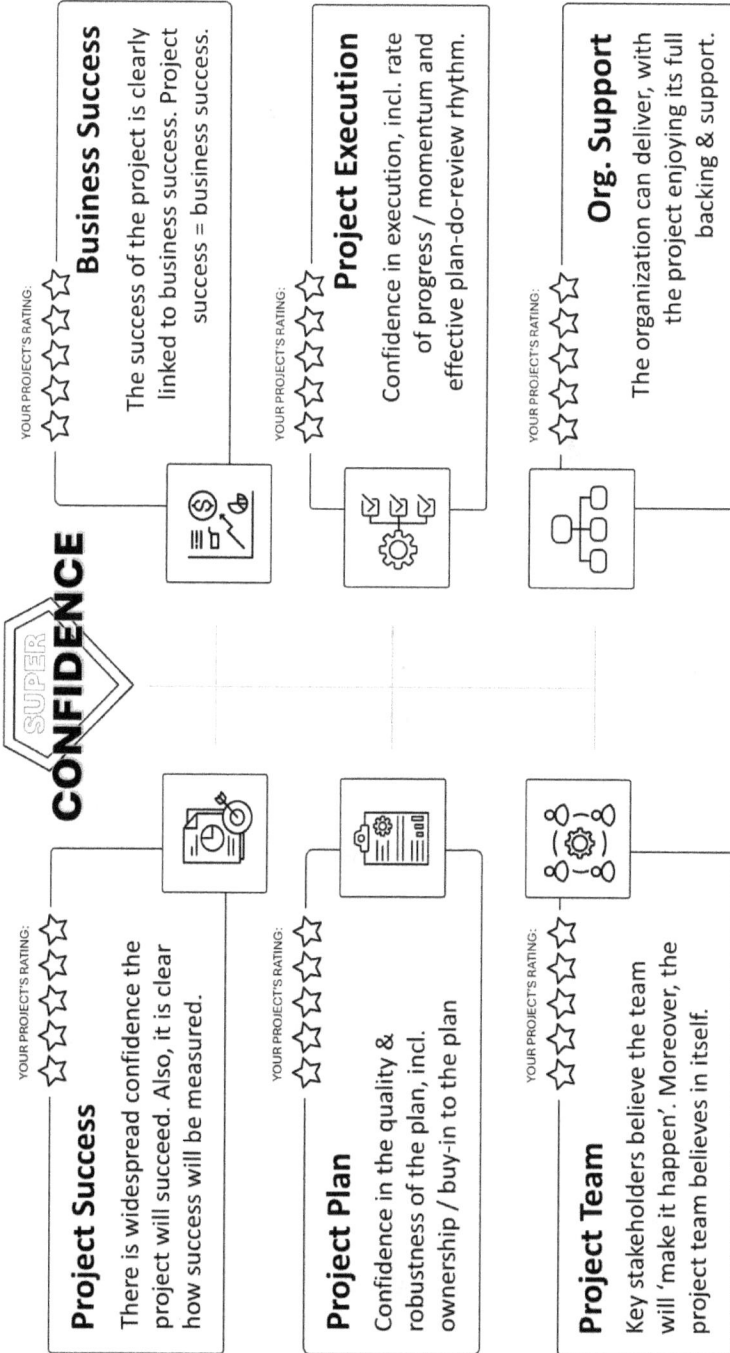

SUPER CONFIDENCE

Project Success

YOUR PROJECT'S RATING: ☆☆☆☆☆

There is widespread confidence the project will succeed. Also, it is clear how success will be measured.

Project Plan

YOUR PROJECT'S RATING: ☆☆☆☆☆

Confidence in the quality & robustness of the plan, incl. ownership / buy-in to the plan

Project Team

YOUR PROJECT'S RATING: ☆☆☆☆☆

Key stakeholders believe the team will 'make it happen'. Moreover, the project team believes in itself.

Business Success

YOUR PROJECT'S RATING: ☆☆☆☆☆

The success of the project is clearly linked to business success. Project success = business success.

Project Execution

YOUR PROJECT'S RATING: ☆☆☆☆☆

Confidence in execution, incl. rate of progress / momentum and effective plan-do-review rhythm.

Org. Support

YOUR PROJECT'S RATING: ☆☆☆☆☆

The organization can deliver, with the project enjoying its full backing & support.

1. What is the level of confidence in Overall Project Success?

Confidence in project success may be a feeling – a sixth sense based on gut instinct, or an assessment based on thoughtful analysis and considered reasoning. Both are worth listening to.

> Imagine a project review where those present, especially those in senior management functions, were required to sign on the dotted line. Personally, attesting to the reality of the project, the veracity of the project update, the accuracy of the project risk register and so on. In the past this may have sounded far-fetched, but not anymore as those in senior management functions are increasingly being held personally accountable[67] for **an expanding definition of compliance** that includes managing risk, ensuring resilience[68] and maybe even delivering 'good outcomes for retail customers.'[69] With this in mind, are you ready to sign your name to your analysis on the previous page?

2. What is the level of confidence in the link to Business Success?

Typically, big projects are a means to an end, rather than an end in themselves. Ultimately, their success is measured in terms of business impact.

Whether the big project is driven by IT, compliance or any other department, business needs and priorities should come first. However, those needs and priorities are continuously changing.

> **Warning for Senior Leaders:** Our data shows that those at the top of the organization are likely to be up to 20% more confident in any big project or ambitious strategy than those who are charged with making it happen. This confidence gap leaves project executives with two choices:
>
> - Increase their confidence to match those at the top.
>
> - Bring those at the top down to their own level.
>
> Some brave leaders see it as their job to rein in expectations and to inject realism into big project conversations with senior management. That is a risky strategy, however. When it comes to talking about risks, obstacles and setbacks, most senior leaders are more likely to shoot the messenger than entertain doubt. That is not the result of any character flaw, but reflects the level of pressure that senior leaders are under.

3. What is the level of confidence in the Project Plan?

Belief in the project plan shapes confidence around a big project, with our data pointing to two inter-related elements:

- Confidence in **delivering against the plan** – that is, in delivering on time, within budget and to scope (in terms of deliverables, quality, etc.).
- Confidence in **the project plan** itself, including:
  o The quality / robustness of the plan.
  o The process of planning that created the plan.
  o Buy-in and the level of consultation / co-creation.
  o How the plan will be reviewed and updated.
  o The plan as 'a sales document.'
  o The plan as a roadmap for effective delivery.

Those running super projects know their plans are good, but their ability to adapt is even better. They are not stuck with a project plan that is no longer working, but can adapt and adjust, navigating around obstacles and learning from setbacks. Moreover, they can do this without endless committee meetings or bureaucratic approval processes.

4. What is the level of confidence in Project Execution?

Without effective execution, the 'best plan in the world' will struggle. But, at a time of accelerating change, confidence in project execution is shaped by many factors, including:

- Access to resources.
- The perceived rate of progress and momentum.
- Levels of visibility and control available to leaders.
- Levels of productivity and efficiency.
- Effectiveness of Plan – Do – Review rhythm.
- Levels of speed, agility, collaboration and innovation.

For super projects, delivering on time, to budget and to scope isn't a matter of faith, but effective ongoing review and adjustment. Regular and effective project reviews enable the dynamic adjustment of static plans in a fast-changing environment. Super project reviews build momentum, celebrate progress, which energizes and builds resilience.

5. What is the level of confidence in the Project Team?

Confidence in a big project is closely linked to confidence in the people who are running it. Our data suggests that Project Team Confidence has two inter-related parts:

- **The project team believes in itself**. A healthy self-concept is important, but it should be based on a realistic appraisal of the team's performance and potential. Pride in belonging to a team and trust among team members are important too.

- **Others believe in the project team**. Key stakeholders believe the team has the capabilities, talent and commitment required to 'make it happen.' This is reflected in team autonomy and broadly positive stakeholder interactions.

'Is there something missing?' asked the director looking over his glasses. 'The forecasts are ambitious – which is good – but **I don't see anything relating to risks and dependencies**. I don't see the underlying assumptions, either' he added. 'What we have here' he continued, 'is only half the picture and I wonder if it is the optimistic half.' Seeing the surprised look on the face of the project leader, the director continued: 'I would like to see those before taking the discussion any further.' At that moment the organization's project leaders had been given license to 'get real' about their projects and strategies in any future conversations with senior leadership.

6. What is the level of confidence in Organizational Support?

Those leading a project may be confident in their own ability, but unsure of the extent of the organization's commitment. Specifically, the ability of the organization's leaders to fully support the initiative, resourcing it adequately and staying the course (despite competing projects and priorities).

> The Head of Strategy was anxious. With the strategy up and running for 6 months, **it was now time for a review**. The date was in the diary and the extended leadership team of 21 people had been invited. But, how to manage the conversation within such a large group? In the past, unmanaged conversations had generated noise and distraction, introduced yet more priorities and unraveled previous decisions. Foremost in the leader's mind was the danger of the CEO emerging from the session frustrated, or even angry. This was sure to happen if there was any hint that the promises made to the board would not be met.
>
> While the Head of Strategy was planning a strategic conversation, she wondered if it would be better to simply **corral people** in line with what was set out in the strategy. Perhaps a presentation, rather than a conversation on the strategy, would be safer, she thought. After much deliberation, the leader chose the 'less safe' route. The reward for her courage was one of the most powerful strategic conversations ever.

CHAPTER 3:

SUPER ALIGNED

INTRODUCTION

Super projects have 5 superpowers (i.e., key factors that make them super). But which of them is the most important? That is a question we are often asked. For example, when it comes to success, is it Super Ambition, Super Confidence or one of the other 3 that matters most? Well, our answer is the focus of this section: Super Alignment.

For many readers our selection of alignment as the most important of the superpowers comes as a surprise. However, that makes this chapter all the more important. Part of the reason why optimizing alignment pays such a dividend is that it is often misunderstood and underappreciated, especially at a time of accelerating change and uncertainty.

SETTING THE SCOPE

Alignment is a big and complex topic, so before we get started let's set out the scope. There is vertical and horizontal alignment, there is the alignment of strategy and execution and the alignment of people and resources too. Yet, our research points to a clear definition of 'super alignment' for any big project. This is alignment with business strategy and success. Upon this, all other alignment depends.

We are going to focus on IT-Business alignment in this section, given the role of IT and its biggest projects. However, the same principles apply to so many other functions, from marketing to compliance. So, don't worry if you're not in IT, the frameworks and tools within this section can serve you too.

WHY ALIGNMENT REALLY MATTERS

The word 'alignment' can lack punch, so let's be clear about why this matters. There are three reasons why alignment deserves to be called a big project 'super power:'

- Alignment secures more **funding**.

- Alignment tackles the No. 1 source of **frustration**.

- Misalignment could steal your project's **glory**.

Let's explore each of these (funding, frustration and glory).

1. Alignment Secures More Funding

Alignment can help **secure more funding**. With so many projects and initiatives competing for scarce resources, leaders need all the leverage that they can get in securing organizational resources and attention. This starts right here – by aligning project goals with business outcomes. Gartner goes as far as to suggest that this could secure and maintain up to 60% more funding.[70] However, for big projects even a fraction of that (e.g., 3% or 5%) would represent a significant boost.

Alignment is linked to resources in other ways too. Specifically, misalignment costs time and money, with people pulling in different directions being a significant drain on resources.

Q: How effectively can you communicate the business impact/value of your big project?

2. Alignment Reduces Friction and Frustration

Alignment is an accelerant, with the potential to make projects go further and faster. However, misalignment has the opposite effect, resulting in friction and frustration. To see this in-action, ask those leading technical projects about **the key challenges they face**. What you will discover is that many of these challenges and frustrations have more to do with business and organizational misalignment than technology. As we will see shortly, that includes issues such as managing internal stakeholders, cross-functional collaboration, changing business needs and competing projects or priorities. These common challenges listed above are symptoms of misalignment that result in big project leaders spending increasing amounts of time pushing and pulling against the rest of the organization.

Some friction and frustration are inevitable in ambitious projects and strategies. It can even be helpful (spurring change and innovation), that is until it starts to hinder progress. The challenges above can **generate noise and interference**, thus distracting from project goals and doing the actual work.

Misalignment drains energy and saps momentum, leaving project leaders and sponsors tired and frustrated. Indeed, many of our coaching colleagues would suggest that misalignment is 'the #1 cause of high blood pressure among project leaders and sponsors.'

Improving alignment can typically save the members of a project leadership team one, two or even four hours per week. However, some would go further to suggest that getting alignment right could save a project many months. However, as we will see next, the link to project success goes beyond saving time or reducing frustration.

Q: Does it sometimes feel like you are pulling and pushing against the rest of the organization?

'It certainly feels like tug-of-war sometimes' proclaimed the leader. He was reviewing the simplest yet most compelling visual in the team's stakeholder data (shown below). The powerful visual suggested his team and its stakeholders were pulling in different directions more than a third of the time (37%). It came as little consolation to the leader that the figure mirrored our benchmark data. What might this figure be for your team and its stakeholders?

Are stakeholders & your team **pulling together** in the same direction?

According to Stakeholders, their priorities & KPIs are 63% consistent with those of the team.

By implication, stakeholders & the team could be pulling in different directions up to 37% of the time.

Consistent, 63%   Inconsistent, 37%

3. Misalignment Could Steal Your Project's Glory

The third, but arguably the most important reason to care about IT-Business alignment is that it could **rob you and your big project of its glory**. A classic symptom of misalignment is divergent perspectives on project performance and success (between the project team and key stakeholders). Indeed, this is a widespread problem, with many C-suite executives putting an

E or an F on IT's big project scorecard. This is evident from the typical survey headlines shown overleaf.

Take a moment to read the headlines on the next page. As an IT leader, how does reading what CEOs and others think of IT make you feel? Moreover, what is the risk that some of these things are being said about your big project?

You may be wondering if the headlines are accurate or fair. Many CIOs will point out that innovation and change are an all-of-organization responsibility. Some of the most aggrieved suggest that the survey data is evidence of **a trend towards 'trash-talking' IT** and its biggest projects.[71]

Regardless, the survey headlines are a worthwhile reminder of the importance of managing the narrative around a big project and, more fundamentally, ensuring our super projects are aligned with the goals and needs of our C-suite stakeholders. That enables them to allocate resources, and it reduces the risk of 'trash-talking' and finger pointing (ensuring that they co-own responsibility for success).

Q: Do you know what the C-suite is saying about your department and its biggest projects?

The percentage of CEOs saying IT is **effective at providing basic technology services** has almost halved.

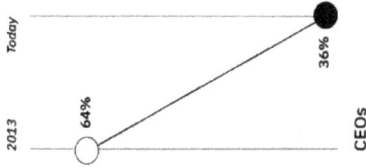

IBM

McKinsey Quarterly

Most organizations achieve less than **30% of the impact** they expect from their digital investments.

McKinsey Quarterly, 2024, Number 2.

...63% of CIOs struggle to communicate **IT's value**...

Only 48% of digital initiatives are **successful**...

Gartner

80% of CIOs & CEOs **are frustrated with IT's inability to deliver value.**

INFO~TECH RESEARCH GROUP

As we will see later, the notion of **perfect and perpetual alignment is an illusion**, especially within large organizations at a time of accelerating change and scarce resources (see **Chapter 3**). Even if perfect alignment were possible, it might not be desirable in the context of rapidly changing business and market needs. Responding to change with speed and agility requires a form of dynamic alignment. This takes nothing for granted, constantly checking to ensure that there is clarity and agreement in respect of business needs and priorities on an ongoing basis.

'Often those leading projects are not senior enough to get inside the C-suite' said the department head. 'They have to download to me (as their boss) and then I go and represent them and their project' he explained, adding: .'..I try to do the best I can, but it often means that the CEO or COO is getting the information second-hand. The result can be an over-simplification of the work being done and what is required for success.' He concluded in a resigned tone 'I guess this is part of the challenge of aligning the C-suite with what teams are doing in IT, engineering or R&D.'

BEYOND TECH INITIATIVES

To understand **the growing importance of alignment** we must look back to the time when a technical project, was just that – a project concerned with technology:

- The focus was on hardware and software, front end and backend, programming languages, etc.

- The project team consisted of programmers, UX designers, data engineers, etc.
- Their work was to build the application, infrastructure, user interface, etc.

Back when tech initiatives were purely tech initiatives, everything other than the technical stuff was considered peripheral to success. It was a distraction from doing the work. However, the age of the 'technology initiative' is at an end.

Today, calling something an 'IT or technical initiative' is a misnomer. Rather, it should be called a **'business initiative led or sponsored by IT**.' This shift in perspective underscores the essential role of technology as a strategic business enabler. Incidentally, there are no HR or Compliance projects either, these are 'business initiatives led or sponsored by HR or compliance.'

Today's big technology projects are first and foremost business initiatives. Their goal is to drive business strategy or success. The shift from 'technology initiative' to 'business initiatives driven by technology' is summarized in the table on the next page. It is a seismic shift in the role and the strategic importance of IT.

Paradoxically, the end of the technology initiative is the beginning of a golden age for IT. This could be **the best time ever to be a CTO, CIO or big project leader**. What happens next depends on alignment, however – indeed, it depends on what we call Super Alignment.

SUPER ALIGNMENT IS B.E.S.T.

The best tech initiatives are super aligned. More specifically, they deliver **Business Efficiency & Success *via* Technology** (BEST).

That **business efficiency and success are the ultimate purpose of any tech project** sounds like a statement of the obvious, yet it cannot be taken for granted. While few would disagree that tech projects are a means to an end, the complexity involved means that the project often becomes the end in itself.

Caught up in the busyness of the day to day, it is **easy to lose sight of business needs and priorities**, even market reality. This is what we call 'project myopia' and it is **the #1 risk facing any big project**.[72] That is worth emphasizing – the biggest danger facing any tech initiative is not the failure to deliver on time, to scope or to budget, but rather the failure to meet the needs of the business and its stakeholders. At a time of accelerating change in uncertainty, this can easily happen because business needs and market reality are in flux. Over the course of a project spanning two to three years, business needs and priorities can change significantly. **Business Efficiency & Success *via* Technology** (BEST) can be a moving target. It is a challenge.

'Over the past 3 years we generated over 100 proposals or RFP responses' said the executive from the global systems vendor. 'Do you know how many of those we had **visibility of the customer's business case or business logic** for?' she asked. Then after a short pause came the answer: 'For just 2 of them! 'For the other 98, we proposed technological solutions with little, if any, understanding of the customers' business or commercial needs' she explained.

> With raised eyebrows, she proclaimed: 'That sounds crazy, but it is true! Today, we obsess on the business logic for our customers. It is a key pre-qualifier and an essential part of our sales pitch.'

Take a moment to read the table on the next page. Use it to explore whether your big project is:

- A technology initiative (as traditionally defined) or

- A BEST initiative enabling Business Efficiency and Success *via* Technology.

Pause to reflect on the implications for your project and any opportunities to leverage the power of super alignment.

BUSINESS EFFICIENCY & SUCCESS

Technology decisions are first and foremost business decisions. In other words, business success and efficiency come first. To invest in technology, it must be clear how it will drive both.

While **Business Efficiency & Success *via* Technology** (BEST) is self-explanatory, it is worth deconstructing its two key parts:

- **Success**: Business success is a broad and general term, allowing for the fact that organizations will have different visions, strategies and goals. For some projects risk management, compliance or financial control may be the connection to business success. For others, it may be customer acquisition or retention, new product development or sales and marketing capability.

	Traditional 'Technical Initiative'	BEST Initiative (Business Efficiency & Success *via* Technology)
Who is involved?	IT	Cross-functional
What kind of decisions(s)?	Technical Decision(s) E.g. which technologies to use?	Business Decisions(s) – Which strategies & projects to invest in?
How is success measured?	Technical Solution to a technical problem	Business Impact / Success
How difficult to manage?	Complicated (many parts) but manageable	Complex (incl. variables difficult to manage and predict, e.g., stakeholders)
What are the key risks?	The technology doesn't deliver	Change / adoption doesn't happen. Business goals not met.
What are the key challenges?	To determine the best architecture, define technical specifications, manage coding and integration, etc.	Building the business justification, Managing Internal Stakeholders, Accessing Resources, Org. Change / Adoption, etc.

- **Efficiency**: Efficiency is a little more specific (than success) and reflects the primary business obsession at this time.

These two together are the perfect combination of short-term performance and longer-term success. The IT project portfolio must enable both. However, the **drive for efficiency is the ace card for today's CIOs and CTOs**. As one of our clients puts it: 'While cost-cutting and efficiency has everybody else running scared, it really adds to the importance of IT.' Meanwhile, the business case for IT has been strengthened in the following ways:

- With accelerating change and uncertainty there is mounting pressure on performance. With cutbacks and a scarcity of resources, leaders are almost universally expected to do more with less.
- The biggest upheaval in ways of working, since the production line, has resulted in widespread paranoia about performance.[73]
- Business leaders are tantalized by the promise of digitization, automation and Ai.

All these factors underscore the importance of IT. Of course, they also add to the pressure on it to deliver projects and solutions with greater speed and efficiency too – for IT to deliver more with less resources and greater speed.

MINDSET SHIFT

This is a great time to be in corporate IT, probably the best time ever. It is a Moses moment – when some fundamental principles are being carved in stone (as shown below).

Before we resume our quest for super alignment, let's pause to take stock – to reflect on the two statements. For many CIOs and CTOs, these principles as set out in the previous pages are commonsense. They are second nature for business-focused IT departments and projects. For others, a **mindset shift** may be necessary.

Some IT leaders may fear that these new principles diminish the role of IT – making it subservient. However, the very opposite is true. What it really means is IT becoming more important, rather than less. Specifically, it means:

- IT moving from being a support function to the role of strategic business enabler.
- IT having a seat at the table when it comes to the direction of the business and the allocation of resources.

- IT commanding and orchestrating more effective cross-functional collaboration. As one CIO puts it: 'IT is no longer a whipping boy' with other department and function heads being required to take their share of the responsibility for project success.

- A clearer link between IT and strategy, making it easier to address the thorny issue of the return on IT spending.

Do you want to realize the above benefits? If so, **are you ready to make the mindset shift** from 'tech initiative' to BEST (Business Efficiency & Success *via* Technology)? The remainder of this section will provide a framework and set of tools to make it happen. Moreover, it will do this in a way that leverages concepts familiar to all.

Knowing the difference between complicated and complex is important. Take for example implementing a CRM system. From an IT point of view, that may be a technically demanding and even complicated project. However, if the objective of the initiative is to deliver a world-class customer experience, **that** is complex. Its success will require:

- Many parts of the organization working together (e.g., marketing, compliance, finance, etc.).

- Not just changes in process, but in organizational behavior and culture too.

As so many leaders have learned, the real challenge regarding CRM and other systems is business impact and even adoption, more than technical performance.

FROM TECH STACK TO TWIN STACK

Transformation initiatives bring together a range of technologies (software, hardware, etc.) to build the optimal solution. But all the parts must work well together. How this happens can be seen by reference to the tech stack.

The tech stack is a great way of visualizing the technical complexity of an initiative. But wouldn't it be great to have a similar way of engaging with the non-technical, too. Specifically, those **business-related and organizational aspects** (such as business justification and internal stakeholders) that play an ever-greater role in project success, take up more and more time and can create a lot of noise and distraction.

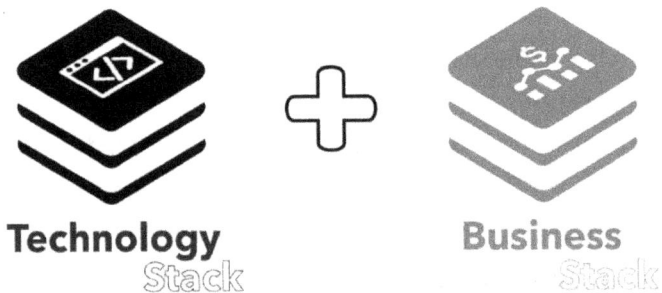

Technology Stack   **Business** Stack

The tech stack is an established concept, while the business stack is not. Thus, while everyone has a framework for managing technical complexity, almost nobody has a business equivalent for **managing the layers of business and organizational complexity**. That is, until now.

To be successful today's technical initiatives don't just need a technical stack. They require a business stack too! Adding a 'business stack' to the tech stack provides a fuller picture of success for those leading any initiative. Such a 'twin stack' provides greater visibility and control of both the technical and business-related key success factors and risks. The business stack is a powerful tool in the quest for super alignment.

> Project leaders were queuing up to tell the newly-appointed division head about their important projects. The new leader was not so keen, however. All he really wanted to know was **the impact on the numbers** and how quickly this would be realized. To his frustration, this essential piece of information was not obvious for most of the 30 or more IT department priorities and initiatives underway. When the division head got over his frustration, he realized the necessity of communicating more clearly the commercial pressures facing the organization.

THE 'BUSINESS STACK' REVEALED

Actively managing the 'business stack' in tandem with the 'tech stack' is essential to delivering business efficiency and success *via* technology (BEST). But, what would the 'business stack' for a big tech project look like? Well, just like the technology stack, the 'business stack' would have many layers (as shown overleaf).

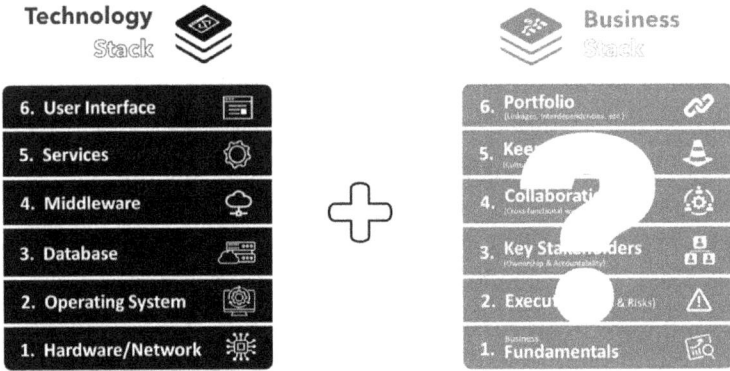

Each layer would be a different piece of the business and strategy jigsaw. While each individual layer would be important, the layers must also work together effectively – just as the different parts of the organization must work together.

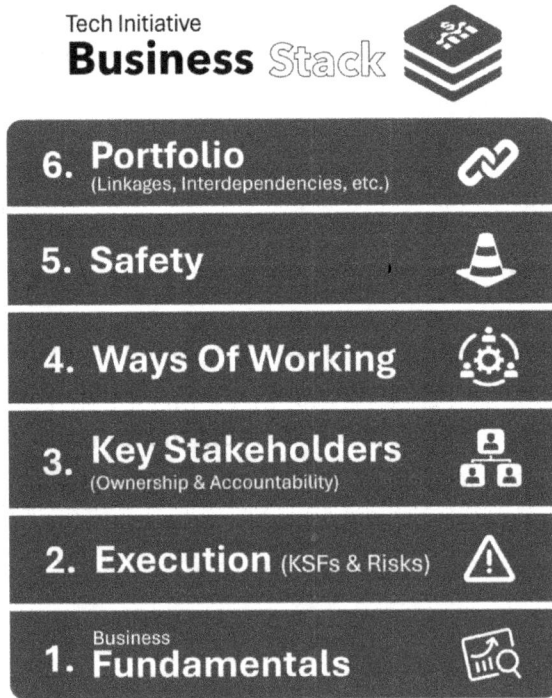

So, what are the layers of the Business Stack? The business stack aims at managing the complexity of the non-technical aspects of a big project. Thus, the layers correspond to those business related and organizational factors that must be aligned and integrated to ensure business, as well as technical success. That gives us **a total of 6 layers** as follows:

1.   **Business Fundamentals Layer:** This is the fundamental business rationale or 'why' behind the big project, including business needs, market reality, business impact and investment. This layer is particularly important in connecting to strategy, aligning cross-functional stakeholders, accessing power and justifying resources. As we will see shortly, it addresses the #1 risk facing any big project.

2.   **Execution Layer:** This layer maps out the Key Success Factors (KSFs) and potential risks for a big project, emphasizing the importance of early identification and mitigation strategies. The objective is to ensure there is a shared view of the road ahead in terms of execution, including often hidden (or undiscussed) KSFs and risks. This is essential to good governance and meeting compliance requirements too.

3.   **Stakeholder Layer:** When everybody pulls together, amazing things can happen, but it is not easy. This layer seeks to align stakeholder needs and expectations with project reality. It maps stakeholders, reveals what they are really thinking, and aims to maximize stakeholder ownership and accountability.

4.   **Collaboration Layer:** Teamwork and cross-functional collaboration are critical to big project success. This often-overlooked layer analyses levels of productivity

and efficiency in respect of ways of working within project teams, between project teams and across the rest of the organization.

5. **Keeping it Real Layer:** Those leading ambitious big projects must walk a tightrope between 'selling the dream' (required to access resources and gain support) and 'keeping it real' (required for effective execution). This layer is aimed at providing leaders with a reality check in terms of project status and project sentiment, including the accuracy of project updates and the likelihood that people will talk openly about risks and setbacks.

6. **Portfolio and Linkages Layer** – no big project happens in isolation; countless other projects and initiatives are planned and underway. With a view of the wider strategic project portfolio, this layer aims to:

    (a) Manage linkages and interdependencies.

    (b) Leverage synergies, shared resources, knowledge and learning.

    (c) Optimize alignment to enable the organization to focus with greater intensity on the projects and priorities that matter most.

The 6 layers of the Business Stack illuminate the complexity of the non-technical or business aspects of a big tech project. Importantly, they are also the means of integrating and aligning the non-technical layers of a project.

Q: What are the most critical layers of your business stack at this time?

WHY THE BUSINESS STACK?

Super Alignment is the tight integration and alignment between the technical execution (tech stack) and the business objectives (business stack) of a project.

The objective of the tech stack is to ensure the alignment of the various technologies to be used, whereas the objective of the 'business stack' is to **ensure alignment with the wider organization and in particular with business strategy and success** (see diagram).

Tech Project Success	Business Success
Tech Project Scope	Business Needs & Priorities
Tech Project Plan	Business Strategy
Tech Project Deliverables	Business Impact
Tech Project Team	Business Leadership
Tech Project Spend	Business ROI

The 'business stack' is about stacking the odds in favor of your project. It does this by integrating and aligning the technical project or initiative with business needs and strategy, the technical team with the C-suite and technical project success with business success. The test of this integration is **the level of clarity and alignment among key internal stakeholders** regarding the different layers of the 'business stack' (e.g., business needs and KSFs or risks). Let's bring this to life by exploring the foundational first layer of the business stack, called 'business fundamentals.'

You may have noticed a pattern regarding the 'why.' It keeps popping up in respect of every aspect of a super project. We saw it first in terms of the 'super why' that fuels super ambition. We will see it again as the means of engaging with super complexity (**Chapter 4** and a factor called project myopia) and as central to super collaboration (**Chapter 5**).

THE FOUNDATIONAL LAYER

The first layer is called the 'business fundamentals' because **it is literally the foundation of everything else**. It is the basis upon which the project or initiative is built. Technical initiatives that are built without a clear business foundation are vulnerable.

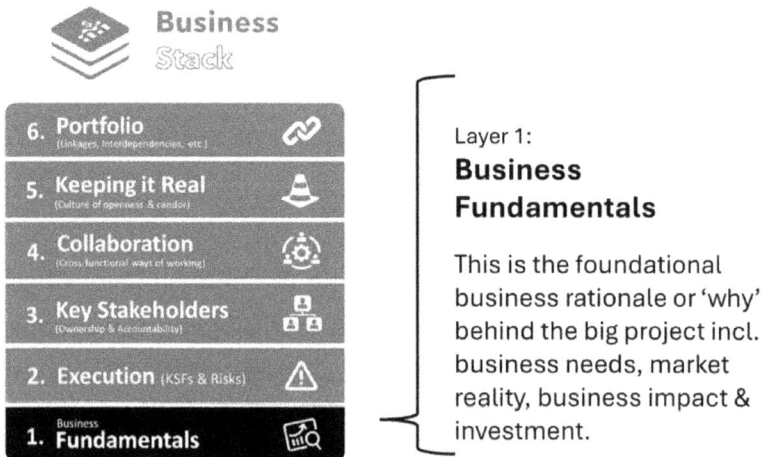

Business Stack

6. **Portfolio**
   (Linkages, Interdependencies, etc.)

5. **Keeping it Real**
   (Culture of openness & candor)

4. **Collaboration**
   (Cross-functional ways of working)

3. **Key Stakeholders**
   (Ownership & Accountability)

2. **Execution** (KSFs & Risks)

1. Business **Fundamentals**

Layer 1:
Business Fundamentals

This is the foundational business rationale or 'why' behind the big project incl. business needs, market reality, business impact & investment.

In contrast to the technical stack, which largely focuses on the 'how' of a project, **the 'business stack' emphasizes the 'why.'**

That is the business (not just the technical) 'why' of a project. This is fundamentally important for 4 reasons:

1.   The success of any technology initiative is increasingly being **measured in business, rather than technical terms**. For a big project, to deliver a technical solution on time and to budget means little if it fails to contribute to business strategy and success.

2.   For the organization to invest in IT, technology must be considered **key to business success**. For an initiative to be strategic, it must be clearly connected to the strategy and success of the business.

3.   There are more projects and priorities than there are available people or resources. For IT initiatives to command **scarce organizational resources,** the business logic or rationale for any technology-related investment decisions must be both compelling and clear.

4.   **Solo-runs by IT are fraught with danger**. For IT's various initiatives to be successful requires the backing and support of other departments and functions – from IT to Compliance. It is vital to have a clear and compelling business rationale around which these otherwise siloed functional interests can be rallied.

Q: What is the level of clarity and alignment regarding the business fundamentals of your project?

To explore the business or organizational 'why,' **the business fundamentals layer** includes 9 factors:

1. Business needs.
2. Market reality.
3. Strategic ambition.
4. Project confidence.
5. Business impact.
6. Business investment.
7. Business urgency.
8. Business unusual.
9. Stakeholders.

Having studied this list of 9 business fundamentals, pause to consider:

Q: Which (if any) of the 9 business fundamentals require greater clarity?

One-page frameworks sheets are very popular – take the business canvas or the beermat business case as examples. Should there be a one-page tool for critical projects or initiatives? We believe the answer is 'yes,' so we created one. Shown overleaf, its goal is to ensure clarity and alignment on the business fundamentals of a big project or initiative. It is a speedy way to ensure that **everybody is on the same page** regarding your initiative.[74] However, there is an even more compelling reason – it could help to access up to 60% more resources (remember the Gartner research at the start of this chapter).

Is everyone on the same page regarding your big project or initiative? Find out by completing the blank fundamentals on the next page.

Market REALITY

What key external market realities (insights, trends, assumptions & predictions):

- Make this project necessary or essential?
- Inform or shape this project/initiative?
- Provide external validation for this initiative?
- Represent uncertainty or risk for this project?

Business URGENCY

What is the level of urgency around the initiative?

- What is the burning platform for this initiative?
- What if the project did not proceed or was delayed?
- How does the approach accelerate the time to results?
- How to appease those who think it's not fast enough?

Budget INVESTMENT

What is the approx. total budget required?

- What is the expected payback or return on project investment?
- Level of confidence in adequacy & accuracy of the numbers?
- Has project got the attention, people & talent that it needs?
- What could be done with 5% or 10% more or less?

Project CONFIDENCE

What is the level of confidence (at this time)?

- What factors underpin confidence in this initiative?
- What factors detract from confidence in this initiative?
- Could there be blind spots, hidden risks or over-confidence in any area?
- What assumptions are we making to arrive at this confidence level?

Business NEEDS

Why does the business need this project/initiative? How much is it needed?

- How does it address key business priorities?
- What problem/opportunity does it address?
- How does it further the strategy/vision?
- How will it build/extend org. capability/capacity?

What is the level of clarity & alignment on the Business Fundamentals of your big project?

SUPER ALIGNED

Business IMPACT

How will success be measured?

- What business outcomes (results & benefits) will result?
- What is the likely long-term impact on the business?
- How robust has analysis/modelling of business impact been?
- How effective has the dialog re business impact been?

Business UNUSUAL

What aspects of the project are 'Business Unusual'?

- What is new or innovative about this project/initiative?
- How much change or disruption is likely/evident?
- Is there any Hidden Complexity? i.e. Factors difficult to manage or predict.
- Are New Ways of Working required? E.g. Speed, agility or collaboration.

Strategic AMBITION

What is the ambition driving the project / initiative?

- Does it aim for modest or massive gains?
- Does it dare to dream big? Will it stand-out or leave a lasting mark?
- How will it stretch / challenge the org. to grow?
- Could any aspect(s) be seen as overly or under ambitious?

Stakeholders

How focused is the project on key stakeholders?

- What needs & expectations are being addressed?
- What are key stakeholders saying about this project?
- How will the project identify & adapt to emerging needs?
- How will this initiative engage & energize stakeholders?

A word of caution: Many leaders zealously fill out the panels on the diagram overleaf and proclaim: '**Yes, the fundamentals are clear!**' But is everybody on the same page regarding the business fundamentals? That is the key question the tool overleaf aims to address for your big project.

ONE-PAGE ALIGNMENT TEST

While managers want and expect alignment, many are using the wrong tools to generate it. This is clear from **the emergence of the super deck** – the set of 100 or more carefully crafted and beautifully presented slides.

> 'Project leaders are spending so much time preparing slide decks ahead of big meetings' warns one of our coaching colleagues. 'These take hundreds of hours and thousands of dollars to create, but in most cases it is folly' they add. 'If it takes 100 slides to communicate why your project matters, then you are lost. Your audience will be lost too. More slides and more information won't necessarily generate better alignment, especially when people are already suffering from information overload.'

Slide decks are an important information resource. But, when it comes to alignment, the one-page tool (i.e., the business fundamentals on a page) is a powerful alternative to the 'super deck.' Moreover, it puts conversations ahead of presentations.

Counselors tell us that the quality of conversations reveals the health of a marriage. For the marriage of science and strategy, that means **the ability to have strategic conversations**. These are conversations about the elements in our strategy table and especially the business fundamentals (on the one-page tool).

The business fundamentals are **an ideal place to start a conversation** with any senior executive regarding your project. Whether it is a project pitch or a project update, start with the why. Then it is not just another project conversation, but the most strategic of conversations. This is infinitely more powerful as a means of engaging and aligning senior executives, as it connects to what is most important to them – business strategy and success.

Super alignment means that all the key people working on a big project (whether they are scientists, engineers or anything else) can explain in a few soundbites 'the why' (i.e., why it matters). The test is straightforward, called **the Elevator Test**:

A project leader steps into the elevator on the first floor and finds the CEO already inside. The CEO immediately asks about their key project. The challenge is: Can they communicate how the project aligns with strategy and success before the CEO exits the lift?

If they can (using some of the language and logic on the one-page 'Super Aligned' tool, the CEO is much more likely to say: 'That sounds interesting, I'd love to hear more.'

Business Fundamentals *versus* Business Case

Some leaders see the words 'business (or strategic) fundamentals' and immediately think 'business case.' However, for most, the concept of business fundamentals goes a lot deeper than the business case. It goes to the very 'why' of a project, which cannot be answered by reference to a spreadsheet or cost-benefit analysis alone.

The business case typically involves writing a document, while the Business Fundamentals is a process of strategic conversation that boosts stakeholder alignment, collaboration and confidence. In this way, it helps secure greater organizational resources and support ahead of competing projects and initiatives.

THE ALIGNMENT TEST

A compelling set of business fundamentals (on paper) means little unless key internal stakeholders are bought into and aligned with what is written. IT-business alignment is **achieved through dialog and engagement**, rather than spreadsheets or prose. Moreover, as it involves dealing with people rather than code or machines, the process involved can be slow and time-consuming, perhaps even frustrating.

On the positive side, the business fundamentals are **the ideal place to start a conversation** with any senior executive regarding your project or initiative. Whether it is a project pitch or a project update, start with the why. Then it is not just another project conversation, but the most strategic of conversations. This is infinitely more powerful as a means of engaging senior executives as it connects to what is most important to them – business strategy and success.

The business fundamentals are critical in getting a project off the ground, providing a clear and compelling business justification, securing executive sponsorship and accessing resources. However, once set, they **must be continually reviewed**.

The business fundamentals of an initiative **cannot be set in stone**. That is because in a dynamic market environment, business needs and priorities are subject to change. If this layer shifts and the others are not adjusted accordingly, the stability of the entire business stack is in question.

'The business fundamentals of this initiative are strong, indeed compelling' said the leader in a tone that indicated that it was time to move the conversation on to something else. Unfazed, the consultant paused and then replied 'Yes, I agree, compelling is the word. What I am curious about is whether everybody else knows how compelling they are and whether that is reflected in their level of commitment to the initiative?' Then she added in a reflective tone, 'Based on my experience, what I am curious about is **the level of clarity and alignment or shared ownership of the business fundamentals** or "the why" across the organization and especially among the senior leadership team.'

BUSINESS STACK COMPLEXITY

We don't have the space here to explore each of the business stack's 6 layers in detail – you can do this online (**www.super-projects.co**). However, having explored just one of the layers (i.e., business fundamentals), you will likely have gathered that the business stack is complex.

For IT leaders, the tech stack is concrete and manageable, even if complicated. After all, it is driven by logic and analysis. Moreover, as the tech stack is easily documented, it is clear for all to see. By contrast **the business stack can seem abstract and vague** – with the flowery words of a vision statement rather than the clarity of a technical specification.

While the tech stack is a matter of fact, the layers of **the business stack can be subjective**. For example, ask people to articulate the business strategy (driving a technology project) and you may not get a clear answer. Ask several people and you may get several different answers. For those trained in IT, the answers may be in a somewhat alien language, called business speak. Moreover, there may be many unknowns (perhaps called scenarios, assumptions or hypotheses).

Importantly, while IT is largely in the driving seat regarding the tech stack, it can find itself **a mere spectator** when it comes to the business stack. Here IT must defer to others. Even if IT could determine the business stack and tell the rest of the organization what it is, that would probably be unwise.

Key stakeholders must be involved in co-creation of the business stack if they are to own it. The immediate implication is that there may be **a lot more meetings and a lot more people involved**. Often that is the very last thing that busy IT leaders want.

If you think you have achieved full clarity and alignment re your project, think again. Here is why: You know the game where one person whispers a message to another, who then whispers it to another, and so on, until it has reached 20 people (or, in the case of a big project, 20 stakeholders). The 20th person then shares what they heard, only to reveal that a simple and clear message such as 'the cat is on the mat' has become 'the bat is on the hat.' Called the telephone game, this provides an insight into a phenomenon that occurs every day in respect of big projects in busy organizations. So, complete the sentence 'This project matters because...' and then **imagine what it sounds like after it has reached the 20th stakeholder**. What has been lost? What has been added? Is it aligned?

Super alignment strives to ensure that the 20th stakeholder still communicates the essence of why a project matters. So, if you think you have spent too much time talking about the strategy or 'the why' of your project, think again!

TWIN STACKS – DOUBLE THE WORK?

It may be the golden age for IT, but **there is a downside to the twin stack and BEST**. To discover what it is, ask tech leaders driving big projects about the key opportunities and challenges they face, and you may be surprised to find that many of the factors have little, if anything, to do with technology. Indeed, within any list of the top 5 you will likely find non-technical factors such as:

- Accessing resources.
- Changing business needs and priorities.
- Building the business case justification.
- Competing projects and priorities.
- Cross-functional collaboration.
- Internal bureaucracy.
- The management of stakeholders.

While these factors may not be prominent in the typical CIO or CTO job description, they are **taking up more and more of the IT leader's time and attention**. These business-related or organizational factors represent an important dependency or risk to the success of any big IT project or initiative. Moreover, they can generate a lot of noise and distraction, even frustration.

The alignment of business and technology is vital. However, if unmanaged, the 'twin stack' (of tech stack and business stack) **could double**:

- The stakeholders.
- The meetings.
- The bureaucracy (e.g., paperwork and reporting).
- The level of noise and interference.
- The project scope.

The non-technical aspects of projects and initiatives have the potential to generate a lot of **noise and interference**. They can be a considerable drain on time and energy, distracting from the important technical work that needs to be done. This is especially true for those leaders who adopt a hands-off approach to the business and stakeholder-related aspects of a technical project. However, **adopting a more proactive**

approach to the management of these factors can save time, as well as frustration. Indeed, our coaching colleagues report that it can save project leaders and their teams at least two hours per week.

A more **proactive approach** to the management of the business stack means dealing with business-related issues up front and early on. It also means leaning into the messy stuff – the tricky business issues, the tough choices, the areas where clarity is lacking, the underlying causes of misalignment and so on.

Managing and even mastering the tech stack is a core competence of technical leaders and their teams. It is something that they have the skills, the frameworks and the tools to do. But, what about the non-technical aspects of success (business logic or justification, internal stakeholders, etc.)? These aspects of a tech project or initiative are every bit as complex as the choice of technical infrastructure or programming language (if not more so). Yet, **tech leaders have few frameworks or tools to manage them efficiently**. This is a deficit we have addressed *via* our research, with the development of a methodology and set of tools to manage and optimize the business stack. There is a sample screenshot from our analytics below – this is a picture you can get for your big project or ambitious strategy.

ANALYSIS & REFLECTION

In this section, we explored the business stack as the means of ensuring clarity and alignment on the business or non-technical aspects of a big project. Let us pause for a moment to explore your big project's business stack. You will find questions for each layer below – read them or select the layer that interests you most:

1. **Business Fundamentals Layer:** What is the level of clarity and alignment regarding the business fundamentals or 'why' behind your big project (including business needs, market reality and business impact)?

    Here you can take a blank copy of the business fundamental framework (see inside back cover) and apply it to an important strategic initiative or super project that you are working on. Use it to rate the level of clarity and alignment on the 9 fundamentals.

2. **Execution Layer:** What is the level of clarity and alignment on the Key Success Factors (KSFs) and potential risks relating to the execution of your big project?

3. **Stakeholder Layer:** How well do you really know what key stakeholders are thinking and saying about the project? What is the level of shared ownership and accountability?

4. **Collaboration Layer:** What is the level of productivity and efficiency in respect of ways of working within project teams, between project teams and across the rest of the organization?

5. **Keeping it Real Layer:** What is the level of clarity on project status and project sentiment, including the accuracy of project updates? How likely are people to talk openly about risks and setbacks?

6. **Portfolio and Linkages Layer** – How well are linkages, synergies, knowledge and learning shared between your big project and the wider strategic portfolio?

Q: What is the level of clarity and alignment regarding the business fundamentals (e.g., business needs and business impact) of your solution?

CHAPTER 4:

SUPER COMPLEX

INTRODUCTION

All big projects are complex. Super projects aren't necessarily any more complex than any other big project. That is not the differentiating factor. What makes super projects 'super' is how they engage with complexity. They turn what is a potential vulnerability into a source of strength. How this happens is explored here.

RE-THINKING COMPLEXITY

Big projects are one of the least routine and predictable aspects of what an organization does. In other words, they are complex, even super complex. This complexity operates on at least 3 levels – you could think of it as **complexity cubed** (C^3):

1. **Project Complexity:** Projects themselves have many moving parts, including people, stakeholders, deliverables, timelines and so on. Moreover, they must be delivered with greater speed, despite constraints on resources.

2. **Internal Complexity:** Big projects don't exist in a bubble, but rather in the context of a wider organization(s). That is another source of complexity, with competing projects and priorities, scarce resources and changing business needs and priorities. Other factors driving complexity include the need for cross-functional collaboration and the challenges of reconciling operations and development or business as usual and business unusual.

Parse our conversations with leaders, and one word continuously emerges: 'Complexity.' However, while Leaders are typically well-attuned to external or market complexity, they may be less aware of internal complexity.[75] That is the real danger because internal complexity determines **how well any big project can adapt** or even profit from external change and uncertainty. In particular, the level of speed, agility, collaboration and innovation that is possible.

3. **External Complexity:** Projects and their organizations cannot stand still. They must adapt to a fast-changing external / market environment or risk being overtaken by accelerating change. That includes changes in terms of technology, competitors, customers and channels, as well as politics, legislation, economics and society.

These 3 levels of complexity explain why big projects are super complex. While the project may be under a project leader's control, the organization and its industry are not. Yet, **high levels of complexity are not the problem**; they can present as many opportunities as challenges. The difficulty arises when big projects are managed in a way that does not reflect the level of complexity involved. In a nutshell, here is what our research reveals:

Because super projects are super complex, those leading them need to be super at engaging with complexity.

Let's get more specific next, outlining 8 ways big project leaders can do this. We are going to reframe complexity, to enable big project leaders to manage, even profit from, it.

In times gone by, the complexity of a project could be defined in terms of the relationship between cost, time and scope. That was the classic Project Triangle (also called the iron triangle), created in the 1960s. But, at a time of accelerating change and uncertainty, **the project triangle struggles in the context of the C3 complexity** involved in today's big projects. As one of our colleagues puts it: 'Today's project triangle is more of a polygon, and it is not made of iron, but of elastic. How projects are managed will never be the same again.'

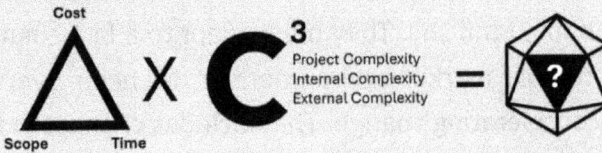

Q: How complex is your big project?

SUPER COMPLEXITY

Naturally, leaders are confident about the success of their ambitious strategies. However, not even super projects are invincible – **they have vulnerabilities too**! Think of these vulnerabilities as metaphorical big project kryptonite.

Kryptonite is the fictional radioactive substance that robs Superman or Superwoman of his or her powers. This is a somewhat light-hearted way of talking about an aspect of big projects that is both very serious and very real. **Reframing project complexity** in this way is important because talking about risks and obstacles, although essential, can be difficult. This is particularly true in organizations that only do good news.[76]

What makes super projects 'super' is their ability to transform potential vulnerabilities (kryptonite) into a source of strength. They do this by **engaging head-on with the real-world complexity** involved, ensuring clarity as well as alignment in the process. The concept of big project vulnerabilities (BPVs) or kryptonite, **depersonalizes and depoliticizes** the issue of project risk and uncertainty. Typically, the result is a more open and honest analysis, dialog too. Without this, engaging with complexity is difficult.

Q: How well does your project engage with or master complexity?

8 TYPES OF PROJECT KRYPTONITE

Complexity is the super project equivalent of kryptonite, and there is a lot of it around! Specifically, our data highlights 8 key sources of complexity, as listed below.

1.   **Business Myopia Kryptonite** occurs when teams get caught up in the project bubble and lose sight of business needs or even market reality. This risk is intensified at a time of change and uncertainty.

2.   **First Mile Kryptonite** recognizes the pressure to get initiatives up and running fast, where some steps may be skipped and some fundamental issues may not be addressed. 'First Mile Kryptonite' emphasizes the importance of getting a big project off on a solid footing, while still ensuring the need for speed.

Don't worry if the list seems intimidating or if you are struggling with the kryptonite metaphor. The message here is simple: **Super projects require acknowledging and embracing complexity**, rather than attempting to avoid it. By the end of this section, you will have a practical and powerful framework to do just that.

3.   **Stakeholder Kryptonite** weakens projects when key stakeholders stay on the sidelines, disengaged or failing to share responsibility for success and risks.

4.   **Pollyanna Kryptonite** is where leaders only do good news and concerns are silenced. This creates a false sense of security and prevents proactive risk mitigation.

5.   **Alignment Kryptonite** undermines projects when there is the illusion of alignment, but teams and stakeholders are not truly united in their understanding of priorities, goals, dependencies and risks.

6.   **Project Proliferation Kryptonite** occurs when organizations juggle too many initiatives, spreading resources thin and thereby hindering progress. Also, when they fail to leverage linkages, synergies and shared resources across different initiatives.

7.   **Business Unusual Kryptonite** is the tension that often arises between the innovative, disruptive nature of 'Business Unusual' projects and established ways of working, planning, budgeting and so on.

8.   **Corporate Kryptonite:** Projects don't happen within a bubble, but within a wider organizational environment. Thus, they are subject to:

   a. Noisy Kryptonite: Where change, politics and other organizational factors distract attention and resources.

   b. Bureaucratic Kryptonite: Where committees, approvals and reporting get in the way of speed, agility and innovation.

These are **8 of the most complex aspects of any project,** yet they rarely get mentioned (if at all) in any project plan. Thus, a whole swathe of project risk gets neglected.

Pause for a moment to reflect on these 8 sources of kryptonite or potential vulnerabilities: Which of the related questions do you feel are most relevant to your big project at this time?

> The consultants' eyes lit up with glee at the amount of amber and red ratings for key aspects of the big project given by its leaders. They were confident of a long stream of future consulting revenue fixing the many factors highlighted as risks and obstacles to project success. Yet, the client's leaders seemed unfazed – taking the reds and ambers in their stride. After all, they had seen it before. Rather than being something to get worked up about, these factors simply revealed **the complexity of working on a big project within a large organization**. Some of the factors could be addressed now, others would need to be lived with, meanwhile work on the big project would continue unabated.

SUPER COMPLEX

YOUR PROJECT'S RATING:
☆☆☆☆☆

BUSINESS MYOPIA ①
kryptonite
We ensure the project never loses sight of business needs & priorities.

YOUR PROJECT'S RATING:
☆☆☆☆☆

FIRST MILE ②
kryptonite
Despite the urgency, we ensure projects are set up for success.

YOUR PROJECT'S RATING:
☆☆☆☆☆

STAKEHOLDER ③
kryptonite
We effectively engage & excite, even challenge stakeholders.

YOUR PROJECT'S RATING:
☆☆☆☆☆

POLLYANNA ④
kryptonite
We can openly talk about risks, obstacles & setbacks.

YOUR PROJECT'S RATING:
☆☆☆☆☆

⑤ **ALIGNMENT**
kryptonite
We continuously work on alignment & never take it for granted.

YOUR PROJECT'S RATING:
☆☆☆☆☆

⑥ **PROLIFERATION**
kryptonite
There are not too many projects competing for time & attention.

YOUR PROJECT'S RATING:
☆☆☆☆☆

⑦ **BUSINESS UNUSUAL**
kryptonite
We don't manage big projects as if they are business as usual.

YOUR PROJECT'S RATING:
☆☆☆☆☆

⑧ **CORPORATE**
kryptonite
Bureaucracy & committees don't kill our speed & agility.

EMBRACING COMPLEXITY

Before exploring each of the 8 big project vulnerabilities or drivers of project complexity (*aka* kryptonite), let's stay high and set the context.

Paradoxically, super projects aren't 'super' because they don't face obstacles or setbacks — but because they do. They derive **strength from engaging with the real-world complexity** of delivering on ambitious strategies. They are super at engaging with complexity.

These 8 forms of big project kryptonite (or big project vulnerabilities) are widespread. Every project has some — normally several of them. That includes even the best projects, so **they are nothing to be ashamed of**.

The 8 vulnerabilities or kryptonite are **no reflection on the leader or the team**, but rather they reflect the complexity of delivering big projects within large organizations at a time of accelerating change and uncertainty. Conversely, the big project that does not have, or is in denial of, them is the project that is most vulnerable.

Super projects minimize hidden complexity — they own their weaknesses and vulnerabilities. In so doing, they are made stronger. **Kryptonite is 8 ways to engage with complexity** and ultimately to turn it to your advantage. So, as you read through this section, the goal is to identify what could make your project stronger.

It is important to remember that the danger is not complexity, but rather **hidden complexity**.

Embracing complexity is key to avoiding:

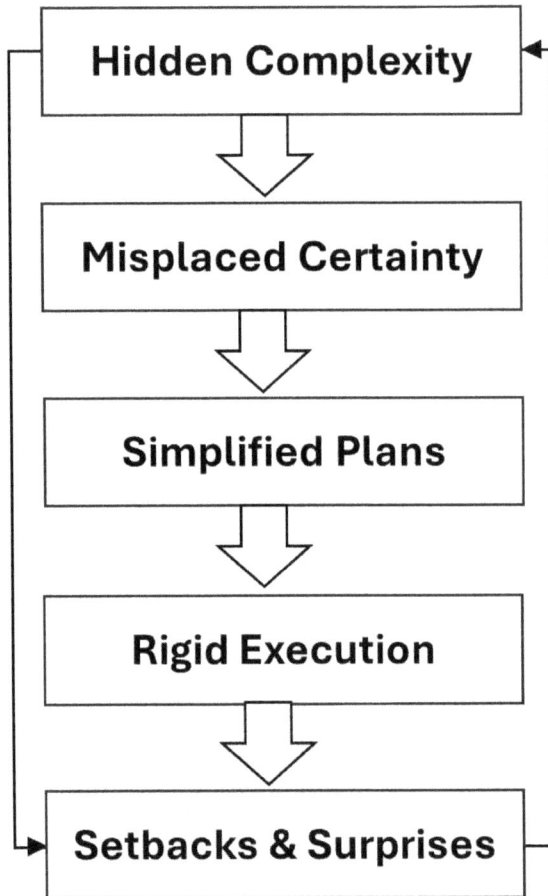

```
┌─────────────────────────────┐
│      Hidden Complexity      │
└─────────────────────────────┘
              ⇓
┌─────────────────────────────┐
│     Misplaced Certainty     │
└─────────────────────────────┘
              ⇓
┌─────────────────────────────┐
│       Simplified Plans      │
└─────────────────────────────┘
              ⇓
┌─────────────────────────────┐
│       Rigid Execution       │
└─────────────────────────────┘
              ⇓
┌─────────────────────────────┐
│    Setbacks & Surprises     │
└─────────────────────────────┘
```

As you read the list of big project vulnerabilities (*aka* kryptonite) you may have felt a bit overwhelmed. You may be thinking: 'That is a list of 8 other things that I need to attend to. Many of which are messy and not actually within my control.' Well, don't worry, that is a natural reaction. Stick with this; by the end of this section, you are likely to be thinking, 'This kryptonite is dynamite!' The goal is to equip you with a **practical and powerful framework to manage project complexity** and a new way to engage with hidden project risk.

To continue the super projects metaphor: As 'super' as Superman or Superwoman is, they still have a vulnerability – that is kryptonite. This makes their character more relatable, interesting and real. Similarly, even well managed projects, with experienced and dedicated teams, have big project vulnerabilities (BPVs). These are **nothing to be ashamed of**, they simply reflect the real-world complexity of delivering big projects within large organizations at a time of accelerating change and uncertainty. How a big project, and the people leading it, deal with challenges and setbacks is a key part of what really makes them super.

1. BUSINESS MYOPIA KRYPTONITE

Ultimately, the success of any big project is measured in business terms. For example, how well does it address a specific business need, further the strategy of the business or impact on its present and future performance? A project may deliver against the project plan, **delivering on time and to budget, yet fail to succeed** from a business perspective. In a complex fast-changing business environment, this happens more often than you might think.

Data shows that **the #1 factor behind project failure and frustration** (perceived or real) is the failure to meet changing business needs or priorities.[77] This is a point worth emphasizing. The #1 cause of project failure is not the skill of the project manager, access to resources, the task list – or any other 'project management' related factor. Rather, it is because, caught up in the busyness of a project, it is easy to lose sight of business needs and priorities. This 'project myopia' is increasingly prevalent in a time of fast-changing business needs and priorities.

Q: To what extent is your big project connected to changing business needs and priorities?

The challenge for any big project, whether it is from IT, HR or any other department, is to put the needs of the business ahead of departmental or project goals. This means putting the 'Business First' (as shown in the table below).[78]

Business First	Project First
Success measured in terms of business impact.	Success measured in terms of project outputs.
Deliver on the business strategy / vision.	Deliver on the project plan.
Adapt to changing business needs and priorities.	Deliver against a set of pre-defined requirements.
C-suite and board level strategy conversation is key.	Project plan and Gantt chart is key.
Cross-functional collaboration is essential.	IT or HR project led by the relevant function.
Focus is on business needs, impact, urgency, etc.	It is about project timeline, budget, tasks, etc.
Ongoing strategic conversations at C-suite are critical.	Traditional project planning and review workshops are enough.

Pause for a moment to reflect on your big project using the table above: **How many of the items in the left-hand column apply?**

Looking at the table, it is not that you don't need the items on the right (i.e., the traditional project-style thinking). These are still important, but to prevent myopia, they must be complemented by the business first factors on the left.

> To prevent project myopia, your big project needs a clear and compelling 'why.' That is what we call a 'Super Why,' as explored in **Chapter 3: Super Ambition**. This is one of the most universal aspects of a super project. In addition to playing a key role in engaging with internal complexity (examined here), it also underpins super ambition, super alignment and super collaboration too.

2. FIRST MILE KRYPTONITE

There is an urgency around strategies for performance and transformation. This is reflected in the rush to get projects speedily off the ground. However, **in the race to get a project up and running**, key issues may be left unaddressed. This could even include such fundamentals as business needs, market reality, business impact or the level of business investment.[79]

The first mile matters because, if you are off course by just a few degrees at the start, you could be out by miles by the time the project is well underway. Meanwhile, **unaddressed issues don't just go away**, but come back to haunt a big project.

Q: Do important issues remain unaddressed for your big project?

Q: To what extent has your project been set up for success?

'I was looking at the Olympic running' said the product team lead. 'The runners were stretching and waiting, then they started to take their places, ready to race and waiting for the starting gun. In the pressure of the moment one runner got the timing wrong and raced off, others hesitantly followed. But the gun had not been shot! Everybody had to return to their positions and wait for a re-start. While I was watching this I was thinking about our approach to big projects – the challenge of managing the urgency around getting a project up and going. Also, the danger of a false starts' he added.

Why do fundamental issues remain unaddressed when starting a big project? Well, our research highlights several reasons:

- There isn't enough time, given the pressure to get up and running. There may not be enough patience, either.

- Some issues or questions may be difficult to address, especially at the outset. Perhaps there is little available information, or opinions are divided.

- Project sponsors may fear that trying to address key issues up front could stall a project or prevent it ever getting off the ground.

- The process of consultation or dialog involved may be difficult and slow. Moreover, there may be a weariness of engaging internal stakeholders given its risks.

- A desire to act with greater speed and agility results in bypassing traditional planning processes and bureaucratic approvals procedures.

- The project cannot see beyond its own narrow technical goals, to engage effectively with business needs and priorities.

Q: Do any of the above apply to your big project?

> **'To speed up, you may need to slow down.'** That's one implication of the first mile, but it is a message that busy leaders may not want to hear. 'Save time' is probably a better message. Our data clearly shows that skipping steps such as clarifying business needs, or market validation, ends up costing a lot more time than it saves.

Leaders or sponsors may hope that outstanding issues will be easier to address once a project is up and running. However, this is often wishful thinking. Addressing difficult issues rarely gets easier, and the pressure to get a project off the ground is quickly replaced by the pressure to deliver results.

> Was it a slip of the tongue or a carefully considered and intentional commitment? Regardless, the division head had promised the board that the platform would be live in Quarter 4. As a result, people **were scrambling to figure out how to make it happen**. Meanwhile, the business fundamentals of the platform initiative were far from clear. The project data showed that only 3 of the 8 business fundamentals were rated 'green.'[80] The project team was divided: should they focus on putting the fundamentals in place, or just focus on the immediate deadline?

The first mile of a project[81] is the time to:

- Address the business fundamentals or strategic rationale.
- Ensure key stakeholders are engaged and aligned.
- Get the prioritization, timing and sequencing of initiatives right. After all, not all initiatives can proceed, and certainly not at the same time.
- Set the project up for success (adopting an approach to project management that balances rigor with agility).[82]

The first mile of a big project is not high speed – and often not very glamorous either. Yet, it serves the vital purpose of **setting a project up for success**. It ensures that projects that get the green light will have the maximum chance of success. A more cautious approach in the initial stages is one of the most effective ways of engaging with big project complexity.[83]

'This initiative was doomed from the start' said the leader of the struggling project. 'I can see clearly now…' she added after a brief pause, '…the obstacles and setbacks we now face can be traced back to the very earliest days of the project.' After multiple missed deadlines and with growing stakeholder disquiet, the project leader's comments, if overhead, could have been incendiary. After all, conversations around the project were already quite tense. As far as many were concerned, the project's success or failure would be laid at her door. But was the project leader seeking to evade responsibility or simply stating the obvious – that, in the rush to get the project up and running, some important fundamentals had not been addressed?

3. STAKEHOLDER KRYPTONITE

The real danger for any project is not that it does not reach the finish line, but that it gets there only to find that **the finish line has moved and that key stakeholders are waiting elsewhere**. In other words, their needs have changed and are not being met. This happens more often than you might expect, especially at a time of accelerating change and uncertainty.

Reaching the finish line becomes a lot more difficult when stakeholders are standing on the sidelines. We call it **the stakeholder-bystander effect**,[84] and it happens when those leading a project keep stakeholders at a distance, or because stakeholders choose to stay on the sidelines. Perhaps they are too busy, or they feel that their input is either unnecessary or unwelcome. Maybe it is just that they were not asked. However, while corporate leadership may delegate responsibility for the execution of a strategic initiative, it cannot abdicate responsibility for its success.

'Stakeholders have a stake in the game' says one of our coaching partners. 'But it is essential that they **share in the responsibility too**' she adds. It is too easy for certain stakeholders to stay on the sidelines:

- Highlighting problems, but not offering solutions.
- Holding the project team to the original budget or timeline, even when the scope of the project has expanded, or resources have been cut.
- Wanting it all and not being prepared to make trade-offs or compromises.
- Commenting on what could or should be, without any responsibility for making or enabling it to happen.

- Looking for written reports and slideshows on what is happening, rather than meaningful project conversations.

Q: Do any of the above apply to your big project?

Those leading projects know that it is dangerous not to involve stakeholders, but they also know that **involving stakeholders has risks too**. For example:

- The process of engaging important internal stakeholders can generate additional complexity, resulting in scope creep or confusion.

- Interactions with stakeholders are not always positive and supportive. Rather than being a relationship of equals, it can sometimes seem like that of a parent talking to a child.

'We are like a deli counter' exclaimed the team leader.[85] 'Stakeholders keep coming to us asking for things! As far as they are concerned, everything is urgent, and it is difficult to say no! The result is that we are being pulled in different directions, with an endless list of priorities competing for scarce time and attention.'

'We need to manage stakeholders proactively' added the team leader. Continuing the deli counter theme, she said: 'To some stakeholders, we need to be able to say: *"Take a ticket and wait in line."* There must be a process whereby any request and its implications are evaluated or at least planned for. When we say yes, we must clarify that other priorities must be put at the bottom of the list.'

When senior stakeholders are on the sidelines, project success is put at risk. Moreover, the people running projects are denied one of the most valuable organizational resources – the experience and foresight of its senior leaders.

Q: To what extent do key internal stakeholders actively share in the responsibility for your big project's success?

Given the importance of a big project, you would imagine that leaders would continually be talking about them (including progress, setbacks, lessons learned, risks and so on). Moreover, you would also expect those driving the projects to seek out every opportunity to tell their leaders what is happening. Sadly, this isn't necessarily true.

Many senior leaders operate a **'don't ask, don't tell'** approach to big projects. Leaders at the top (e.g., the CEO or the board) don't ask, while leaders in the middle (e.g., project leaders) don't tell. This is a trap that those leading super projects are keen to avoid.

4. POLLYANNA KRYPTONITE

Naturally, leaders are expected to be confident and ambitious regarding their projects and plans. However, too many organizations only do good news when it comes to projects and initiatives. This is a form of Project Pollyanna – a culture of excessive optimism where **people have learned to silence their doubts and concerns**. This is the result of a lack of psychological safety, respectful challenge or sufficient diversity of opinion.[86]

Q: Some leaders only want good news. What about you?

The result is that many project decisions are based on limited information – that is, only positive information. Ultimately, this leaves a big project vulnerable to setbacks and surprises. Rather than talking about risks, obstacles and setbacks, people stay silent or simply nod in agreement (the 'nodding dog' syndrome).[87]

Q: Can people talk openly about risks, obstacles and dependencies?

'Are we being overly ambitious?' asked the newest member of the leadership team. It was a question prompted by genuine concerns about the ability to deliver against target, given results to date and deteriorating market conditions. The question could have spurred a good debate at the leadership table. Instead, the result was a tirade by the CEO followed by stunned silence among the rest of the team. Clearly, the leader wasn't interested in dialog given the pressure to deliver. All but the very courageous would stay silent or nod in agreement.[88] That the project could become a super project was immediately in doubt.

For most surprises and setbacks that befall a big project or ambitious strategy, someone saw the danger but either didn't speak out or was not listened to. Enabling people to speak openly about risks, obstacles and setbacks is a key priority for those leading and sponsoring big projects and transformation initiatives. If the regulator (or anybody else comes knocking) they won't be able to say, 'Nobody told me' or 'It was not my responsibility.'

Q: Can people talk openly about risks, obstacles and dependencies?

How organizations engage with risk (as well as obstacles, dependencies and setbacks) varies greatly depending on the culture of the organization, the style of the leader and many other factors. However, 4 key patterns emerge as shown in the diagram.

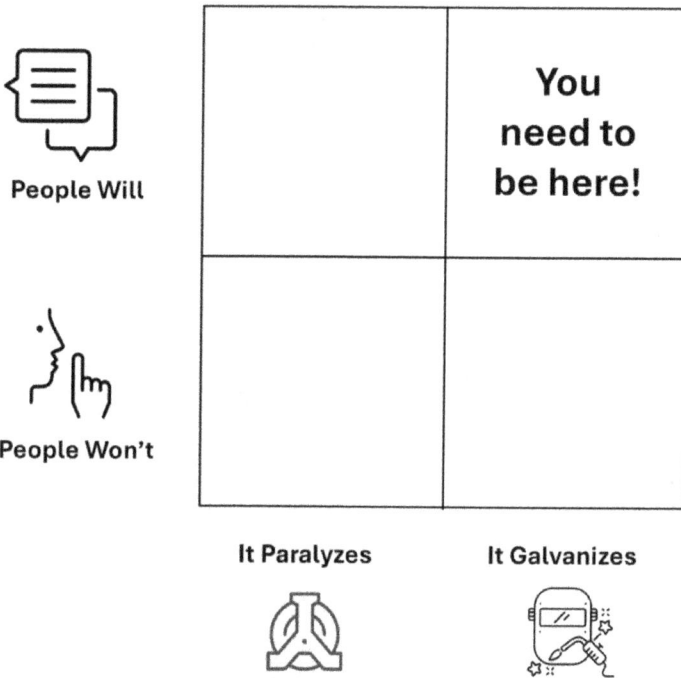

People Will

People Won't

You need to be here!

It Paralyzes   **It Galvanizes**

Galvanized or Paralyzed?

In some organizations people will talk openly about risks and obstacles, in others they won't (it is not safe or rewarding to do so). Even more important, however, is what happens when conversations about risk and resilience do happen. Will they have the effect of paralyzing or galvanizing the project, its stakeholders and team? That, according to our data, is the ultimate test.

Paradoxically, Super Confidence means being sufficiently confident to be able to talk about risks, obstacles and setbacks. But, if that does not sound like common sense, then there is an even more compelling reason to do it – to ensure compliance (as the next panel explores).

It was a banking systems migration that stole the headlines,[89] costing the CEO his job, the CIO almost $100,000 in personal fines and the bank over $400 million in penalties and other costs. In an assessment of the TSB systems migration debacle, the warning is clear: *.'..do not allow for risk to be lost or censored as it is summarized for senior audiences. This is central to the due care, skill and diligence expected of company directors and officers.'*[90] Regulators have made risk management mandatory in respect of big projects that impact on operational resilience and ICT systems or security.[91] Leaders cannot say they were not aware or were not told. They cannot simply point their fingers at vendors or suppliers either. They own risk management.

5. ALIGNMENT KRYPTONITE

As leaders, we may think: 'The strategy has been talked about for long enough, surely everybody knows what needs to happen!' Moreover, as we are so invested in our strategies and plans, we can be reluctant to entertain the idea that others are not similarly bought in or committed. Yet, as much as we want alignment to exist, **perfect and perpetual alignment is an illusion**.[92]

Q: Are people really as aligned as you think?

On paper, the organization's strategy makes its priorities clear, yet how resources are allocated is the true indicator of what really matters. On the surface there may appear to be alignment, yet people often say what the leader wants to hear, **stay silent or simply nod in agreement**. The illusion of alignment is a cognitive bias and an easy mistake to make. It persists for many reasons:

- We assume people think like we do.
- We expect people to speak up if they disagree.
- We believe misalignment is somebody's fault (with a lack of alignment reflecting on the leader or others).
- We think alignment is black and white, as in you're either aligned or you're not!

Q: Do any of the above apply to you or your big project?

As a senior leader, you are what is called a **'high status individual.'** That has benefits and perks, but it has drawbacks too. Being prone to the illusion of alignment is one of the potential downsides. It means you can easily lose touch with what is happening on the ground, or even with reality. Your high status means people are likely to tell you what you want to hear rather than telling you the truth, especially where it is potentially bad news. Moreover, the fact that you are busy and under pressure means that you have little time or patience to be involved in lots of conversations or lots of detail.

As leaders, we want alignment, we expect alignment and, based on the available data, we assume alignment. Occasionally, however, we get a glimpse of an alternative reality of competing priorities and people pulling in different directions. Rather than being disappointed or frustrated, **misalignment presents leaders with a great opportunity** – the opportunity to re-align people in terms of priorities, strategy and success. It presents leaders with an opportunity to have some of the most powerful of all big project conversations.

A household consumer brand decided to implement a new technology platform to enhance customer service. The leadership assumed that announcing the strategic benefits would ensure departmental alignment. However, the frontline staff who interacted with customers daily felt the new system complicated their workflows, leading to resistance and slower adoption. However, they were reluctant to speak up, fearing that it would be seen as a sign of disengagement. While many wondered if it would ever change, new leadership at the top of the organization ushered in a new era of open and honest two-way communication. The outlook for the project was suddenly much more positive, as well as more real.

6. PROLIFERATION KRYPTONITE

BIG projects are resource and bandwidth-intensive. They will struggle to thrive in an environment where there are many other projects and initiatives competing for scarce resources. Yet, our data suggests that there **are on average 7 transformation initiatives underway simultaneously** within any organization – each one of these could have up to 10 projects. The diagram overleaf estimates how resource intensive that could be.

Transformation Initiatives	Constituent Projects
7	**70**
Average per leader.	Average per Initiative = 10.
780	**242**
Emails per week.	Hours spent in meetings per week.

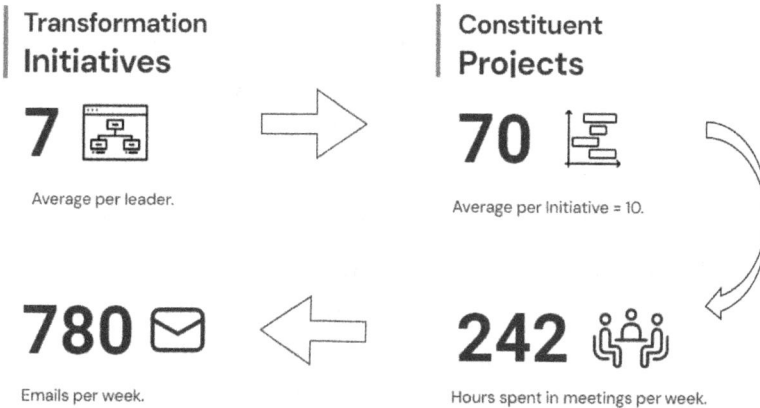

In ambitious organizations there will always be **more projects and initiatives than available resources**. When this stops to be the case, leaders will have reason to be concerned about their organization's commitment to change, innovation and transformation. Meanwhile, a proliferation of projects and initiatives presents challenges, as well as opportunities:

- Leaders find themselves juggling multiple priorities on top of their everyday responsibilities. Many risk burnout.

- Scarce resources are spread thinly over a long list of priorities and projects, with those that matter most being starved of sufficient time and investment.

- No sooner do organizations scrap one project, but another appears. In their efforts at consolidation, organizations have been playing 'whack-a-mole' with projects and initiatives.[93]

- Siloed or stand-alone project decisions and solo runs that result in little synergy, coordination or integration across the project portfolio.[94]

Q: Do any of the above apply to your big project?

> Two-thirds of leaders (66%) tell us they have had
> projects or initiatives scrapped or stalled, with the
> average number of projects affected being 3.7.[95] That
> sounds impressive, doesn't it? With that rate of
> consolidation, you would **expect project proliferation
> to be a thing of the past**. Yet, the numbers tell a very
> different story! Most leaders (84%) still believe there
> are too many projects and initiatives competing for
> time, attention and resources.[96] Yet, the reality is that
> most projects or initiatives are not a 'nice to have,' but
> a commercial necessity.

A more disciplined approach to prioritization should enable organizations to **focus with a new intensity on what matters most**. However, it is not easy. Greater discipline alone won't cut it. Prioritization is also driven by clarity, alignment, purpose and passion.[97]

Q: Has your organization mastered the art of disciplined prioritization?

Tackling project proliferation requires **greater focus and alignment** on key business needs and priorities. Ultimately, this is reflected in a (strategic) portfolio mindset,[98] where:

- Synergies are leveraged with knowledge and resources shared across the portfolio.
- Linkages, connections and dependencies between projects are managed.

- There is effective sequencing and timing of projects and initiatives (e.g., they cannot and should not all start at the same time).

In July 2022, Meta (formerly Facebook) announced plans for **'disciplined prioritization** and work with a high level of intensity to reach its goals.'[99] It was part of a global trend of consolidation that started in the tech sector following its pandemic-related boom. Although, a variety of words are used, 'Disciplined Prioritization' remains a key priority for many of today's CEOs. That big projects might have to wait in line for resources is one of the key factors that can prevent them from becoming super.

7. 'BUSINESS UNUSUAL' KRYPTONITE

Business Unusual is exactly what it says on the tin: Unusual. It is not the usual ways of working, organizing, managing or executing on strategy. Indeed, your big project will likely **challenge the way your organization works**, perhaps even the way it thinks.

Ensuring the peaceful co-existence of your 'business unusual' big project with the rest of the organization can be a real challenge. Especially, when it pits short-term performance against long-term transformation, innovation against bureaucracy, and operations against development.

Business as usual and business unusual are often seen as opposites (as per the table overleaf). In reality, however, projects are to be found on **a continuum from business as usual, to business unusual**. With this in mind, where would you place your big project on the business unusual continuum? Give it a number from 1 to 10, where 10 is completely business unusual and 1 is completely business as usual. A score of 5 would be half business as usual and half business unusual. A scale is important because it is not enough to say, 'business unusual is what the project team located in the far corner of the 3rd floor are doing.' Business Unusual cannot be boxed away like that.

Business As Usual	Business Unusual
Short-term	Longer-term
Performance	Transformation
Lower risk and uncertainty	High risk and uncertainty
Visibility and control	Speed, agility, collaboration and innovation
Bureaucracy, hierarchy and functional silos	Cross-functional matrix or network of teams

If an organization is 99% business as usual and 1% business unusual then what will happen to that rare and precious 1%? Like a diseased cell in the body, it will be **attacked by the organization's immune system**.[100] The goal should be to simulate innovation and fresh thinking in all the activities of the organization.

It is popular to talk about 'moonshots,' 'inflection points,' and 'blue ocean strategies.' But **what does blue ocean project management look like**? How does project managing transformation differ from project managing something more straightforward (e.g., a routine IT systems upgrade)? One thing is clear – you cannot manage business unusual initiatives like they are business as usual.

> **'Do we have permission to do that?'** asked the manager in all sincerity. For those unfamiliar with the organization's bureaucratic ways, the question may have seemed strange, perhaps even child-like in its subservience. Yet, it revealed how the group of long-tenured managers charged with delivering on transformation had become cynical of the prospects of change and weary of fighting with corporate.
>
> Of course, seeking permission does not sound very 'corporate,' but needing to get sign-off or approval certainly does. There is a host of formal 'business as usual' processes and procedures to be followed, as well as the informal norms to be adhered to. The result is organizational rigidity in an age that demands speed and agility – at a time when innovation is paramount.[101]
>
> On a positive note, our research shows that many teams fail to fully exploit the autonomy that they have. By contrast, those leading super projects **push the limits** in terms of what they are allowed to do.

Business Unusual is a by-word for many of the most complex challenges of modern leadership and strategy.[102] The problem is that the structures, processes and ways of working suited to BAU don't deal with the unusual very well. Thus, big projects that are managed as 'business as usual' will inevitably struggle when it comes to speed and agility, collaboration and innovation.[103] As one of our colleagues likes to say about complex projects – 'the U in Business Unusual stands for uphill struggle.' Yet, this can be a positive thing. Indeed, if there isn't **some tension or conflict**, maybe your big project isn't being innovative or ambitious enough.

> Some predictions put **Platform Teams as the future of IT**.[104] Consider a growth platform initiative aimed at enabling the next generation of financial products. It requires leaders from all functions – IT, operations, finance, compliance and marketing – to collaborate effectively. Operating outside traditional structures allows for bypassing conventional reporting lines, functional boundaries, and short-term performance targets. However, despite the potential offered by the platform team, it soon found itself wrestling with the rest of the organization to get things done. Its determination in doing so marked the platform initiative out as a super project.

Q: How successfully is your organization balancing the tension between business unusual and business as usual?

8. CORPORATE KRYPTONITE

Projects don't happen in a vacuum, but rather in the context of the wider organization. This can result in two forms of corporate project kryptonite. The first relates to the level of bureaucracy and the second to the level of noise within the corporate environment.

(a) Bureaucratic Kryptonite

There is 'the work,' and then **there is the 'work about the work.'** The latter can account for more than 50% of the busy executive's working week and includes internal meetings, procedures, reporting and so on.[105] Despite an organizational obsession with cost-cutting and efficiency, this major drain on productivity is typically overlooked.[106]

For every project or initiative, there is an **administrative and collaborative overhead**, including approvals, meetings, emails, documents and so on.[107] The more projects and priorities the greater the overhead and the less time there is for doing the work, especially the value creating or strategic work. Although rarely discussed, this is a bigger Issue regarding executive productivity than the usual suspects, such as quiet quitting or remote working. It directly impacts on levels of speed, agility, collaboration and innovation.

Think of the innovative potential of a group of 7 intelligent, experienced, and worldly-wise middle managers brought together from across the organization to drive a strategic initiative. With an average of 19 years per leader, the combined experience of the team amounts to a whopping 171 years. Such a team is likely to have **unbounded creativity and problem-solving potential** in response to the challenges or obstacles that emerge within the project. That this potential will be exploited cannot be taken for granted, however. It could all hinge on the requirements of getting new ideas or solutions approved, for example:

- How many committee meetings will be required?
- How many people must be convinced?
- How much paperwork will be required?

- How long will that take (e.g., weeks or months)?
- Will it need to go in front of a committee?
- What obstacles or blockers are likely to be faced?

Pause for a moment to apply these questions to your big project.

Faced with accelerated change, leaders are calling for more innovation. But calling for innovation is not enough. Nothing hampers speed and agility like top-down approvals or signoffs, rigid plans and traditional reporting. For innovation to happen, leaders need to ease bureaucracy and empower teams. This is reflected in an updated approach to project management that we call 3.0.[108]

Project Management 1.0	Project Management 3.0
Rigor	Agility + Rigor
Waterfall / bureaucratic	Agile / iterative
Top-down	Bottom-up
Task-centered	Talent and team-centric
Occasional project reviews	Regular project adjustments
Bureaucracy and control	Innovation and creativity
Project outputs	Business outcomes / impact
Removed from strategy	Connected to strategy

Q: How can approvals and reporting requirements be streamlined?

Traditional project management may be at a low point in its popularity, seen as an instrument of bureaucracy and control.[109] However, please don't mistake these paragraphs as a justification for bypassing **the key basics of project rigor** such as the Gantt Chart, project scope and budget, etc. Those leading super projects know that these are still essential. However, they use them in a way that enables the level of agility and innovation required for success in an increasingly complex and fast-changing world.[110]

(b) Noisy Kryptonite

If only those leading big projects could focus on their work, without sideshows and distractions, imagine how productive they would be. Unfortunately, that is not always possible.

With so much going on within organizations, it can be difficult to **keep the full focus and attention on a big project**. The endless cycle of strategy refresh, organizational restructuring and cost-cutting or efficiency drives has the potential to generate lots of noise and interference, thereby distracting from the focus on delivering a big project. Some implications highlighted by our research include:

- In an environment of cost-cutting and consolidation, people are naturally anxious to protect themselves – their position, even their job. Moreover, many executives have become cynical of the latest corporate initiative.

- With so much organizational change, people can become internally focused, thereby losing sight of what is happening with customers, competitors and so on.

- With increased pressure on short-term performance, and cost-cutting in particular, it can be difficult to maintain the focus on those initiatives aimed at growth and longer-term value creation.[111]

- It does not help that there can be a lot of uncertainty and speculation, as well as politics involved in transformation.

Q: Do any of the above apply to your big project?

In the words of business coach Timothy Gallwey, 'Performance is potential minus interference.'[112] Thus, a key role of the big project leader is to keep people focused and on purpose, despite everything else that is happening in the background. That is to stay focused on what they can control, rather than what they cannot.

> 'If you sat in the reception you would get the impression of calmness and order' said the senior leader. 'As a 70-year-old business, that is the image behind our brand. Yet, beneath the surface we are undergoing **massive change**. At times, it can start to feel chaotic, with yet another change initiative being announced' he added. Yet, those leading super projects can turn down the level of noise and interference, so people can 'keep their head in the game.'

Q: As a big project leader or sponsor, how can you buffer against organizational noise and distraction?

Organizational politics has the potential to amplify the level of noise and interference, especially if it is unmanaged. Here some re-think may be required.

Politics often has negative connotations. Yet, it is an essential element of how organizations work and how big projects access the support they need to succeed. Like any other aspect of a big project, it needs to be managed effectively. However, that requires navigating two extremes:

- **Politics Obsessed:** Some leaders are great at promoting themselves and their work – at managing upwards. However, being so caught up in what is happening in the organization, they risk losing sight of what is happening in the marketplace or at the front lines of the organization.

- **Politics Averse:** Other leaders turn their backs on organizational politics. They are closely connected to their customers and to the people serving them, but risk becoming disconnected from corporate and what is happening at the C-suite.

Q: How well is your project's leadership managing the issues of politics and power?

To answer this question please use a scale from 1 to 10, where 10 = 'politics obsessed' and 1 = 'politically averse.'

Next, pause for a moment to reflect on the implications. Is this the ideal position? If not, what should the number be, and how might it be achieved?

'What we are asking...' said the co-leader of the cross-functional project team, .'..is that you don't go to your boss alone talking about this project. Bring myself or somebody else from the project team with you, please. We need to present a united 'front to our key stakeholders.' It was, of course, a difficult situation given that each member of the project team had their own departmental boss. **Where should team member loyalties lie?** Well, naturally with those who would write their annual review and determine their next promotion. Yet, the co-leaders fear was that the interests of departmental bosses and the interests of the project were not necessarily aligned.

TACKLING KRYPTONITE

In tackling any of the hidden sources of complexity or potential vulnerabilities, here are some tips to follow:

- **Don't deny or run from it.** Rather, embrace the complexity. When one of these factors surface, it is an opportunity to reconnect with the super potential of your project. Talking about these vulnerabilities means that a project can be 'improved, rather than autopsied.'[113]

- **Don't take any of these vulnerabilities personally.** That may sound strange, but this happens all too often. For example, where a lack of alignment is seen by the leader as a personal slight or failing.

- **Avoid blame.** Don't scold the project leader or team. It isn't anybody's fault. These factors are systemic; they often have more to do with the environment than with any particular stakeholder or project team member.

- **Enlist others in finding a solution.** One person cannot fix these things alone. They can set the process in motion, but it requires a collaborative effort. Moreover, it requires open and honest dialog about strategy and success. For many of these issues, there is an important conversation not being had.

- **It is not just about fixing these things.** Indeed, many are not easy or straightforward. They are, after all, the stuff of strategy, culture and even structure. The challenge is to engage people with them. It is as much about asking the right questions as it is having the correct answer.

- **Go deeper, seek the root of the problem.** Not surprisingly, given the complexity involved in a big project, the 8 big project vulnerabilities (BPVs) can be both causes and effects. For example, Project Pollyanna (where a big project only does good news) can lead to the illusion of alignment and *vice versa*. Moreover, a big project vulnerability could signal a deeper issue.[114]

- **Re-examine mindsets and behaviors.** The solution to these factors is adaptive, not just technical. That is to say, learning a new skill won't be enough. A change of mindset or behavior is likely to be required. Take, for example, the curiosity, candor and courage required to embrace complexity (**Chapter 2: Super Confidence**).

- **'Complexity conscious'** leaders[115] require greater curiosity and humility. They must approach business opportunities and challenges with more creative approaches to problem-solving (including experiments, iteration and fast learning).

Q: Which of the tips for engaging complexity can you apply?

> We often think of successful projects as well-oiled
> machines – smooth, structured, and predictable. Yet,
> our latest research tells a different story: **big projects
> and transformation initiatives were 11% 'messier'** in
> April 2025 than a year earlier.[116] Of course, messiness is
> another way of talking about complexity (kryptonite or
> big project vulnerabilities). However, there's a twist—
> messiness isn't necessarily a bad thing. Indeed, there is
> money in the mess! Tackling the factors driving
> complexity and messiness (e.g., competing projects or
> priorities) can significantly boost project confidence and
> momentum.

EMBRACING COMPLEXITY

Big Projects are where organizations face the greatest
complexity. The classic response to complexity or danger is
'threat rigidity.'[117] This happens where leaders **double-down on
existing Business as Usual strategies**, structures, ways of
working, planning, budgeting and so on. Instead of adapting, the
organization becomes more rigid, as:

- Leaders hold ever tighter to the reins and adhere more
  rigidly to their plans.
- Decisions become more risk-adverse and short-term
  focused.
- Budgets are cut, with future-focused investments being
  most affected.

- Bureaucratic procedures and controls multiply, with more committees and approvals required.
- Short-term financial results become the primary obsession.

Q: Do any of the above apply to your big project?

Embracing complexity requires organizations to do what is almost counterintuitive – to **become more agile when the temptation is to become more rigid** (as in the table below).

Rigidity	Agility
Top-down bureaucratic control	Empowered teams with greater autonomy
Hierarchy and functional silos	Matrix or network of cross-functional teams
Rigid budgeting and planning cycles	Resource fluidity
Strategy is divorced from execution	Strategy and execution are aligned and agile
Risk averse / 'Play it safe'	Balanced risk-taking – high trust / learning environment

At times of change and uncertainty, **the lure of control** is great. But when speed, agility, collaboration and innovation are required, control could actually be the problem, rather than the solution. To profit from complexity, those at the top should loosen their grip, rather than wrestle for greater control. If they don't, complexity can start to feel like chaos.[118]

BUREAUCRATIC **C**ONTROLS

HIERARCHY

BUSINESS **A**S USUAL

WAYS **O**F WORKING

SILOS

In responding with agility, the organization sees both opportunities and threats and is primed to adapt to capitalize and **profit from change and uncertainty**:

- It adopts ways of working that enable speed, agility, collaboration and innovation.
- It updates its plan to reflect changing business needs and priorities.
- It empowers people and teams to act, giving them greater autonomy.
- It fluidly allocates resources to where they are needed most.[119]
- It stays connected to its purpose.

Q: How many of the above strategies can be applied to your big project?

Greater **speed, agility, collaboration and innovation** are required to profit from complexity. But it requires empowering leaders and teams closest to the action, giving them the resources and the power and autonomy required to adapt and innovate.

ANALYSIS & REFLECTION

Please indicate the extent to which you agree or disagree with the statements below. Add your rating to the right column, using a scale of 1 to 5, where 1 = 'Absolutely Disagree' and 5 = 'Absolutely Agree.'

Vulnerability	Statement	Rating
1. Business Myopia Kryptonite	Our big project is clearly connected to business needs and priorities.	
	There is no risk of our big project operating in a bubble and losing sight of business / market needs.	
2. First Mile Kryptonite	Our big project has been carefully set up for success.	
	In the rush to get started, no important issues were left unaddressed.	
3. Stakeholder Kryptonite	There are no key project internal stakeholders on the sidelines or disengaged.	
4. Pollyanna Kryptonite	People regularly discuss risks, obstacles and setbacks.	
5. Alignment Kryptonite	People are pulling in the same direction, being clearly focused on shared priorities and results.	

Vulnerability	Statement	Rating
6. Project Proliferation Kryptonite	There are <u>not</u> too many projects or initiatives competing for scarce resources.	
	Projects are <u>not</u> being managed in silos; linkages, synergies and shared resources are leveraged.	
7. Business Unusual Kryptonite	We don't apply business as usual methods or mindsets to the execution of innovative projects.	
8. Corporate Noise Kryptonite	The project team is <u>not</u> getting distracted by what is happening in the wider organization.	
	People are empowered to make it happen, without bureaucracy and reporting getting in the way.	

Pause for a moment to reflect on the 8 sources of kryptonite or potential vulnerabilities.

CHAPTER 5:

SUPER COLLABORATION

INTRODUCTION

Do you start a big project thinking **'Let the magic begin'** or simply 'Here we go again!' That is an instinctive test of super collaboration. However, when it comes to teamwork and collaboration on most big projects, there are a lot more meetings than there is magic!

Super projects succeed in transforming collaboration from a major drain on productivity into a force multiplier in terms of performance, innovation and momentum. This is what we call Super Collaboration and while it sounds magical, it is something that most projects can aspire to.

THE COLLABORATION IMPERATIVE

Big projects cannot be delivered in silos or by solo runs. Cross-functional collaboration is essential to deliver:

- The products that will beat the competition.
- The type of service that multi-generational customers expect.
- The technologies that drive efficiency and future-proof the business.
- The level of oversight that meets the needs of regulators and boards.

The essential strategies to drive today's performance or tomorrow's transformation require effective collaboration between IT, finance, operations, compliance, marketing, and more. Moreover, at a time of accelerating change and uncertainty, sequential handovers and sign-offs between departments or functions won't be enough. **Speed, agility and**

innovation require dynamic and efficient cross-functional collaboration. But is that what big projects presently enjoy?

> While trends such as remote working and the adoption of Ai steal the headlines, one of the biggest workplace shifts has gone unnoticed. That is the rise and rise of collaborative work and the explosion in the number of internal meetings. We call it a 'Tsunami of Collaboration' because of its sweeping effects – impacting on all aspects of work and the work experience. The result is a **new 70:30 reality**, where collaboration accounts for 70% of all work![120] The implications are huge, and leaders are still grappling with them.

THE STATE OF COLLABORATION

'One united team' – that is the refrain from so many visionary Chief Executives. They know that today's ambitious strategies require bringing people together from a diversity of backgrounds and functional specialisms. Yet, the **'one team ideal'** is far removed from the reality of cross-functional collaboration within most large organizations and many smaller ones too.

Two pieces of data from our research are sufficient to illuminate the state of collaboration:[121]

- 70% – the percentage of time executives are spending on internal collaboration. This is collaborative **overload**.

- 50% – the percentage of internal collaboration that 'adds little or no value.' This is collaborative **inefficiency**.

As these numbers reveal, collaboration on most big projects could hardly be described as 'super.' Indeed, second-rate might be a better term for it.

Pause for a moment: What % of your time is spent on internal collaboration? What % of that collaboration adds value?

It is difficult to put the words collaboration and efficiency in the same sentence. Indeed, for many organizations, **collaborative overload (i.e., the 70%) and inefficiency (i.e., the 50%)** are the key factors draining executive performance and productivity. This is especially true for the many leaders who:

- Start the week with up to 30 hours of internal meetings in their calendars.

- Get interrupted, on average, every 15 minutes, leaving less than one hour of uninterrupted time in a typical day. The primary casualty is 'focus time' to complete deep / complex work or even time to think – and especially to think strategically.[122] And add to that a higher risk of burnout due to run-away multitasking.[123]

As one of our colleagues jokes: 'What is a knowledge worker? It is a person who spends most of their time in meetings (mostly internal meetings)!' Given the portrait of internal collaboration above, this is perhaps not just a joke! Poor internal collaboration is **a critical bandwidth issue** and a key barrier to 'getting stuff done,' especially value creating work. This is particularly important at a time when resources are in short supply and cost-cutting, or efficiency dominate the business agenda.

'If meetings are the heartbeat of the organization, then we are at risk of congestive heart failure' joked the leader. But the humor masked a serious underlying frustration. Over the past week, the leader had 16 meetings. When they reflected on how many of them added real value, the answer was just 4! Moreover, as intelligent, experienced and senior as the leader was, they felt powerless to do anything about it! The problem is that to achieve super collaboration you have to believe it is possible.

COLLABORATION: A SIREN'S CALL

In times gone by collaboration may have been considered a 'nice-to-have.' Today, making collaboration more effective is one of the **greatest opportunities or challenges** for any big project.

Let's explore this with our key data points from the start of the chapter. With executives spending over 70% of their time on collaboration (i.e., overload) and 50% of that adding little or no value (i.e., inefficiency), the total waste **could be as much as 35% of all executive time** (i.e., 70% x 50%). That is a staggering figure, yet it is the data given by executives themselves. The implication is that up to a third of all the work taking place in meeting rooms, open-plan offices and in Zoom, Teams or Slack may be wasteful or inefficient. That is a siren's call for leaders everywhere.

The volume of inefficiency or waste inherent in poor collaboration likely **dwarfs the gains of most productivity drives** or cost-cutting programs. However, it is not just a challenge, but a big opportunity too. The 35% of executive time lost due to poor collaboration (as calculated earlier) is a heck of a prize. Imagine if only 10% or 20% of that waste was saved, it could:

- Boost project capacity or resources by between 3.5% and 7%.
- Increase the budget or number of people deployed by up to 7%.
- Save executives over half an hour per day, or almost 3 hours per week (every week).

These numbers make poor collaboration **bigger than all the hot topics of the last number of years**, including quiet quitting, performance paranoia and even remote working. Moreover, it can deliver much of the gains promised by Ai and automation.

> Shocked by the team's collaboration data, the leader had told his team: 'If meetings are not adding value then you can decline them and if somebody asked why you can point them to me.' Little had changed, however. The volume of meetings stayed the same and people still complained about having so little time to do their work. The leader was baffled, asking: 'Why are people going **"lemming like" from one unproductive meeting** to another?' FOMO was one of the answers, that is fear of missing out. More specifically:
> - Fear of what would be talked about or said if / when they were not present.
> - Fear that they would be out of the loop.
> - Fear that they would be sidestepped or overstepped.

HOW DID WE GET HERE?

While you have been busy tied up in internal meetings, something monumental has been happening. There has been a fundamental shift in how work gets done and organizations are run.

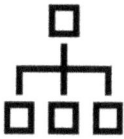

OLD Traditional Hierarchy

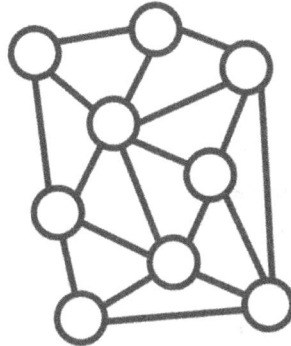

new **Network of Teams**

Organizations were built to master this:	Today, we expect them to master this:
Production line / Routine work	Knowledge work and project work
Predictability, efficiency and control	Speed, agility and innovation
Top-down functional hierarchy	Cross-functional matrix or network of teams
Business As Usual	Business Unusual (projects)

This is the reason you spend so much time on internal meetings and get frustrated as a result. You may think meeting overload is unique to your organization and its culture, but it is connected to something much bigger that has its origins in megatrends such as globalization, **the 4ᵗʰ industrial revolution and the rise of the information economy**. Meanwhile, our organizations are struggling to adapt. Here is why you are feeling the pain:

Big projects require a form of collaboration that most organizations were neither designed nor built to provide. Thus, while big projects require effective cross-functional collaboration, **the system is (in some ways) rigged against it**. For example:

- Traditionally organizations have been structured along **hierarchical lines**, with each function having its own leadership, budget and targets. This is more likely to foster silos and solo runs than effective cross-functional collaboration.

- As a fix, big projects are increasingly happening outside the traditional structure in a **matrix or network of cross-functional teams**. It can get confusing, since executives may be working on multiple projects and teams with different priorities and goals, and reporting to people who are not their direct boss.

- Traditionally, people have been hired, promoted and rewarded based on **individual (rather than collective) performance**. This is as likely to foster competition as collaboration.

- As a fix, organizations are starting to adopt a team-centric approach to talent. Yet, organizations may not know how many teams they have, how many are performing or not, and most important of all, what makes the difference between the two.

Organizations have mastered complexity before – take the production line or the global supply chain. Next is the need to master collaboration and the matrix too.

There is a whole new **science emerging around teams and teaming** that is only slowly being discovered within many industries. Traditionally, how organizations recruited, managed, motivated and rewarded people was largely focused on individual, rather than team performance. Moreover, the distinction between a team, a group or even a crowd is lost on most leaders. All this means that many leaders will be amazed as they discover the new science of teaming and the power of super collaboration.

STRIVING FOR MATRIX MAGIC

'*Teach an Elephant to Dance*' was a popular management book some years ago. It was a warning to large organizations that are too big and too slow that they cannot compete with new entrants in terms of speed and innovation. What our research shows, however, is that many large organizations have found a work-around. Although the org. chart shows a hierarchy, with functional lines of reporting, they know that not how you map innovation today. Rather, innovation is happening in a matrix or network of teams that span boundaries and functions. In this way, large organizations are increasingly adopting **a dual operating model** that enables:

- The highest levels of stability, predictability and control in its core business as the market and the regulator expect of any large institution.

- Innovation to be delivered with surprising levels of speed, agility and collaboration by cross-functional teams of extraordinarily talented and committed people.

As managers, we have been perfecting the hierarchical organization for a long time. But as today's leaders we have a new role. **The hierarchical structure has reached the limits of what it is capable of**. We see this in the fact that much of the important work – the truly strategic work – now happens in a network of teams that spans traditional boundaries and functions. Empowering and enabling these teams to succeed is our new role as leaders.

'Matrix magic is great when it happens' says one of our project coaching colleagues. 'But, in reality, there is more madness than magic' she adds, explaining:

- 'The **madness** is where people start their week with 20 or 30 hours of meetings in the diary and hundreds of unread emails – most internally generated.'

- 'The **magic** is when teams have all the expertise and power they need to make things happen with greater speed, agility, collaboration and innovation.'

Most organizations are still trying to make sense of the shift from departments and functions to cross functional teams. But, where is your organization on the **spectrum from matrix madness to matrix magic**?

Collaboration is the primary vehicle for knowledge work. It is the means of realizing the speed, agility and innovation required at a time of accelerating change and uncertainty.

Super Collaboration is what we call 'matrix magic.' It is the magic of teamwork and collaboration where it is needed most – that is in a cross-functional matrix (or network of teams). It has the potential to transform collaboration from a major drain on productivity into a force multiplier in terms of performance, innovation and momentum.

STANDARD SOLUTIONS FALL SHORT

Attempts to cut waste and optimize collaboration have ranged from the complex (re-organization, restructuring and cultural change programs) to the simple (new communications platforms and tools). However, the results are at best only mixed. The Return on Collaboration™ (this is the metric we use to measure the effectiveness of internal collaboration) has remained stubbornly low – it hovers around 63% based on our multi-year data.

Many organizations have focused on **cutting the number of internal meetings** (e.g., 20% to 30% reduction), the duration of meetings and the number of meeting attendees. Also, constraints in terms of the days on which meetings can take place (e.g., no meetings on Fridays). The aim is to enable people to get more stuff done, especially more strategic or value-adding work. It is also to remove an important source of frustration.

Cutting the number of meetings or the time spent in meetings is an obvious strategy, but it is not enough to deliver super collaboration.

Many organizations proudly proclaim that all development is done 'in-house.' But attend any big project update and you are in for a surprise – there are staff, contractors, consultants and more besides spread across multiple time zones. The new 'in-house' is 'a house without walls' – it is global (both near shore and far shore), it is hybrid and it is networked. It includes employees, contractors, partners, associates and so on.

There will always be more projects than people. Thus, organizations need to take talent everywhere they find it – orchestrating talent in new ways to deliver big projects with greater speed and agility.

Naturally, however, this 'talent everywhere' model presents control and co-ordination challenges. It requires a new operating model, with a focus on teams that are empowered to optimize the way that they work, interact and prioritize on an ongoing basis.

TOWARDS SUPER COLLABORATION

To succeed, big projects require super collaboration. This isn't just about fewer meetings or new communication tools or platforms. It goes much deeper than that, to include:

1. The Way We **Measure**: How a big project team (or network of teams) tracks and reviews its collaborative performance and potential.

2.   The Way We **Work**: How a big project team organizes its work (ensuring that the right people are in the right roles, doing the right work, etc.).

3.   The Way We **Interact**: The quality of interactions within a big project team, also called team dynamics.

4.   The Way We **Prioritize**: How a team dynamically focuses its energies, efforts and resources on what matters – ensuring clarity (in the now) around results, priorities and purpose.

You could think of the above as 'the Way of the Super Collaborator.' It is the path to matrix magic. More importantly, it has the potential to transform collaboration from **a major drain on time and productivity to a force multiplier in terms of performance, energy and innovation.**

Let's explore each of the 4 ways to super collaboration next but, before we do that, pause for a moment to reflect on the following question.

Known for his love of coffee, the manager's mug proclaimed in big letters: 'I survived another meeting that should have been an email.' It was evidence of mounting frustration with **the time consumed by meetings and other forms of internal collaboration.** Fast-forward eight months and the leaders of other departments and functions were starting to talk about the team as 'Super Collaborators!' The team had taken ownership for its own collaboration, moreover it had sent a signal to the wider organization – showing that there was a better way.

Q: Which of the 4 aspects of Super Collaboration are you most curious about for your big project?

Super projects are 'super soft' or to be more precise they are super at the 'soft' stuff. They have the ability to transform Individual high performers into high performing teams and silos into synergy. Let's explore how.

THE WAY WE MEASURE

Traditionally, teamwork and collaboration were considered 'unmeasurable,' 'messy,' and 'soft.' However, given their importance, they require the same science and sophistication as any other area of business. This starts with how they are measured. After all, **'what gets measured gets managed.'**[124]

Q: How well does your project measure or track team performance?

For the collective performance and potential of those working on a big project there are 5 big numbers. These are **5 next-generation metrics** used by leaders to illuminate the collaborative performance and potential, as well as the productivity and efficiency of a cross-functional team. You can see the numbers in the table overleaf, with an explanation on the next page.

What are your team's Big Numbers? Why not enter them. In the table you will see benchmark data covering 1,000 executives – it will help you compare your team to its peers.

Balanced Scorecard:	Benchmark	Your Team

Confidence in Performance	71%	
% Full Potential Exploited	65%	
Level of Pressure on People	74%	
Vitality / Well-being	73%	
Effectiveness of Collaboration	58%	

Just as your big project needs metrics and numbers, so does the team that is running it. Like the 5 vital signs for a patient, these numbers illuminate the collective health, as well as the collaborative performance and potential of a team (or network of teams). They are the **KPIs for effective cross-functional collaboration** – the key metrics for any team charged with delivering critical projects or initiatives:

1. **Performance** – What is the level of confidence in meeting target / delivering key results?

2. **Potential** - What % of your team's full potential is presently being utilized / exploited?

3. **Pressure** – What is the level of pressure (where 100% = peak pressure) on your team and its members?

4. **Vitality/Well-being** – To what extent is your project team and its members thriving (100% = thriving)?

5. **Collaboration** – How effective (where 100% = very effective) is collaboration within your team / organization?

Pause for a moment to answer the questions above.

Q: Which of the 5 big numbers matters most to your project team at this time?

We refer to these 5 Big numbers as KPPIs (key performance **potential** indicators) as they relate not just to today's collaborative performance, but to **the sustainability of performance** into the future.[125] They are, in essence, a balanced scorecard for teamwork and collaboration that address the twin 'better work — better life' goals. The 5 big numbers serve the needs of the team, as much as they do the needs of the project / organization. Thus, teams have a reason to be curious, rather than cautious, about these metrics.

The mere act of putting numbers on the collaborative performance of teams and networks of teams signifies that they matter. Also, that teams matter, and **super collaboration or peak performance doesn't just naturally evolve**.[126] This is particularly true in respect of high performing individuals – they often face the greatest challenges when it comes to collaboration.

> Naturally, as leaders we focus on the result (especially short-term results). However, we may pay little attention to **how the results were achieved**. For example, we ask whether the project deadline was met, without any consideration as to the price paid in terms of employee productivity, engagement or other factors that could impact longer-term results. Super projects use the 5 numbers to provide a more holistic view of performance. Using the numbers at the start of every project review signals that **the team matters as much as the task(s)**.

What is interesting about the big numbers is that there are 5 numbers, not just one. Like the numbers on a combination lock, you cannot just change one number in isolation. **Collaboration**

is situational and is connected to many other things (performance, pressure and so on).

The BIG numbers **set the leadership agenda**, shaping priorities and goals. For some teams the focus may be on managing pressure; for others it may be on vitality or collaboration. Importantly, these BIG numbers are not fixed. Leaders and their teams **can improve collaboration** and the other related numbers by attending to the 4 elements of super collaboration. That includes the Way We Work, examined next.

When we talk about *Super Collaboration*, it's important to make a key distinction: we're focused on **super teams**, not super groups – and definitely not super crowds. The team is the core unit of performance, but only when it's kept to a manageable size. Smaller teams collaborate better, move faster, and deliver more. If you want to make collaboration harder, just add more people. A group of 14 or 18 isn't a team – it's a group. The real teams are often smaller and hidden within. Find them, back them, and help them work well together. And above all, don't ask a group to do the work of a team.[127]

THE WAY WE WORK

If teams had a superpower, it would be the ability to optimize and refine the way they work.[128] This **self-organizing and self-optimizing potential** is vast, but largely untapped. Changing this situation is essential to becoming a super project.

Super projects are complex and business unusual. They demand greater levels of speed, agility, collaboration and innovation. That requires working in a **cross-functional matrix**, rather than a departmental hierarchy. Thus, super projects challenge traditional role definitions, reporting relationships, ways of working, and so on. Most important of all, they demand that teams take (and are given) greater control over the way that they work.

Q: Does your team 'own' the way that it works?

There's a lot that teams have little control over – for example, the corporate strategy, structure, or culture. But teams have **more control than they think** over how they organize themselves and their work. Without re-drawing the organization chart or changing job titles, they can find the best way of working together. This can enable them to get more stuff done, taking productivity and efficiency to new levels. It also enables them to bring out the best in each other.

'Ways of Working' is a hot topic with many buzzwords. But, while it is an interesting subject for a business blog or HR conference, it is largely the territory of business writers, consultants and academics. By contrast, **'the Way We Work'** is an actionable agenda. It is specific – the 'WE' is your own unit, group or team. The focus is on how WE (i.e., your unit or team) work today and how WE will work tomorrow, given the priorities, projects, work streams and tasks before us.[129] Most importantly, it is about how as individuals and teams WE will benefit.

The 'way we work' is about those who are closest to the work taking greater ownership and accountability for literally the 'way that they work.' It involves teams planning and reviewing, not just the work that is done, but **how it gets done**. It means approaching projects, tasks and even meetings with a performance mantra or checklist (called the 9 Rights) in mind:[130]

- Are all the **Right People**?
- In the **Right Roles**?
- Doing the **Right Work**?
- At the **Right Time**?
- Working together in the **Right Way**?
- In the **Right Place** (e.g., WFH / WFO)?
- With the **Right Resources**?
- And the **Right Rewards**?
- To achieve the **Right Results**?

In the real world it is not possible to get all the 9 Rights 'right' all the time. What leaders and their teams can aim for, however, is to progressively optimize them over time, thereby finding the source of **the next 2%, 5% or even more** in terms of performance.

Q: How can your team optimize the way that it works?

Productivity and efficiency have topped the list of business priorities in recent years. Terms such as productivity theater, quiet quitting and performance paranoia have dominated the headlines. For ourselves, we have long held the view that **it is OK to be paranoid about performance** and that some paranoia is a good thing.[131] However, productivity and performance are no simple matter.

Our data suggests that all but 1 in 20 organizations have recently undertaken a productivity or efficiency drive. Yet, the level of executive productivity has stubbornly remained below 70%.[132] Why the disappointing results? Well, all evidence points to the need for **a re-think of productivity in the era of the knowledge worker**.[133] That is exactly what the 9 Rights is. As it can be used by anyone, almost anywhere, we call it the 'Swiss Army knife' of performance and efficiency.[134]

The graph shows an analysis of 7 of the 9 Rights for 1000 executives using data gathered by our Pitstop Analytics™ platform. It illuminates the complexity of working on a cross-functional team within large organizations to deliver ambitious projects and strategies.

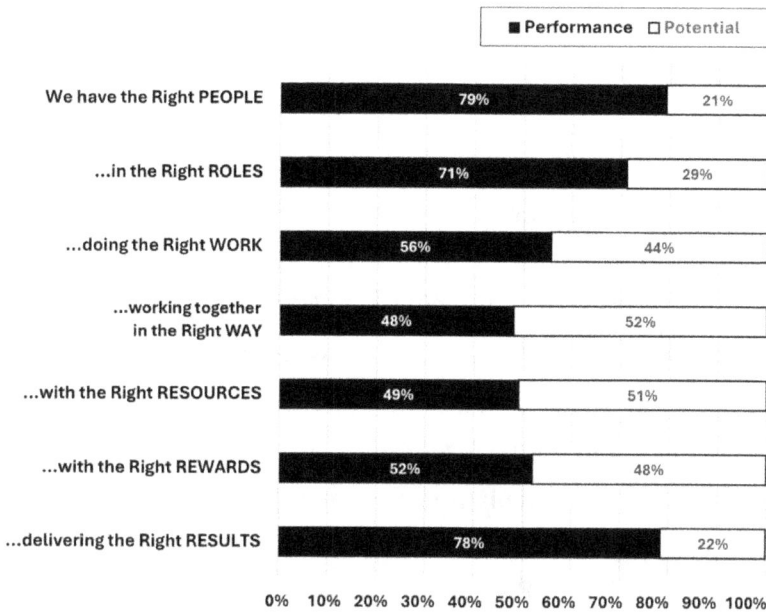

	Performance	Potential
We have the Right PEOPLE	79%	21%
...in the Right ROLES	71%	29%
...doing the Right WORK	56%	44%
...working together in the Right WAY	48%	52%
...with the Right RESOURCES	49%	51%
...with the Right REWARDS	52%	48%
...delivering the Right RESULTS	78%	22%

0%   10%   20%   30%   40%   50%   60%   70%   80%   90%   100%

There is a 'glass half full' and a 'glass half empty' way of interpreting this analysis. Thus, for each of the 7 factors, the graph shows two scores. The first is the performance score, for example a figure of 79% for 'the Right PEOPLE' and then the potential score of 21% (i.e. 100% - 79%).

The 7 Rights is a powerful proxy for **team productivity and efficiency**, with the average score being 62% (based on the 7 factors shown in the previous graph). However, it is even more powerful in terms of illuminating the potential to boost productivity and efficiency.

From our perspective, it is difficult not to look at the graph and get excited about the opportunity that exists within most teams. Specifically, the potential to boost productivity and efficiency by up to 38% (based on the average of the percentages shown in white). However, let's be more modest and practical in our goals.

Pause for a moment to reflect on the Way We Work (the 9 Rights) for your team. Can you use the diagram overleaf to find the next 3%, 5% or more for your team?

The analysis on the previous page has a direct impact, not just on performance or productivity, but on all of your team's big numbers (potential, pressure, vitality and collaboration). Moreover, optimizing the Way We Work has the potential to benefit not just the organization but its people too.

The Way We Work helps teams to get into 'the zone' (or what we call the Zone of Peak Performance™).[135] Think of the flow state – the immersive high-performance state where a person is simultaneously getting the most out of, and giving the most to, their work.[136] **The 9 Rights is the flow state for teams**, with the potential to deliver productivity and performance gains that are much greater. The 9 Rights is where the magic of teamwork and collaboration happens. Thus, it is the essence of matrix magic for cross-functional teams.

The Way We Work:

Where will your team find the next 3%, 5% or more?
Use the stars below to explore your project team's performance & potential.

Right ROLES?
YOUR PROJECT'S RATING:
☆☆☆☆☆

Right WORK?
YOUR PROJECT'S RATING:
☆☆☆☆☆

(working together)
Right WAY?
YOUR PROJECT'S RATING:
☆☆☆☆☆

Right REWARDS?
YOUR PROJECT'S RATING:
☆☆☆☆☆

Right RESOURCES?
YOUR PROJECT'S RATING:
☆☆☆☆☆

Right RESULTS?
YOUR PROJECT'S RATING:
☆☆☆☆☆

Right PEOPLE?
YOUR PROJECT'S RATING:
☆☆☆☆☆

Right PLACE?
☆☆☆☆☆

Right TIME?
☆☆☆☆☆

The pharma industry shone during the pandemic, bringing new vaccines to the market in rapid time. However, the process of drug development is a commercial form of high stakes gambling, with 8 out of 10 drugs in development failing to reach the market. Obviously, science is the key factor, but what about the people in the lab and elsewhere – what role do they play in success? For example, if the same drug candidate was given to two different teams (within the same organization and using the same scientific methods), would the result be the same? Our research suggests that the difference between product development teams (and more specifically the Way We Work or 9 Rights) could boost the level of R&D Productivity (and ultimately drug success) by 2% to 6% directly and by many times that indirectly. That could amount to savings of millions per drug and billions across a drug pipeline or portfolio. Industry-wide it could result in **an additional 100 new drugs every 12 to 15 years**, with the impact on people's lives being more difficult to measure.[137]

Empowering teams to optimize the way they work (and interact) using the 9 Rights can **save teams 2 to 4 hours per week** per team member. Given the constraints on resources, that is a major boost to any project. Moreover, given the cost of any team, the business case for even single figure gains can be significant. However, that is not all! Given that teams are the primary vehicle through which people experience their work, this is an area with an outsized impact on our working lives. All told, the 9 Rights could have a greater practical impact than the latest corporate strategy or re-structure.[138]

According to pop psychology, we feel good about things to the extent that they seem within our control.' Moreover, a sense of **empowerment and autonomy** can really bring out the best in teams. The 9 Rights 'puts people in the driver's seat,' resulting in greater ownership and accountability. It reduces the number of **'IF ONLY' moments** within a team. Those are moments when your team feels disempowered and not in control – when it is looking for others to fix its problems or giving its power away. In those moments a project either moves closer to or further away from being a super project.

> Many leaders have a strangely hands-off or *'laissez-faire'* approach to teams. There is an assumption that teams will rise to the level of their ability, achieve a high level of productivity and efficiency, while also bringing out the best in each other. It is as if bringing talented people together is enough to create a high performing team. However, high performing teams are not naturally occurring and are far from the norm. Indeed, depending on how you define a high performing team, they are as rare as 1 in 10 or even 1 in 20. Those leading super projects know that a peak performing team requires getting a lot of things right – specifically the 9 Rights (right people in the right roles and so on).[139]

Q: Is yours a peak performing team?

Productivity and efficiency are important, but they aren't everything. Efficient, but soulless, interactions can only take a project so far. The **quality of the interactions also matters**. So, creating an environment that brings out the best in each other also matters. That leads us to the next dimension of super collaboration, called the Way We Interact.

THE WAY WE INTERACT

Normally, we describe a team in terms of the work it does, who is on it and where it sits on the organizational chart. We might also talk about the number of people, their key responsibilities and focus or expertise. But there is another way to think of a team – it is to see it as a bundle of interactions. For example, **one team equals approx. 1,000 interactions** (i.e., emails, calls, IMs and so on) per month.[140] Each interaction can either be positive and efficient, or it could be an unwarranted and unmanaged interruption.[141]

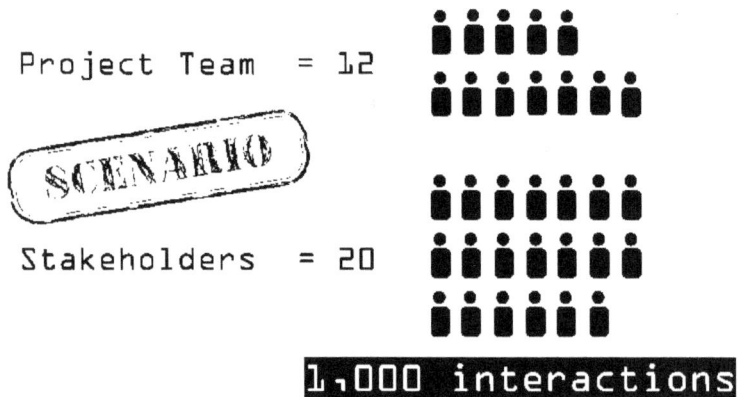

Project Team = 12

SCENARIO

Stakeholders = 20

1,000 interactions

The 'way we interact' is defined in terms of **8 specific team dynamics or behaviors:**[142]

1. Sense of urgency.
2. Trust and respect.
3. Excitement and adrenaline.
4. Tension and cohesion.
5. Communication.
6. Discipline and persistence.
7. Continuous improvement.
8. Everybody wins.

Pause for a moment to reflect: Are there any of the 8 dynamics shown here that you feel can be optimized for your team(s)?

The eight team dynamics often evolve without conscious consideration, but with awareness and dialog, they come within a team's direct control.

When we optimize the 'way we work' and the 'way we interact' together, we can **simultaneously boost organizational performance and organizational health**. The latter, which is typically called culture, has a significant impact on performance. Indeed, some research suggests that it could account for half of success. But that is not all, the Way We Interact is also a significant new strategy in terms of cultural change.

Many organizations are struggling with the issue of **cultural change**. There is a growing realization that the traditional methods used to transform culture (i.e., training programs, organizational restructuring and executive mandates) are coming up short. However, 'no sooner does one door close than another opens' when it comes to cultural change. As Roger L. Martin ('the world's #1 management thinker') puts it: 'Culture – you can only change it by altering how individuals work with one another.'[143]

While direct attempts at cultural change are struggling, new strategies are proving to be surprisingly effective. These strategies are aimed at **changing culture by enabling people to optimize how they work and interact** at the level of the team. This shifts the focus to the dynamics of specific teams, rather than the overall culture of the organization. The result is an operational definition of culture, that makes it more actionable and real (as can be seen from the table below).

Shifting the focus away from the culture of the organization to the dynamics of a team(s), illuminates specific critical behaviors **within a team's control**. Here, the means of change is to generate front-of-mind awareness and intentionality as to how leaders and their teams interact.

Organizational Culture	Team Dynamics
• Expansive (organization-wide).	• Focused (group or team).
• Vague, abstract and nebulous.	• Specific 'critical' behaviors.
• Messy, unmeasurable and soft.	• It can be measured and managed.
• Difficult to change.	• Dynamic – changeable.
• Often simplistic ('the organization as a machine').	• Embraces complexity (the organization as a complex social system).

If you have been to the movies recently, you will probably have noticed that today's heroes are team players. For example, there are the Avengers, the Justice League, The Fantastic Four and the Guardians of the Galaxy. When it comes to saving the world or delivering a big project, the heroic solo run is no longer enough. **It takes a group or a team to win.** The ability to turn individual high performance into a high-performing team is the ultimate superpower.

THE WAY WE PRIORITIZE

When people pull together, amazing things can happen. However, with multiple priorities and projects, people often find themselves being pulled in different directions. The result is waste, inefficiency and frustration.

'Today I have 21 KPIs' complained the leader in a perplexed tone. 'Next month I could have 23!' he quipped. Those leaders running super projects must master the skill of 'disciplined prioritization.'[144]

That brings us to the 4th element of super collaboration, prioritization, or to give it its full title **'disciplined prioritization.'** This enables leaders to focus with a new intensity on those priorities and projects that matter most. It requires leaders, stakeholders and teams to be focused and aligned in respect of:

1. **Priorities**: Is there a laser-like focus on the key priorities at this time?

2.   **Projects**: Are key projects getting sufficient time and attention? Remember: 'Projects are the new way of working... organize around projects not jobs.'[145]

3.   **Results**: What is the level of confidence in meeting key targets or deliverables?

4.   **Purpose**: Are people fired up by a clear and compelling purpose (especially for the next 3 to 6 months)?[146]

A clear and compelling 'why,' or 'super why,' is at the core of super collaboration – just as it is essential to super ambition, super alignment and super complexity. The above are **4 ways of defining the 'why'** – right results, right priorities, right projects and right purpose. This is important because if the 'why' is compelling enough, people will find a 'how.' Moreover, if the 'why' is a shared 'why,' teamwork and collaboration become a natural act. However, in a dynamic environment, the 'why' is often in flux and requires ongoing attention.

'It is beginning to feel a bit chaotic around here' said the member of the transformation Leadership Team. From the nodding heads, it was clear others were thinking the same. 'The busier we get, the more difficult it is to make real progress, and the more we seem to be **pulled in different directions**' she continued. 'The uncertainty in the market seems to be amplified by a lack of clarity and alignment on key priorities (rated 67% and 71% respectively)' she added. 'This is an opportunity to clarify what is really important and what is not. Thereby aligning resources and focus with greater intensity on the key priorities and initiatives that matter most.'[147]

Disciplined prioritization (revisiting results, priorities, projects and purpose) is one of the most powerful ways to boost performance, engagement too. However, it doesn't come naturally – it is typically **hard won and easily lost**. This is especially true at a time of accelerating change. However, a new approach makes focus and alignment easier. It has 3 essential elements:

1. An agile approach with **dynamic adjustment** as business needs and priorities change.[148] This contrasts with rigid plans that are quickly invalidated by changing events.[149]

2. A **bottom-up** approach, involving those closer to the work in the setting of priorities and goals. This contrasts with the traditional approach of cascading goals from the top of the hierarchy.

3. **Smarter goals** that are more actionable, measurable and real. In particular, linking priorities to quantifiable results and distinguishing inputs and activities from outputs and outcomes (also explored in **Chapter 1**).

For a business unit to have 50 or more 'live' projects is not unusual. If the average budget is $1.5 million, that represents a total investment of $75 million. For large organizations the number of projects and initiatives could be many times that. Then, of course, there are the 'projects in waiting' – those that are being planned or are seeking approval. Maintaining oversight of such an 'army' of projects is no easy job. Yet, it is essential if the organization is to focus on what matters most. **Disciplined Prioritization** is essential for super projects.

Q: When is the last time your big project team reviewed its results, priorities and purpose?

> 'In this organization everything is urgent – everything is a priority' said the jaded business unit leader. 'As for the last time **a priority was removed from the list** – off the top of my head I would have to say *"Never!"*

A NEW OPERATING MODEL

There is growing frustration with the time spent in meetings and other forms of internal collaboration. Often, we can put a name and a face against it, pointing to a particular leader, department or team that is impossible or frustrating to work with. But the collaboration challenge is bigger than any or all of us. It is the result of **a monumental shift in ways of working** and the emergence of knowledge work.

It is the result of a workplace revolution bigger than remote working or even Ai, yet it has happened unnoticed. That is a **Tsunami of Collaboration** and resulting flood of internal meetings. The implications are huge and leaders are still grappling with them. Many argue for a fundamental re-think of the model of work, the workforce and even the workplace.[150]

Talk of a new operating model sounds complex, yet the solution may be closer to hand than you think. It is to practice the 4 ways to achieve super collaboration (as explored in this section).

'Let go of the old:

WORK   ⊕   **WORKFORCE**   ⊕   **WORKPLACE**

Operating Models of the past.'

Deloitte Human Capital Report, 2023.

Super collaboration has the potential to accelerate progress and momentum, like little else. Moreover, it **requires little if any investment in terms of additional resources or technology**. Importantly, it does not depend on organizational change and restructuring either.

> Investing in talent is a key pillar of business strategy, with the competition for A-players and key skills being constant concerns.[151] However, the scarcity of talent, is only a part of the problem, especially if the best talent is being hired to be put into environments that are just 62% productive or efficient (as shown earlier). Moreover, hiring individual high performers fails to take account of the importance of teamwork and collaboration. In particular, the 9 Rights analysis challenges the assumption that bringing individual high performers together is enough to generate a high performing team.

ANALYSIS & REFLECTION

Having explored the 4 ways in which leaders and their teams can realize super collaboration, which one represents the greatest opportunity for your team? Use the diagram overleaf to recap.

Once you have selected one or more of the 4 'ways of the super collaborator,' return to the page(s) in question and explore the various aspects involved – for example, the 9 Rights of the Way We Work or the 8 Dynamics for the Way We Interact.

Remember, nobody is in a better position to tackle the barriers to driving productivity than the people who are planning, managing and doing the work. Highly productive teams take greater control of the way they work, interact and prioritize – this is their hidden superpower.

'If the senior leadership is out of alignment by 2%, what impact does that have two levels down in the organization?' asked the consultant. 'Well, 10% to 15%, I guess.' replied the CEO. 'And it probably gets exponential after that!' he added. In so doing, the leader underlined the consultant's message: 'Nothing signals the importance of alignment more than the behavior of those at the top of the organization. When the senior leadership team masters alignment, much of the rest of the organization magically follows.'

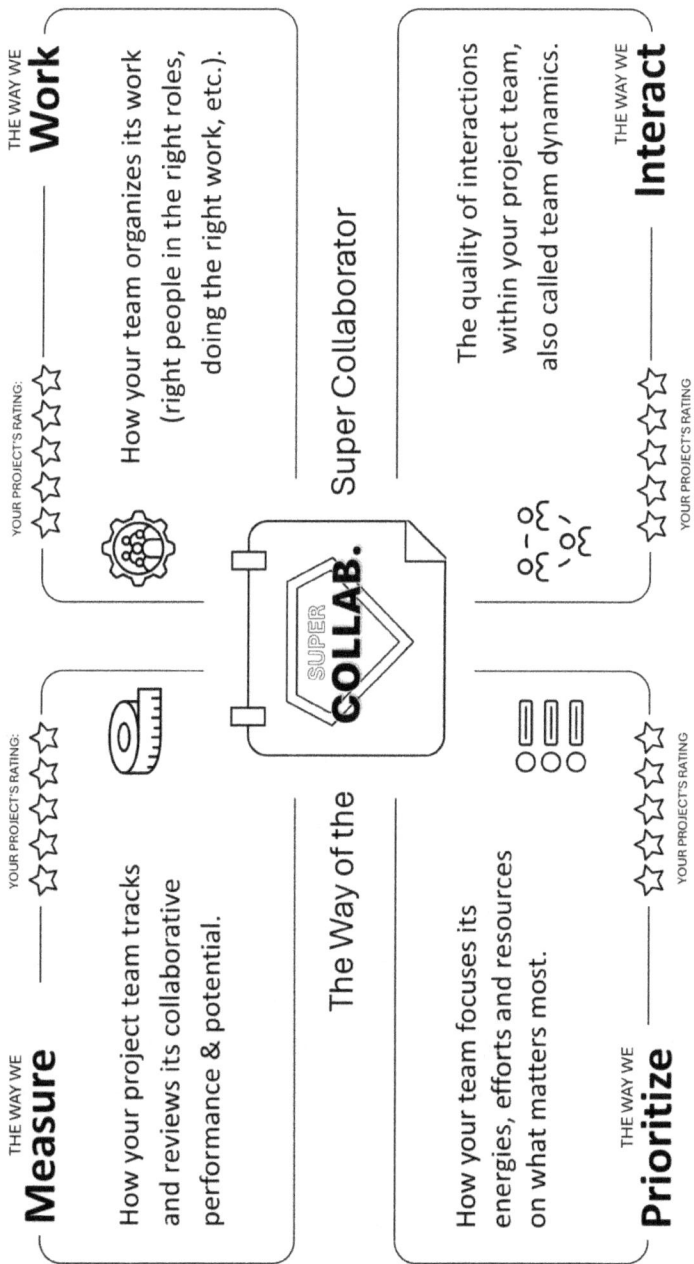

THE WAY WE
Work

YOUR PROJECT'S RATING:
☆☆☆☆☆

How your team organizes its work
(right people in the right roles,
doing the right work, etc.).

Super Collaborator

THE WAY WE
Interact

The quality of interactions
within your project team,
also called team dynamics.

☆☆☆☆☆
YOUR PROJECT'S RATING

SUPER
COLLAB.

THE WAY WE
Measure

YOUR PROJECT'S RATING:
☆☆☆☆☆

How your project team tracks
and reviews its collaborative
performance & potential.

The Way of the

How your team focuses its
energies, efforts and resources
on what matters most.

☆☆☆☆☆
YOUR PROJECT'S RATING

THE WAY WE
Prioritize

Some may say that the present environment in many organizations is NOT ideal for enabling teams to thrive. That is because of the focus is on re-structuring, cost-cutting or efficiency, and little else! However, **some teams are thriving despite all the noise and distraction** in their environment. As one big project leader put it: 'As a project team, there are many things that we cannot control and plenty of potential distractions. What we can control, however, is how we organize our work and how we interact with the rest of the organization. What our numbers show is just how powerful this can be.'[152]

A few decades ago, the message was KISS – 'Keep it simple stupid!' Today, it is the opposite: **Embrace Complexity**! But first you must be aware of it. Our data warns that senior leaders may be up to 20% less complexity aware than those who are charged with 'making it happen.'[153] This is a surprise risk to the execution of ambitious strategies and plans. It is also a key reason why super projects engage and empower those closest to the action.

CHAPTER 6:

ACTION HEROES

INTRODUCTION

Super projects are powered by people. So, while most of this book has focused on 5 superpowers (super ambition, etc.) super projects ultimately derived their strength from their people.

This chapter is about the people who bring strategies to life, often against the odds. These are the new organizational heroes. The goal is to enable you to recognize, foster and support them.

SUPER PROJECT

ACTION
HERO

Latent ├──────┼──────┼──────┼──────┤ Manifest

OPENNESS
(esp. to challenging ideas)

THE NEW ORGANIZATIONAL HEROES

Everyone needs heroes – people we can look up to and be inspired by. This is especially true in difficult times when danger surrounds us, and the future seems uncertain. We need people that point the way forward and give us hope for the future.

Every organization and industry faces challenges – including regulation, competition and technology. That is why heroes are needed. But where to find them? Well, what our research shows is that **they are to be found in surprising places.**

Traditionally, corporate heroes were pictured in the annual report, named in the press release or featured in a business magazine. They were visionary leaders with ambitious strategies – they were to be found at the top of the org. chart. However, **a new definition of corporate heroism** is emerging. It is of the action hero – the people who bring ambitious strategies to life. They are to be found at the coalface, as the leaders of cross-functional teams driving ambitious projects and initiatives.

Look closely and every organization has its action heroes. They are not always in the limelight and often go unnoticed but are essential to '**making things happen**' and bringing ambitious strategies to life.

These new action heroes possess **extraordinary talent, passion and determination**. They need to because our big organizations don't always make it easy. Our action heroes must wrestle with competing priorities and scarce resources. They also wrestle with aligning stakeholders, cross-functional collaboration and managing internal bureaucracy. But these obstacles don't stop them! Our action heroes go through bureaucratic walls and functional silos to make it happen and are capable of surprising speed, agility and innovation.

> *'..you don't have to be able to fly like Superman, scale walls like Batman or become green and super strong like the Incredible Hulk to turn a great strategy into great performance. You need performance-driven managers who master Strategy Execution.'*
> **Jeroen De Flander**, *'Business Strategy Heroes'*[154]

WHAT MAKES A HERO?

The message is: *'Today's corporate heroes aren't just visionaries, but "actionaries" too.'* They are the action heroes who make things happen. But, what is it that makes some project and portfolio leaders heroes? Well, there are 4 heroic attitudes and behaviors that form the acronym HERO:

1. **Honesty** – even when it hurts.
2. **Empowerment** – despite constraints.
3. **Relentlessness** – despite obstacles and setbacks.
4. **Openness** – even to challenging ideas.

These 4 qualities are not a value judgement on the people involved but **reflect the environment** within which they are working and a project is happening. These **latent heroic qualities exist within every project.** However, the extent to which they are manifest will likely depend on the culture of the organization and situational factors such as the level of pressure that people are under.

The good news is that these 4 heroic qualities **can be fostered and developed**. Yet, in many organizations, they go unrecognized and unrewarded. Indeed, some may even see them as vices, rather than virtues. This is particularly true in bureaucratic and slow-moving organizations, where getting things done requires shaking things up.

Q: How good is your organization at recognizing and celebrating its project heroes?

The 4 heroic qualities **challenge the traditional definition of corporate heroism** and may require a mindset shift. For example, in some organizational environments talking about risks and obstacles can be mistaken as a sign of disloyalty or a lack of commitment. Yet, staying silent is what really can harm a project.

Not surprisingly, there is a link between the 4 heroic qualities and the 5 superpowers. For example, super confidence and super complexity require honesty and openness.

With these factors in mind, let's explore what it means to be a project or portfolio hero, providing you with a framework to help you recognize and celebrate your organization's project and portfolio heroes.

HONESTY
(even when it hurts)

RELENTLESSNESS
(despite setbacks)

SUPER PROJECT

ACTION HERO

EMPOWERMENT
(despite constraints)

OPENNESS
(esp. to challenging ideas)

HONESTY (even when it hurts)

The defining trait of heroic project and program leaders is **honesty**, not just as an idealized virtue, but as an essential requirement for navigating complex projects.

Honesty isn't just about telling the truth and telling no lies. It is also about speaking up, rather than staying silent. It is about a willingness to have difficult conversations and being fully transparent in project proposals, updates and so on.

However, honesty and transparency require courage, especially in organizations that only 'do good news.' Specifically, it takes courage to challenge assumptions, and talk about risks, obstacles and setbacks.

Pause for a moment and use the checklist on the next page to explore the extent your big project(s) fosters honesty. Then, use the scale below to explore the extent to which honesty is manifest or evident within your project. If you like, you can map the checkboxes in the table to the scale below.

SUPER PROJECT

ACTION

HERO

Latent ├────┼────┼────┼────┤ Manifest

HONESTY
(even when it hurts)

HONESTY Checklist

	Strongly Disagree	Disagree	Neutral	Agree	Strongly Agree
1. Risks and challenges are openly discussed in this project.	☐	☐	☐	☐	☐
2. Stakeholders are updated with full transparency, without filtering information.	☐	☐	☐	☐	☐
3. Our team regularly challenges assumptions behind our strategy.	☐	☐	☐	☐	☐
4. People feel safe speaking up, even when it's uncomfortable.	☐	☐	☐	☐	☐
5. As a leader, I have openly admitted mistakes or uncertainty recently.	☐	☐	☐	☐	☐
6. We are honest and realistic about what it will take to achieve ambitious targets set.	☐	☐	☐	☐	☐
7. Bad news is addressed head-on rather than ignored or hidden.	☐	☐	☐	☐	☐
8. We acknowledge and discuss difficult truths about this project.	☐	☐	☐	☐	☐
9. Pre-mortems – we openly discuss what could cause our project to fail and how to prevent it.	☐	☐	☐	☐	☐

Updating project status and communicating the reality of a project through its ups and downs can be a courageous act. The challenge for project leaders is to be honest even when it hurts. That includes being totally honest about progress and prospects.

That may involve 'calling it' on a project or strategy that isn't working or project goals that are unrealistic. Such a courageous act puts the organization's needs ahead of any specific project and may involve a personal sacrifice in terms of loss of prestige, budget and resources.

Too many organizations run their projects and portfolios using a patchwork of spreadsheets and other tools. It requires courage for organizations to implement systems to manage big projects and project portfolios. Similarly, putting information into any of these systems can be a courageous act.

EMPOWERMENT (despite constraints)

In a large organization, it's easy to feel disempowered. After all, much of strategy gets dictated from the top, and key decisions often come down to the numbers on a spreadsheet. Yet, heroic project leaders **don't let that define them**:

- They are 'corporate entrepreneurs' – they seize the initiative and don't wait to be told.

- They take ownership and make it happen, even when there are many factors beyond their control.

- They creatively navigate constraints including rigid plans, bureaucracy and scarce resources.

- They shape the strategy and its execution, even in small ways.

Use the following checklist to explore the extent to which your big project(s) empowers its people.

EMPOWERMENT Checklist

	Strongly Disagree	Disagree	Neutral	Agree	Strongly Agree
1. We take ownership rather than waiting for permission.	☐	☐	☐	☐	☐
2. We actively make things happen instead of just reacting to events.	☐	☐	☐	☐	☐
3. We connect this project to a deeper purpose beyond efficiency and targets.	☐	☐	☐	☐	☐
4. We take responsibility for outcomes, even when external factors are beyond our control.	☐	☐	☐	☐	☐
5. We navigate organizational barriers instead of allowing them to stop us.	☐	☐	☐	☐	☐
6. We focus on what we **can** do right now, despite any constraints.	☐	☐	☐	☐	☐
7. We prioritize overall business success over simply delivering a project.	☐	☐	☐	☐	☐
8. We foster a **no-blame, no-hiding** culture within our team.	☐	☐	☐	☐	☐
9. We actively identify and address barriers to full ownership of the project.	☐	☐	☐	☐	☐

Based on the checklist above, place your project on the scale below to reflect the extent to which empowerment is fully manifest.

SUPER PROJECT

ACTION HERO

Latent ├────┼────┼────┼────┤ Manifest

EMPOWERMENT
(despite constraints)

RELENTLESSNESS (despite setbacks)

Being at the forefront of change isn't easy. Project and program leaders must wrestle with a long list of challenges – internal bureaucracy, scarce resources, changing business needs or priorities and misaligned stakeholders. Yet, **despite everything that is thrown at them, they keep on going**. Being undaunted by challenges and setbacks is what really makes projects super and the teams running them heroic.

Use the checklist on the next page to explore the extent your big project(s) fosters relentlessness.

RELENTLESNESS Checklist:

	Strongly Disagree	Disagree	Neutral	Agree	Strongly Agree
1. We clearly identify our greatest challenges and take decisive action to overcome them.	☐	☐	☐	☐	☐
2. We push forward boldly rather than hesitating or being overly cautious.	☐	☐	☐	☐	☐
3. We act with a sense of urgency rather than getting bogged down by bureaucracy.	☐	☐	☐	☐	☐
4. We know when to apply pressure and when to be patient in the project.	☐	☐	☐	☐	☐
5. We actively manage competing priorities to prevent them from slowing us down.	☐	☐	☐	☐	☐
6. We take deliberate steps to maintain momentum, even in the face of setbacks.	☐	☐	☐	☐	☐
7. We are willing to challenge resistance from other parts of the organization to drive progress.	☐	☐	☐	☐	☐
8. We recognize and accept the personal or organizational sacrifices needed for success.	☐	☐	☐	☐	☐
9. We hold ourselves accountable for pushing past excuses and obstacles.	☐	☐	☐	☐	☐

Based on the checklist on the previous page, place your project on the scale below to reflect the level of relentlessness evident.

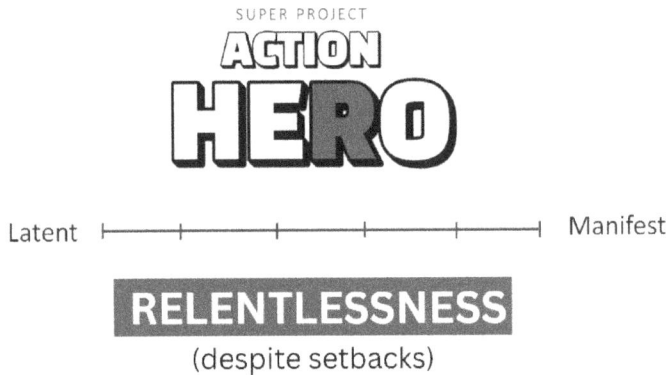

SUPER PROJECT

ACTION

HERO

Latent ├──────┼────────┼────────┼────────┤ Manifest

RELENTLESSNESS
(despite setbacks)

OPENNESS (even to challenging ideas)

Nobody likes to think of themselves as closed-minded, yet **challenging convention and traditional thinking can be difficult**. It takes courage to be open, as well as curiosity and humility. This is especially true when plans, targets, and assumptions are already in place.

Use the checklist on the next page to explore the extent your organization and its big project(s) fosters openness.

OPENNESS Checklist:	Strongly Disagree	Disagree	Neutral	Agree	Strongly Agree
1. We actively challenge our assumptions to ensure they are valid.	☐	☐	☐	☐	☐
2. In meetings, everyone contributes, rather than a few people doing all the talking.	☐	☐	☐	☐	☐
3. We are open to contrary information rather than filtering out what we don't want to hear.	☐	☐	☐	☐	☐
4. We proactively identify and acknowledge potential risks.	☐	☐	☐	☐	☐
5. We create space for cynics and skeptics to contribute constructively.	☐	☐	☐	☐	☐
6. We engage compliance early rather than as an afterthought.	☐	☐	☐	☐	☐
7. We have changed our minds based on new insights within the last six months.	☐	☐	☐	☐	☐
8. We ask thoughtful, challenging questions rather than seeking confirmation of what we already believe.	☐	☐	☐	☐	☐
9. We balance gathering input with making timely, decisive choices.	☐	☐	☐	☐	☐

Based on your answers to the questions on the previous page, where would you place your project on the scale below?

SUPER PROJECT

ACTION HERO

Latent |———+———+———+———+———| Manifest

OPENNESS
(esp. to challenging ideas)

CONCLUSIONS & REFLECTIONS

Every Super Projects has its heroes – these are the action heroes that make it happen. But there is more heroism waiting to be unlocked, where project leaders and sponsors create the right environment.

Pause for a moment to reflect: How will you both demonstrate and foster **honesty**, **empowerment**, **relentlessness** and **openness**? Use the diagram overleaf to note your answers.

RELENTLESSNESS

How will you (a) foster and (b) demonstrate it:

OPENNESS

How will you (a) foster and (b) demonstrate it:

SUPER PROJECT **ACTION HERO**

HONESTY

How will you (a) foster and (b) demonstrate it:

EMPOWERMENT

How will you (a) foster and (b) demonstrate it:

CHAPTER 7:

AI: THE ULTIMATE SUPER PROJECT

SUPER AMBITIOUS

SUPER COMPLEX

SUPER COLLAB.

SUPER CONFIDENT

SUPER ALIGNED

INTRODUCTION

It is the biggest thing in business right now – fueling so many conversations and stealing the headlines. That, of course, is Ai and its potential to drive business performance and transformation. But, what is it going to take to deliver on the promise and potential of Ai? Well, the answer (or at least part of the answer) is Super Projects!

LET'S MAKE Ai SUPER!

Nowhere are super projects more necessary than in respect of Ai. That is not just because of the technical leaps involved, or even the transformative potential. But because of the level of organizational and societal change required, the extent of hyped expectations and likely challenges around adoption, ethics and trust.

Soon, we expect Ai to account for 20% of all projects underway within large organizations. For the rest, we expect there to be a significant Ai component too. So, that is another reason why combining Super Projects with Ai is key.

Given its role and importance, it is essential to apply everything that we have learned about projects (technological and otherwise) to the implementation of Ai. We need to leverage the 5 superpowers – Super Ambition, Super Confidence, Super Alignment, Super Complexity and Super Collaboration. We also need heroism and courage to embrace this major transformational change in our organizations and our societies.

Everything that applies to other important projects applies to Ai projects. In this way, all the tools in the book are Ai-ready, so to speak. However, Ai projects bring some additional opportunities and challenges. Hence, this chapter, with additional context in terms of each of the superpowers for Ai. Let's get started with Super Ambition.

SUPER AMBITION

'Super' is hardly a big enough word to describe the level of ambition around Ai. Indeed, there are predictions that the global economic impact of Ai could equal that of the world's 6th largest economy (i.e. the UK).[155] Some are even going as far as to suggest that Ai is humanity's greatest discovery since fire or electricity.[156]

Today, Ai is at the peak of inflated expectations (to use the Gartner language). So, let's start by calibrating the level of Ai-fueled ambition within your organization:

*Q.1: What is your **hypothesis regarding Ai's likely impact** on your organization?*

Please express it in percentage terms e.g. <1%, 1-3%, 3-5%, 5-10% using the table below.

	Next year?	Next 3 years?	Longer Term?
a. Revenue			
b. Profitability			
c. Operating Costs			
d. Productivity			
e. Organizational Health / Culture			

It all starts with a hypothesis of business value or impact. This is essential to ensuring the success of Ai, and in particular its ROI. We use the term hypothesis rather than target or forecast, given that the technology is new, and its impact is as yet uncertain. However, as more data becomes available, we can update hypothesis to better reflect the emergent reality.

Q.2: Is there a Super Why for Ai in your organization?

The table below is a typical list of expected benefits; how would you rank the top 5 (in order of importance to your organization)?

Expected Benefits from Ai	Rating
Improve efficiency and productivity	
Reduce costs	
New / improved products and services	
Encourage innovation and growth	
Shift workers from lower to higher value tasks	
Speed / ease of developing new systems and software	
Increase revenue	
Enhance relationships with clients / customers	
Uncover new ideas and insights / Improve Decisions	
Detect fraud, cyber security and manage risk	
Enable hyper-personalization	
Other:	

Not surprisingly, the #1 expected benefit for most leaders is **efficiency and productivity**. Indeed, 9 out of 10 leaders select this and cost-cutting (i.e., the first 2 items from the table).[157] Of course, that is an obvious place to start, and it helps tackle an issue that has long dogged IT investments – the ability to demonstrate business value / impact. However, most analysts would argue that Ai's real game-changing ability is in generating value, growing revenue and reinventing the business.

Moreover, as explored in **Chapter 1**, Super Ambition goes beyond spreadsheets to connect more deeply and more widely. The challenge for leaders is to expand the debate around Ai to include:

Q.3: Why does Ai matter?

    (a)   What is the **vision of success** with Ai (e.g., how will it enable the organization to thrive as well as to perform)?

    (b)   How will any Ai project connect to **purpose and passion**?

    (c)   How will any Ai project **create value**?

    (d)   How **widely** will the benefits of Ai be distributed?

Ai project leaders and sponsors may not have the answer to all these questions. However, the goal should be to engage stakeholders in finding the answers – that is a powerful means of generating ownership and buy-in. It also connects to the impact on people, as we will explore next.

Q.4: What is the likely 'people impact'?

Leaders talk about why Ai matters to the business – that is its business impact. Rarely discussed is **the 'people impact.'**[158] However, leaders need to watch their language when talking about Ai to avoid triggering negative reactions and emotions. For example, when leaders say 'efficiency' or 'productivity,' their people often hear 'job cuts.'

Ensuring the adoption of Ai requires balancing corporate ambition on the one hand and employee anxiety on the other. That means using the words on the right of the table overleaf, as well as the left. A recent survey warns about what can happen if they don't: 41% of Millennial and Gen Z employees admit to sabotaging their company's Ai strategy.[159]

Business Impact What Matters to the Business	**People Impact** What Matters to the People
Growth	Job security
Profitability	Pay and benefits
Efficiency	Status
Lean	Recognition
Productivity	Pride
Performance	Belonging
Consolidation	Acceptance
Cost-reduction	Appreciation
Change	Being valued
Innovation	Personal well-being
Transformation	Learning and personal growth
Competitive advantage	Career progression
Optimization	Rewarding and meaningful work
Automation	Seeing the results of your efforts
Standardization	Making progress
Speed	Reducing stress and overwork
Agility	Job satisfaction
Headcount	Working with interesting people
	Social connections
	Friends at work

SUPER CONFIDENCE

Ai is presently **at the top of the hype curve**, or what Gartner calls the 'peak of inflated expectations.' This can be seen in the behavior of the stock market, where:

- Ai chipmaker NVIDIA's stock market valuation is the equivalent of the top six players in Big Pharma.[160]

- One Ai stock placement raises the same funding as 15 biotech players.[161]

Experienced leaders know that every hype curve inevitably slopes downward. Thus, while confidence is necessary for action, Ai leaders must strike a balance between 'selling the dream' and 'keeping it real.' That means being both a:

- **Cheerleader**: Excited, optimistic and eager to accelerate Ai.

- **Challenger**: Cautious, even fearful, and asking hard questions about Ai.

Intelligence has been defined as 'the ability to hold two opposing ideas in mind at the same time.'[162] Nowhere is that more true – or more necessary – than with AI. With something that is so new, so hyped and evolving so fast, it is difficult to be totally confident or definitive. The challenge for leaders and teams implementing Ai is to **embrace both Cheerleader and Challenger** perspectives, as shown in this table:

Ai Challenger	Ai Cheerleader
Anxiety	Excitement
Risks	Benefits
People	Technology
Ethics	Economics
Good for society?	Good for business!
Slow down	Speed up
Regulate	Free up
Take jobs	Make jobs
Stripped of autonomy	Super autonomy
Protect the vulnerable	Survival of the fittest

Q: Where are you on the Challenger / Cheerleader Scale?

Mark your position on the scale below.

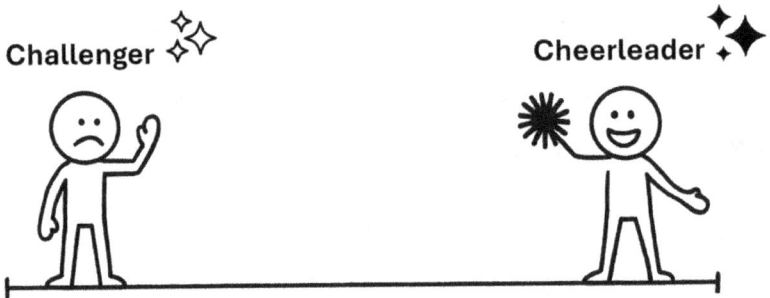

Interestingly, this scale can also be applied on a conversation-by-conversation basis, so think of your last internal meeting about Ai: Where were people on the scale? If you find yourself at either end, you may need to embrace those qualities that distinguish super confidence from over-confidence, including courage, candor and curiosity (see **Chapter 2**).

Organizations and their Ai teams need people and conversations at all points of the Challenger / Cheerleader spectrum. However, **getting the balance right** may not be easy.

Q: How effectively is your organization balancing both Challenger and Cheerleader perspectives on Ai?

Holding the inherent tension between excitement and anxiety, between progress and prudence, will be the real test of leadership in respect of AI. For some organizations, the tension will paralyze, while for others it will galvanize people in the pursuit of Ai-related business advantages.

How to balance the cheerleader with the challenger? Moreover, how to do this without being left behind in the race to adopt Ai and realize its benefits?

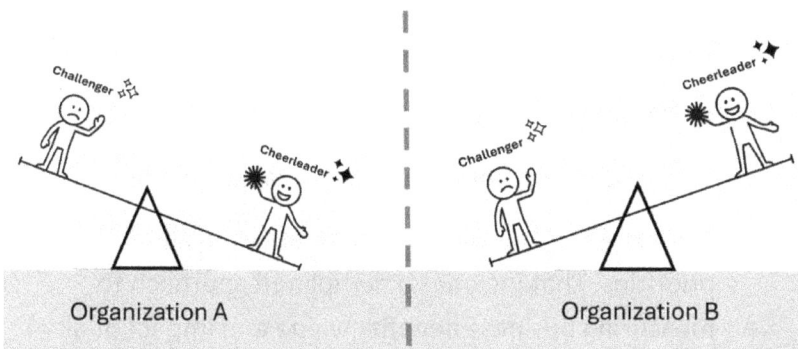

Organization A   Organization B

Well, here is a list of some **strategies leaders can employ**. It can also help ensure your Ai projects and strategies don't overpromise and underdeliver:

1. **Embrace both perspectives**

   - Ensuring that Ai teams have a **mix** of cheerleaders (e.g., IT) and challengers (e.g., Compliance).

- Engage **cynics and skeptics**, making it safe for people to express their concerns or doubts.

- Ensure sponsors and key cross-functional stakeholders can **own** their exuberance and their anxieties too.

- Set out alternative **scenarios and assumptions**, accepting that the future cannot be predicted with certainty.

- Acknowledge **optimism bias**: As humans, we are prone to overestimate benefits and underestimate effort and cost.

2. **Build a solid foundation** for your Ai strategy, including:

- Scope out **the journey** (or at least this phase).

- Required **infrastructure**, Ai-ready data and automation ready processes.

- Oversight and **governance** structures.

- Capabilities, **competence** and talent pipeline.

3. **Anchor Ai to fundamental business needs** and priorities. That includes a disciplined approach to measuring business benefits, value and impact of all Ai investments (with the CFO and others).

4. **Ensure an integrated approach.** With so many pilots and projects, take care to prevent a fragmented or uncoordinated approach.

5. **Review projects regularly,** enabling people to 'call it' where necessary. Support the leaders and teams involved in delivering key projects.

6. **Accelerate learning:** Make it safe for people to experiment, stop or redirect when needed, and share lessons. Accumulate quick wins to build confidence and knowledge.

7. **Set out the principles** to which the organization aims to adhere. For example:

    - People positive and human-centered.
    - Customer-centric.
    - Value creating.
    - Ethical, transparent and fair.
    - Secure, protecting customer data and org. IP.
    - Shared ownership and active engagement with risk, governance and compliance.

8. **Put resilience and risk on the agenda** and keep it there. There will be setbacks and failures; put a system in place to handle them.

Ai requires Super Trust, not just in the technology, but in the intent of those implementing it. So, the 6 Levels of Confidence explored in **Chapter 2** are still very relevant, but should be applied in reverse order, as follows:

1. Confidence (and trust) in Organization and its Leaders.

2. Confidence (and trust) in the Ai Project Team.

3. Confidence in Ai Implementation.

4. Confidence in the Ai Project Plan / Roadmap.

5. Confidence in the Ai project delivering business impact (driving Business Success).

6. Confidence in Ai Project Success (overall).

SUPER ALIGNMENT

Ai (especially Gen Ai) has spread faster and wider than any technology that has gone before. So many people – from board directors to frontline staff, including their kids – have used and marveled at it. Indeed, this universality is one of Ai's greatest strengths. However, there is a potential downside – the danger of misalignment in respect of business strategy and success. Specifically, two the two key challenges of Ai-business alignment are:

- Managing the volume of Ai pilots and projects.
- Capturing and communicating their value.

Let's address these in turn.

1.   Managing the Volume of Ai Pilots and Projects

The level of ambition around Ai is reflected in the number of projects and pilots planned and underway. But, what about your organization?

*Q: What is the number of **use cases, pilots and projects:***

a.   *Planned, approved or underway at this time?*

b.   *What is the expected or likely number next year?*

At conferences and events, leaders often boast of hundreds and even thousands of pilots or use cases for Ai. However, managing, integrating and coordinating the masses of Ai use cases, pilots and projects is key to alignment.

Q: What is the level of coordination / integration across your organization's Ai-related pilots and projects?

Nobody wants to be left behind, but what if the leader in your industry has a truly game-changing Ai strategy? What if their goal is 'Ai being used by EVERYONE EVERY DAY?' How will you keep up? How wide and how fast Ai spreads across organizations will vary greatly.

Should organizations let everyone do their own thing regarding Ai? The challenge is to find the right balance between centralized management or control and an organizational free-for-all. So, is your organization striking the right balance? Before you answer, take a moment to reflect on the factors listed in the table on the next page to answer the following question:

Q: Do any of these factors represent a risk to your organization's Ai Strategy and its implementation?

Given the level of ambition and excitement around Ai, there will be more projects and pilots than people or resources. Thus, the need for:

- A transparent, robust and fair **process to prioritize and sequence** pilots and projects based on business needs and priorities.

- Absolute **clarity on the problems or pain points** being addressed and how both project success and business impact will be measured.

- **A portfolio approach** that balances big bets with small bets, and short-term results with longer-term investments.

- An **integrated approach** to leverage synergies, manage dependences and share resources / learning across Ai pilots and projects (and other projects too).

FACTOR:	Place your organization's Ai on the scale between the statements (left & right).		
Resource Allocation	Spreading resources thinly over many projects	1 2 3 4 5	Focusing resources on key priorities
Clarity of Focus	Fragmented or scattergun approach	1 2 3 4 5	Clear priorities tied to business needs
Balance of Coordination & Autonomy	Bureaucratic control stifles innovation	1 2 3 4 5	Too little oversight, chaotic experimentation
Infrastructure & Data Strategy	Disconnected efforts, missed integration	1 2 3 4 5	Building scalable, shared AI infrastructure
Knowledge & Capability	Silos and duplication	1 2 3 4 5	Shared learning, data and best practices
Risk & Compliance	Inconsistent, patchy oversight	1 2 3 4 5	Clear, consistent management across teams
Access to Tools	People lack tools or procure/create their own	1 2 3 4 5	Standard tools are accessible & supported
Ownership & Adoption	Adoption is hindered by suspicion and lack of ownership / co-creation	1 2 3 4 5	Consultation and involvement generate shared ownership, adoption and buy-in.

Pause for a moment:

- *Do any of the above represent opportunities for your organization's Ai strategy?*

- *If you are running an Ai project, what are the implications for you?*

Not all pilots or projects can or should get the go-ahead, and certainly not at the same time. A set of **decision criteria** is required to ensure that the most important projects get priority. Below is a checklist including some of the most used criteria in evaluating Ai priorities for funding. Such a checklist can be used to transform a long list of proposals into a short list, a pilot list and then ultimately a project or scaling list.

Heading	Questions
Problem & Solution	What is the problem, pain point, bottleneck, or frustration? How confident are we that Ai can solve it?
Strategic Fit	How well does this align with business needs, priorities, and strategy?
Business Impact	What is the potential business impact (e.g., revenue growth, cost savings, efficiency gains)?
Customer Value	Who will benefit and how? Is the value likely to be internal (e.g., teams) or external (e.g., customers, partners)?
Technical Feasibility	Do we have Ai-ready data, automation-ready processes, and infrastructure?

Heading	Questions
Cost & Complexity	What is the estimated cost and complexity? Can we buy *versus* build the solution?
Scalability	Can this be scaled or adapted across other teams, functions, or geographies?
Time to Impact	How quickly can measurable benefits be delivered? What factors could slow progress / results? What quick wins are there?
Sponsorship	Is there a strong business sponsor?
Risk & Ethics	What are the implications in terms of ethics, regulation, and governance?
Confidence & Capability	Do we have the required skills and capabilities today? Will this build internal capability and confidence for future Ai use?
People & Adoption	Are people likely to adopt it? What concerns or resistance might arise?
Pilot & Proof	What will the pilot involve (cost, duration, scope, steps and success)?

2. Capturing & Communicating the Value of Ai Pilots and Projects

Already warnings are emerging regarding the failure of Ai investments to demonstrate business impact. This is a repeat of what happened with Digital Transformation and most other new areas of IT spending. Although, it is an issue that goes much deeper than technology, IT often gets saddled with the blame. Not super projects, however. They progressively capture and communicate business benefits and impact, as follows:

- **Hypothesize the benefits.** Resolving this problem begins with a hypothesis of business impact (as at the start of this chapter) – one that resists being prematurely baked into financial projections, but can keep pace with emerging reality.

- **Describe and detail the benefits or value.** Here we use words to communicate use cases and tell real-world stories of how customers, staff and others have benefited. In particular, customer testimonials and before/after comparisons can be powerful.

- **Quantify the benefits or value.** Here we use numbers and metrics – tying down the benefits and making them tangible or real. For example, the number of hours saved, costs reduced, customer queries handled, or the errors prevented.

- **Monetize the benefits or value.** Here we put a monetary value on the benefits, expressing them in dollars, euro or yen.

- **Strategize the benefits or value.** Linking the benefits to business strategy, business outcomes and results. This means showing how the initiative contributes to goals, such as market expansion, and to drivers of long-term growth.

Capturing and communicating the value of investments in Ai has to be a key priority. Moreover, it is an all-of-organization responsibility – an opportunity for all departments, users and stakeholders to share their use cases, communicate the before/after, quantify the impact on key metrics and monetize the benefits. This isn't just an exercise in PR, but an essential aspect of benefits realization and connecting Ai to business strategy.

Q: How effectively are you capturing and communicating business benefits and impact for your various Ai initiatives?

SUPER COLLABORATION

Who will own or drive Ai? That is a question that often gets asked. Will it be the IT department or some new cross-functional unit or team? Well, perhaps that is outmoded thinking. Ai as a business enabler and game-changer is too important and too much responsibility for any one department or team. Rather, it must be seen as an all-of-organization responsibility (AOR). This underscores the importance of consultation and engagement. All too often IT has been left 'carrying the can' for failures in Digital Transformation that stem, not from technological factors, but the organization's ability to embrace change. This is something that those driving Ai must avoid.

Ai requires effective cross-functional collaboration, including:

- Compliance.
- Legal.
- Technical.

- Commercial.
- Operations.
- HR.

How important is the team? As with any project, it is difficult to say what proportion of Ai project success (or failure) can be attributed to the project team. However, it is significant, even if it is difficult to quantify and is often overlooked. This is particularly true with respect to AI where the skill, innovativeness and determination of the team is particularly important and the process of consultation and engagement is essential to overall Ai project success.

Working to deliver Ai at speed will require **effective real-time collaboration**. Sequential handovers between these functions won't cut it. Thus, the need to:

- Build **high performing teams** around Ai that are cohesive and resilient. These teams are likely to face intense pressure to deliver and must be able to 'pull together to pull it off.'

- Empower those teams responsible for Ai to take control over **the way that they work**. In this way, they can leverage their self-optimizing potential (as explored in **Chapter 5**). After all, they will need to work with greater speed, agility, collaboration and innovation than most of the rest of the organization.

- Provide teams with **political cover and support** where they meet organizational lethargy or resistance. Already we are seeing that many of the challenges being faced by Ai teams have more to do with internal factors (e.g. organizational culture, cross-functional collaboration and so on) than technology and related factors. Hence, Ai teams must have senior executive sponsorship and backing at the highest levels.

What are the characteristics of great Ai teams? Well, in many ways, they are the same as any other great team doing important complex work. However, Ai is not like any other project or initiative. It is bigger than anything that has gone before – with higher stakes and greater uncertainty. That puts additional pressure on those who are charged with making it happen.

Use the table below to explore the following question:

Q: *Has your Ai strategy got a Super Team?*

Ai Super Team Characteristics	Rating 1 = low, 5 = high
Effectively embrace the tension between Ai Cheerleader and Challenger (explored earlier).	
They are **super collaborators**, communicators and listeners. They energize and engage their stakeholders, helping them to win.	
Leap silos and boundaries, being **truly cross-functional** and bridging data science, operations, ethics, and strategy.	
Put the organization (and its needs) first – seeing Ai as the means to an end (i.e., business success).	
Share the credit for success, but don't point the finger when things go wrong.	
They are **passionate**, determined and resilient. They lead and inspire the organization.	
They are **highly curious**, they experiment, iterate and learn fast,	
Balance confidence with humility, being able to say, 'we got it wrong' and 'we don't have all the information.'	
Balance project rigor (plans, budgets, etc.) **with agility** – launching with enthusiasm and being prepared to adapt / adjust their plans as needed	
Relentless, despite obstacles and setbacks.	
Seize the initiative (rather than waiting to be told). They are savvy at navigating internal bureaucracy and getting stuff done.	

Q: Which skills or characteristics (from the list) will your Ai team need to develop?

> The word **deployment** is often used with Ai as well as any other technology. It's a word that perfectly describes an army going into battle or a crack commando team, but what is it the best language for Ai? The real challenge for organizations and their people is to **embrace rather than to deploy**. Similarly, we use the word term scaling Ai, like scaling a wall. Well, for many organizations, that wall is – adoption. Poor adoption rates, even resistance, are a key risk.

REFLECTION

Ai is not just another project. It is *the* Super Project of our time - demanding not only new technologies but super ambition, super confidence, super alignment and super collaboration.

Put another way: Ai is potentially bigger than anything we have done before. It presents bigger opportunities and challenges than we have ever faced before. Let's not mess it up! Let's apply the lessons we have learned from digital transformation and other technologies to make Ai super!

QUICK RECAP WITH TOOLS

It is going to take a super project to deliver on your ambitious strategy. But have you got one? That is the question at the center of this research.

Most super projects are big projects, but not all big projects are super projects. There are 5 factors that make some big projects super. We call these superpowers, as shown in the visual below:

For each of the 5 superpowers there is a chapter and a tool. So, where to focus for your big project? To guide you, here is a quick recap – on a step by step or tool by tool basis. You can get started by rating your project against the 5 superpowers and describing what is super about your project.

What is super about your big project or ambitious strategy?

Use the panels to describe your project.

AMBITION

What is the ambition driving your big project? How does it propel the project forward?

YOUR PROJECT'S RATING: ☆☆☆☆☆

COMPLEXITY

What aspects of your project are difficult to control or predict? How is this managed?

YOUR PROJECT'S RATING: ☆☆☆☆☆

CONFIDENCE

How confident are people in your project? How does this show up?

YOUR PROJECT'S RATING: ☆☆☆☆☆

COLLABORATION

What words would you use to describe teamwork & collaboration on your big project?

YOUR PROJECT'S RATING: ☆☆☆☆☆

ALIGNMENT

Are there any signs of cross-functional misalignment? Where?

YOUR PROJECT'S RATING: ☆☆☆☆☆

Q: What propels projects further and faster?

A: Super Ambition – that is the type of ambition that goes deeper and connects more widely. **Chapter 1** has a tool that taps into the power of super ambition.

SUPER AMBITION

See how 'super' your project's ambition is by filling out the panels:

Why ❓
What is the clear & compelling 'why' for your project?

conviction 🤜
How is the conviction driving the project evident?

visions ◉
What is the vision of success?

for many 👥
How widely will the benefits be distributed?

bold 🚀
What makes this project bold and daring?

transform 🐦
What is transformative about this project?

value ✨
How will this project create value?

SMART plus
How will project progress & business impact be measured?

can (compliance) 📸
What are the compliance constraints on ambition?

of meaningful 🤍
How does it connect to purpose & passion?

Q: What is required to double down on project success?

A: Super Confidence. Prevents overconfidence and under confidence by leveraging the factors shown in the tool below.

strategic **Clarity**

YOUR PROJECT'S RATING:
☆☆☆☆☆

Where / when might **greater clarity** be required?

strategic **Courage**

Where / when might **greater courage** be needed?

YOUR PROJECT'S RATING:
☆☆☆☆☆

SUPER CONFIDENCE

Bridging the gap between confidence & certainty of success

Credit

YOUR PROJECT'S RATING:
☆☆☆☆

Where/when might we **recognize progress?**

strategic **Curiosity** - YOUR PROJECT'S RATING: ☆☆☆☆☆

Where / when **greater curiosity** may be needed?

strategic **Candor** YOUR PROJECT'S RATING: ☆☆☆☆☆

Where / when might **greater candor** be required?

Super confidence has 6 levels (shown in the tool here), which help balance selling the dream with keeping it real.

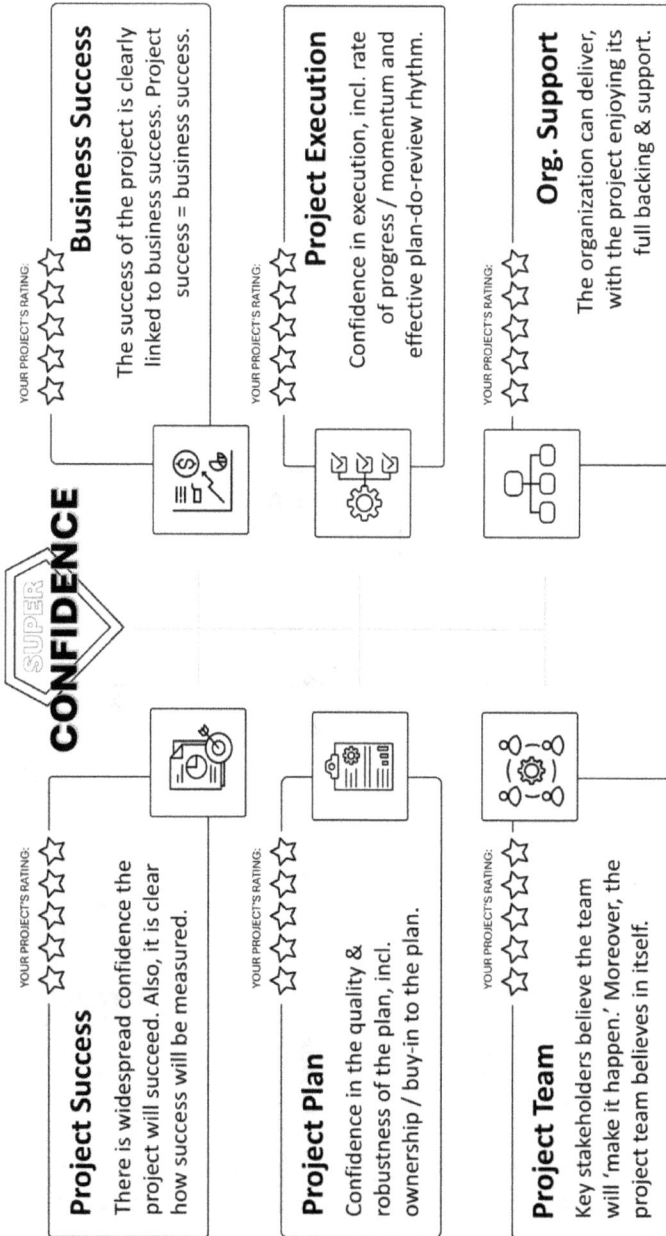

SUPER CONFIDENCE

Business Success

YOUR PROJECT'S RATING:

The success of the project is clearly linked to business success. Project success = business success.

Project Execution

YOUR PROJECT'S RATING:

Confidence in execution, incl. rate of progress / momentum and effective plan-do-review rhythm.

Org. Support

YOUR PROJECT'S RATING:

The organization can deliver, with the project enjoying its full backing & support.

Project Success

YOUR PROJECT'S RATING:

There is widespread confidence the project will succeed. Also, it is clear how success will be measured.

Project Plan

YOUR PROJECT'S RATING:

Confidence in the quality & robustness of the plan, incl. ownership / buy-in to the plan.

Project Team

YOUR PROJECT'S RATING:

Key stakeholders believe the team will 'make it happen.' Moreover, the project team believes in itself.

Q: How to ensure full organizational backing for a big project?

A: Super Alignment. Here is the tool from **Chapter 3**.

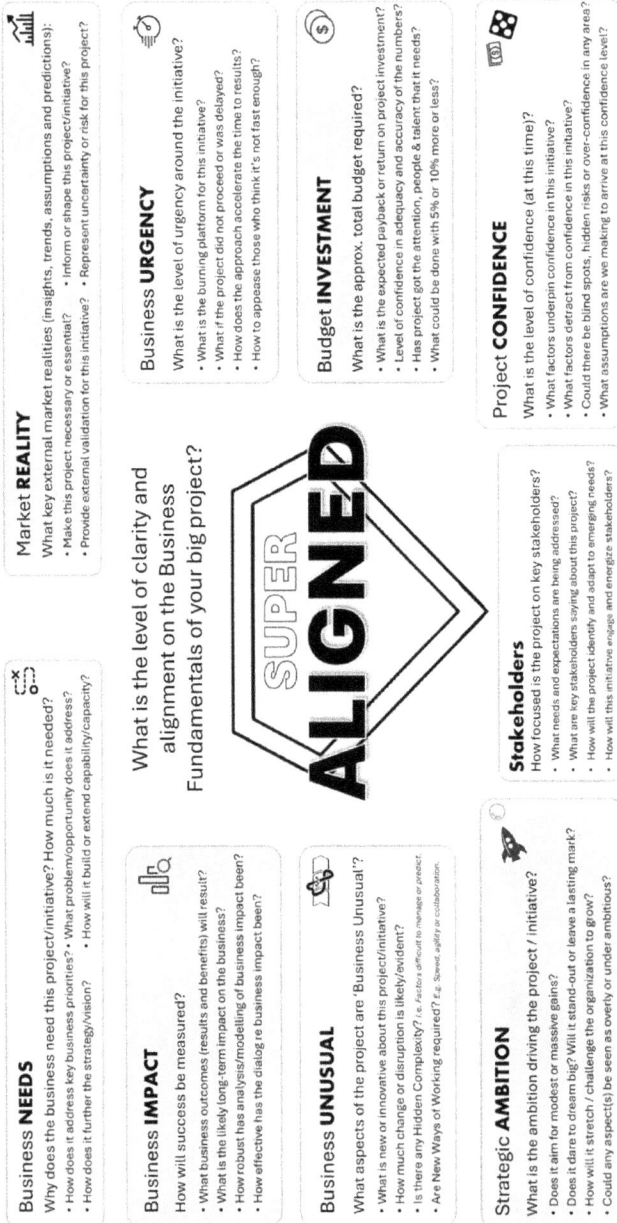

What is the level of clarity and alignment on the Business Fundamentals of your big project?

Market REALITY

What key external market realities (insights, trends, assumptions and predictions):

- Make this project necessary or essential?
- Inform or shape this project/initiative?
- Provide external validation for this initiative?
- Represent uncertainty or risk for this project?

Business URGENCY

What is the level of urgency around the initiative?

- What is the burning platform for this initiative?
- What if the project did not proceed or was delayed?
- How does the approach accelerate the time to results?
- How to appease those who think it's not fast enough?

Budget INVESTMENT

What is the approx. total budget required?

- What is the expected payback or return on project investment?
- Level of confidence in adequacy and accuracy of the numbers?
- Has project got the attention, people & talent that it needs?
- What could be done with 5% or 10% more or less?

Project CONFIDENCE

What is the level of confidence (at this time)?

- What factors underpin confidence in this initiative?
- What factors detract from confidence in this initiative?
- Could there be blind spots, hidden risks or over-confidence in any area?
- What assumptions are we making to arrive at this confidence level?

Stakeholders

How focused is the project on key stakeholders?

- What needs and expectations are being addressed?
- What are key stakeholders saying about this project?
- How will the project identify and adapt to emerging needs?
- How will this initiative engage and energize stakeholders?

Business NEEDS

Why does the business need this project/initiative? How much is it needed?

- How does it address key business priorities?
- What problem/opportunity does it address?
- How does it further the strategy/vision?
- How will it build or extend capability/capacity?

Business IMPACT

How will success be measured?

- What business outcomes (results and benefits) will result?
- What is the likely long-term impact on the business?
- How robust has analysis/modeling of business impact been?
- How effective has the dialog re business impact been?

Business UNUSUAL

What aspects of the project are 'Business Unusual'?

- What is new or innovative about this project/initiative?
- How much change or disruption is likely/evident?
- Is there any Hidden Complexity? I.e. Factors difficult to manage or predict.
- Are New Ways of Working required? E.g. Speed, agility or collaboration.

Strategic AMBITION

What is the ambition driving the project / initiative?

- Does it aim for modest or massive gains?
- Does it dare to dream big? Will it stand-out or leave a lasting mark?
- How will it stretch / challenge the organization to grow?
- Could any aspect(s) be seen as overly or under ambitious?

SUPER ALIGNED

Q: How to master / profit from change and uncertainty?

A: Super at complexity (metaphorical kryptonite – **Chapter 4**).

SUPER COMPLEX

⑤ ALIGNMENT
YOUR PROJECT'S RATING:
☆☆☆☆☆
kryptonite
We continuously work on alignment & never take it for granted.

⑥ PROLIFERATION
YOUR PROJECT'S RATING:
☆☆☆☆☆
kryptonite
There are not too many projects competing for time & attention.

⑦ BUSINESS UNUSUAL
YOUR PROJECT'S RATING:
☆☆☆☆☆
kryptonite
We don't manage big projects as if they are business as usual.

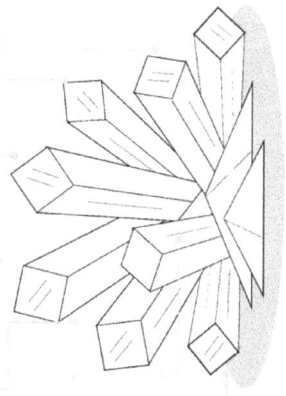

⑧ CORPORATE
YOUR PROJECT'S RATING:
☆☆☆☆☆
kryptonite
Bureaucracy & committees don't kill our speed & agility.

POLLYANNA ④
YOUR PROJECT'S RATING:
☆☆☆☆☆
kryptonite
We can openly talk about risks, obstacles & setbacks.

STAKEHOLDER ③
YOUR PROJECT'S RATING:
☆☆☆☆☆
kryptonite
We effectively engage & excite, even challenge stakeholders.

FIRST MILE ②
YOUR PROJECT'S RATING:
☆☆☆☆☆
kryptonite
Despite the urgency, we ensure projects are set up for success.

BUSINESS MYOPIA ①
YOUR PROJECT'S RATING:
☆☆☆☆☆
kryptonite
We ensure the project never loses sight of business needs & priorities.

Q: How to maximize productivity and optimize resources?

A: Super Collaboration. Chapter 5 includes a framework to turn the #1 drain on productivity for many big projects into a force multiplier in terms of productivity and efficiency.

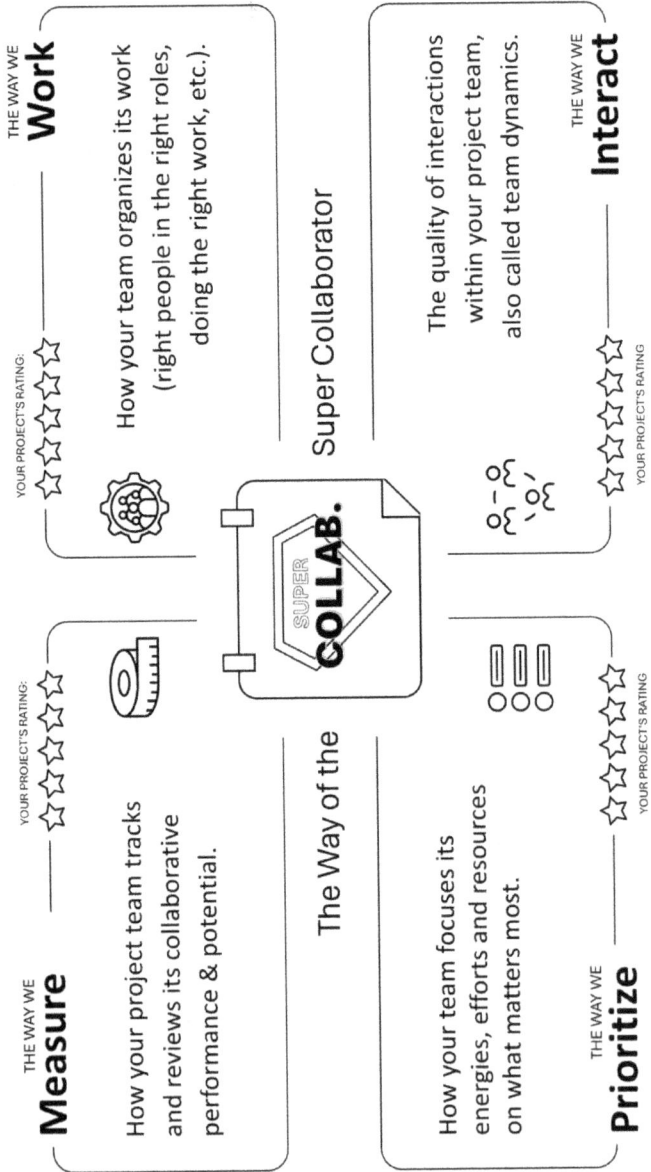

THE WAY WE
Work

How your team organizes its work (right people in the right roles, doing the right work, etc.).

YOUR PROJECT'S RATING:
☆☆☆☆☆

THE WAY WE
Interact

The quality of interactions within your project team, also called team dynamics.

☆☆☆☆☆
YOUR PROJECT'S RATING

Super Collaborator

SUPER COLLAB.

THE WAY WE
Measure

How your project team tracks and reviews its collaborative performance & potential.

YOUR PROJECT'S RATING:
☆☆☆☆☆

The Way of the

THE WAY WE
Prioritize

How your team focuses its energies, efforts and resources on what matters most.

☆☆☆☆☆
YOUR PROJECT'S RATING

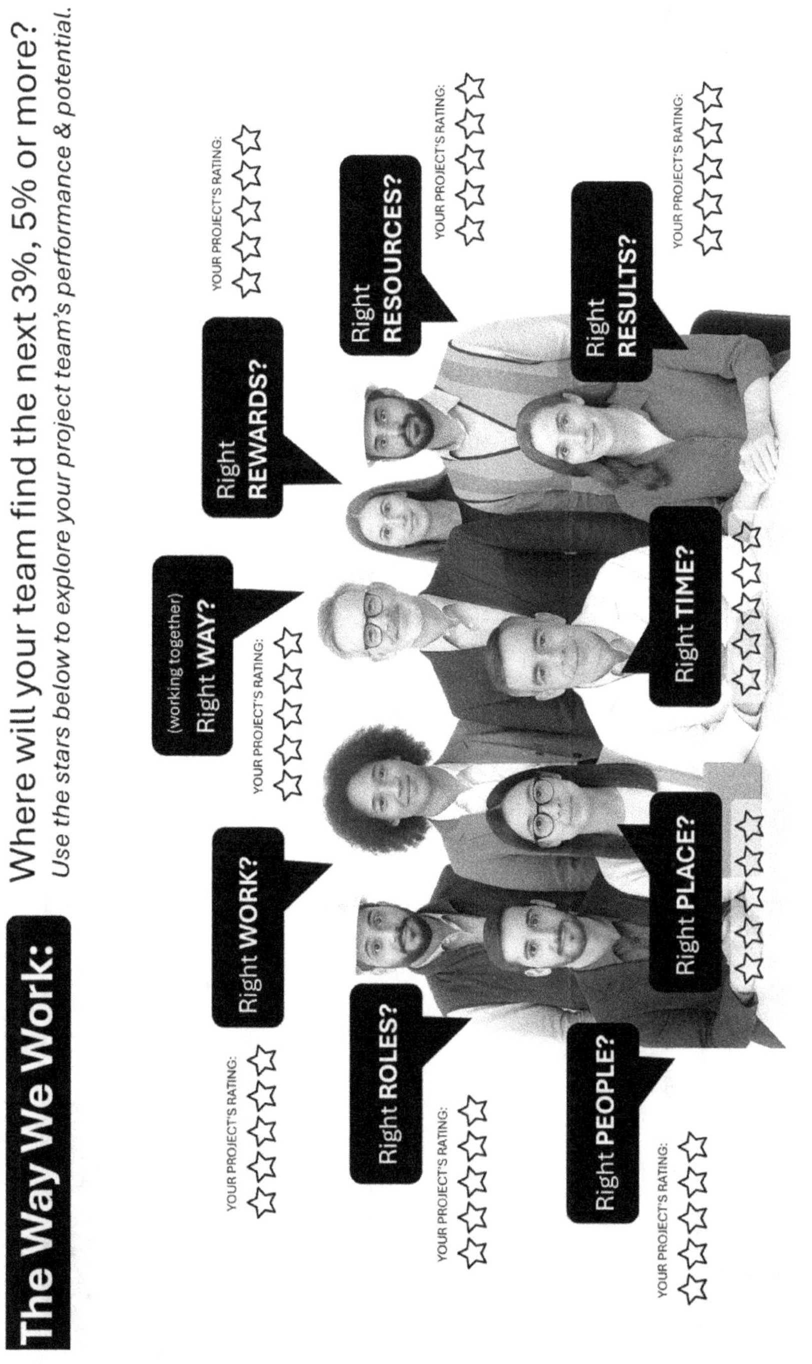

The Way We Work:

Where will your team find the next 3%, 5% or more?
Use the stars below to explore your project team's performance & potential.

Right **ROLES?**
YOUR PROJECT'S RATING:
☆☆☆☆☆

Right **WORK?**

(working together)
Right **WAY?**
YOUR PROJECT'S RATING:
☆☆☆☆☆

Right **REWARDS?**
YOUR PROJECT'S RATING:
☆☆☆☆☆

Right **RESOURCES?**
YOUR PROJECT'S RATING:
☆☆☆☆☆

Right **RESULTS?**
YOUR PROJECT'S RATING:
☆☆☆☆☆

Right **TIME?**
☆☆☆☆☆

Right **PLACE?**
☆☆☆☆☆

Right **PEOPLE?**
YOUR PROJECT'S RATING:
☆☆☆☆☆

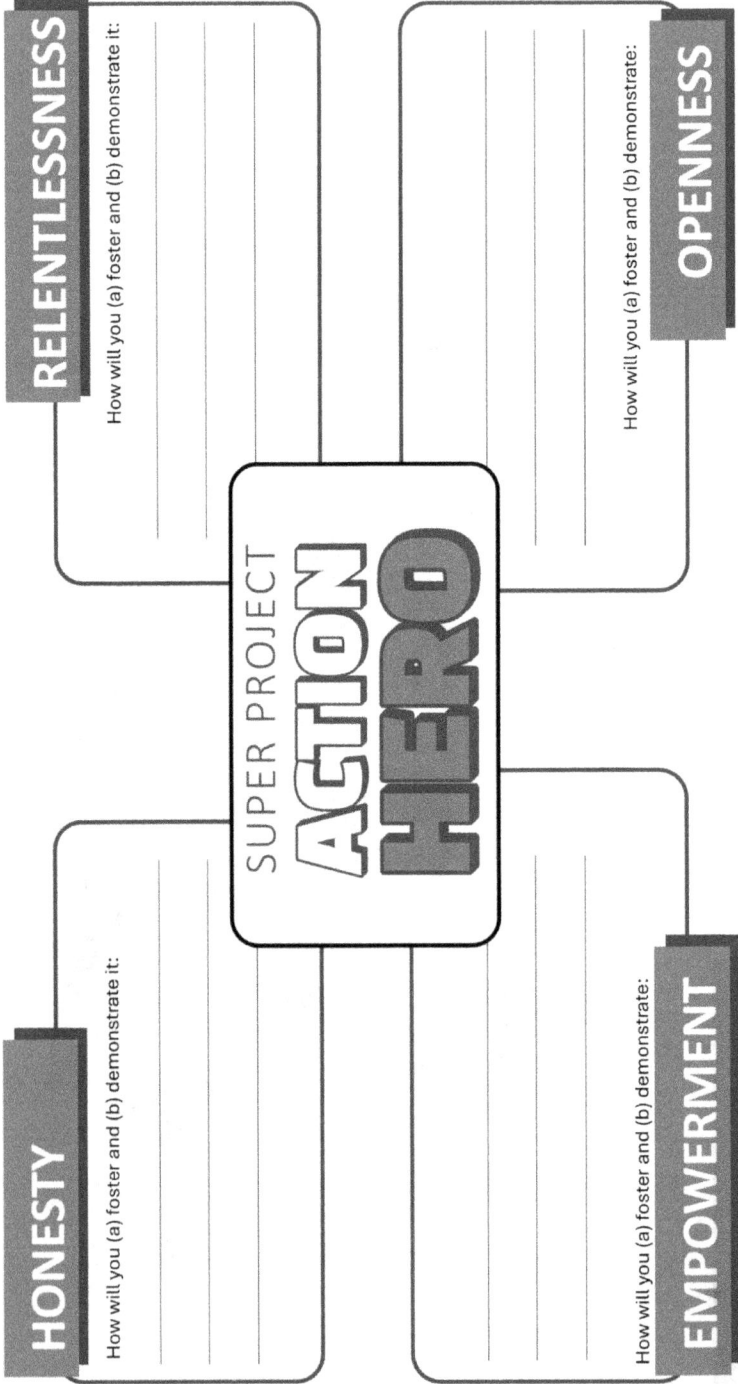

RELENTLESSNESS

How will you (a) foster and (b) demonstrate it:

OPENNESS

How will you (a) foster and (b) demonstrate:

SUPER PROJECT
ACTION HERO

HONESTY

How will you (a) foster and (b) demonstrate it:

EMPOWERMENT

How will you (a) foster and (b) demonstrate:

Here is an overview of the key tool for each of the 5 superpowers:

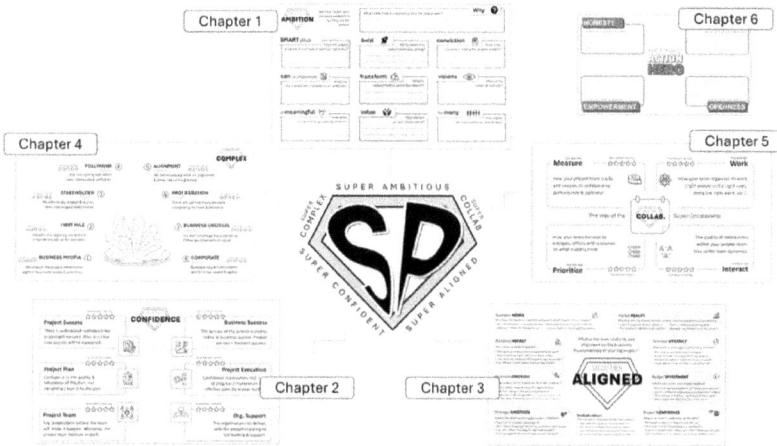

When using these tools, it is important to gather a diversity of perspectives across your project community (project team, stakeholders, etc.). You can find the tools to do this at **www.superprojects.co**.

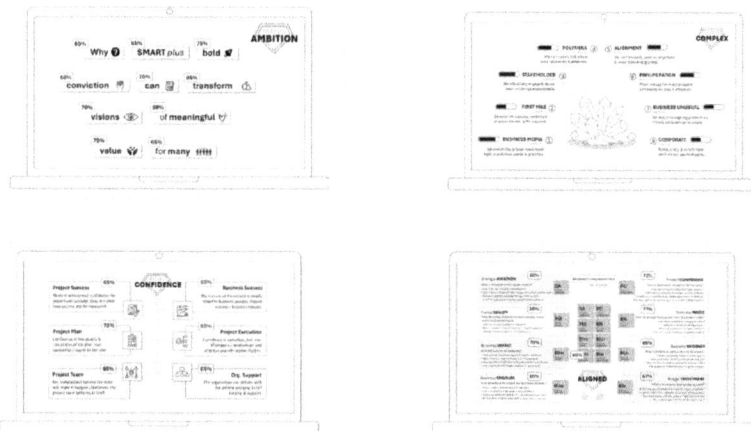

THE SCIENCE, THE AUTHORS
& THE CAUSE

THE SCIENCE BEHIND THIS BOOK

Super Projects is based on **extensive data analysis** involving billions of dollars of projects for some of the world's biggest and best organizations (gathered through our analytics platform). This was supported by qualitative research spanning 371 transformation initiatives, 129 project consolidations and 50 productivity drives.

As a data analysis company, we have unparalleled insight to the reality of big projects and ambitious strategies in large organizations. Indeed, we often know more about many transformation initiatives and big projects than the organization's CEO or their boards.

Mining our datasets (anonymized, of course) provided an essential input to the super projects research. That included qualitative and quantitative data on real-world super projects from multiple perspectives – project leaders and sponsors, internal stakeholders and project teams.

Super Projects is another step on our **14-year journey of research** into the real-world complexity of big project technology decisions. Way back in 2010, we wrote our first book, providing a behind-the-scenes look at how big project technology decisions are really made within large organizations.[163] That included the process (i.e., how), the rationale (i.e., why) and the people involved (i.e., who). It was groundbreaking research we had the pleasure of sharing in places such as the IBM University.

RAY COLLIS

This is a book about super projects and organizational heroes, and the style of Ray's profile reflects this.

Most superheroes have a trusty sidekick – a support person in the background helping them succeed. That is Ray's role too.

Batman has Alfred the butler and Iron Man has his high-powered and glamorous assistant Pepper. These sidekicks play various roles, including **assistant, confidant and coach**. Although, not always in the spotlight, they:

- Ensure that their heroes are set up for success. For example, providing some cool gadgets and tools like James Bond's Q. That is what Ray does – with the tools and analytics in this book and the analytics company of which he is a co-founder (Pitstop Analytics).

- Even heroes have times when doubt sets in, and success is called into question. At those times, they turn to a Ray, a Q or an Alfred, for encouragement and support.

Ray's role, and the role of this book, are the same: To help the new organizational superheroes and their big projects to shine.

Ray is always delighted to connect *via* LinkedIn. There you will also see his more traditional professional profile, including his many books, academic credentials and professional achievements. Also details of his big project coaching companies Growth Pitstop and Pitstop Analytics.

JOHN O'GORMAN

- Six times author, 26 years exploring performance potential across 12 industries including Pharma, Financial Services, Sport, and Technology.

- Managing Partner, Growth Pitstop. My focus is on helping leaders and teams: measure, model and unlock the performance potential of critical growth projects and vital teams.

- Passionate about the subject of teaming. Finding methods to apply metrics to performance and potential fascinates me.

- My current executive and team coaching clients include Bank of Ireland, Merck, Citco and Pfizer.

- Adjunct Faculty – Program Director: Diploma in High Performance Business Development and Sales in UCD Smurfit Executive Development.

- PCC Certified Coach – one of just over 13,000 coaches certified to this level globally.

- Avid reader and naturally curious about collective performance, complex systems, and sport.

- Currently focused on the learning elite sport can give to business and what business can bring to sport.

John is always delighted to connect *via* LinkedIn

Join the 'Super' Cause

We want to **change the narrative.** We want to put the "super' back in big projects, ambitious strategies and transformation initiatives.

We want to **celebrate the new organizational heroes** – those who are making it happen – who are leading and sponsoring big projects.

Will you join us in finding, sharing and celebrating the 'super' in big projects, ambitious strategies and transformation initiatives? Find out how by visiting us at:

www.super-projects.co

ENDNOTES

1. Jim Collins' best-selling book of that title contained timeless wisdom, but it didn't talk about how organizations should execute on their strategies.

2. Ervebo is one of the greatest medical breakthroughs of the last decade. It the first Ebola vaccine and was approved by the FDA in 2019.

3. Kim, W.C. & Mauborgne, R. (2005). *Blue Ocean Strategy: How to Create Uncontested Market Space and Make the Competition Irrelevant.* Harvard Business School Press.

4. Collins, J.C. & Porras, J.I. (1994). *Built to Last: Successful Habits of Visionary Companies.* HarperBusiness.

5. Many senior leaders operate a 'don't ask, don't tell' approach to strategic priorities and projects. Leaders at the top (e.g., the CEO or the board) don't ask, while leaders in the middle (e.g., project leaders) don't tell. This two-way silence has major implications, as explored here: https://shorturl.at/36jo4.

6. Bemoaning the lack of innovation, while common, has little practical value. Let's switch the narrative by seeking out innovation and exploring the organization's portfolio of projects, programs and initiatives. More here: https://shorturl.at/kdBaR.

7. For many people, the words 'projects' and 'project management' have negative associations. Indeed, rightly or wrongly, project management has gotten a bad reputation within many organizations. Find out more: https://shorturl.at/nDBkp.

8. No doubt you have read the gloomy reports on the state of project management and the rates of failure and disappointment surrounding project delivery. But just how helpful or even realistic are they? Moreover, do they help in writing the prescription for success? We argue that a re-think and a new narrative is required. Find out more here: https://shorturl.at/u66N4.

9. With a view to greater openness and engagement, we would rather focus on super, rather than failed or failing, projects – on success rather than failure. The technical term for this is 'Appreciative Inquiry,' see: https://shorturl.at/u66N4.

10. Terms like strategy, innovation and change can seem abstract and vague. It is only when the underlying projects and initiatives are revealed that a strategy is laid bare. Only then can you really predict how successful the strategy is likely to be. Find out more here: https://shorturl.at/rRJ34.

11. Quote from the book *Metaphorically Selling* by Anne Miller, 2024.

[12] What 3 words come to mind when you think about organizational restructuring? That question is one approach to revealing the extent of weariness that surrounds the issue. Another is to turn to studies from the big consulting houses that point to failure levels of 70% and higher. In the search for a better way, there is a growing focus on changing how people and teams work together as the practical vehicle to embed cultural and structural change. This is explored in more detail in **Chapter 5**.

[13] Discussions on leadership over the past 14 months have been dominated by topics such as engagement, productivity and hybrid working. So much so that you could be forgiven for thinking that these subjects define the current era of leadership. What is much less talked about, but more significant in defining the present era of leaders, is ambition. See: https://shorturl.at/IzO0B.

[14] Leaders say their organizations have on average 7 transformation initiatives. One in 5 leaders has 10 or more initiatives. It is worth noting that some initiatives have up to 20 projects. See: https://shorturl.at/EoFuX.

[15] Our research into the 'why' of big projects began way back in 2010 with the publication of *The B2B Sales Revolution* (ISBN 9781907725005), revealing the changes in corporate buying decisions regarding IT.

[16] Brent Flyvbjerg & Dan Gardner, *How Big Things Get Done*, Macmillan Business (February 7, 2023).

[17] The advent of Ai powered tools for generating project names doesn't help. See, for example, **namify.tech** where you enter a description and are provided with a range of project name options, together with domain name availability.

[18] As every experienced leader knows, if people are not energized and engaged when they talk about their big project, they are unlikely to be energized or engaged when they go to work on it. Moreover, levels of energy, engagement and exploration could account for as much as 50% of the difference between the lowest and highest performing organizations according to Alex "Sandy" Pentland, 'The New Science of Building Great Teams,' *HBR*, April 2012.

[19] One of our partners – a global portfolio management systems vendor – estimates that cost-cutting and efficiency-related projects account for up to 80% of all projects managed globally on their platform.

[20] Ensuring that big projects deliver as expected isn't easy. It doesn't help that there is often confusion regarding results and how they will be measured. Ending that confusion has to be a priority; there is a tool – called the results chain – that can really help. See: https://shorturl.at/b7SpE.

[21] Psychologists point to two dominant motivations: 'playing not to lose' (i.e., to protect what they already have, maintain the *status quo*, or to prevent / avoid something happening) and 'playing to win' (i.e., the prospect of achieving a goal, or otherwise making progress). See: Heidi Grant Halvorson Ph.D. & E. Tory Higgins Ph.D., *Focus: Use Different Ways of Seeing the World for Success & Influence*, Hudson Street Press, 2013.

[22] There can be a lot of cynicism regarding strategic initiatives and critical projects. Once we saw this as something negative... preferring to engage with

those who dreamed big and saw few obstacles. How our views have changed! Today, we value the corporate cynic, seeing cynicism as a potentially powerful input to the process of de-risking strategic initiatives. See: https://shorturl.at/cvfj2.

23   Faced with the need to deliver ever-more ambitious projects, with even greater speed, organizations are looking to a new way of working. The hallmarks are collaboration and agility. See: https://shorturl.at/qVfHu.

24   Richard Rumelt, *The Crux: How Leaders Become Strategists*, PublicAffairs (May 3, 2022).

25   As strategy gurus Johnson & Suskewicz put it: '...if you want to understand a company's strategy, don't listen to what it says; look at where it spends its money.' See: Mark W. Johnson & Josh Suskewicz, *Lead from the Future: How to Turn Visionary Thinking into Breakthrough Growth*, HBR Press 2020.

26   Peter Senge, *The Fifth Discipline: The Art and Practice of the Learning Organization* (1990)

27   '$400M fine reinforces view of Citi's expensive stay in regulatory doghouse,' by Harry Terris on S&P Global. Link: https://www.spglobal.com/marketintelligence/en/news-insights/latest-news-headlines/400m-fine-reinforces-view-of-citi-s-expensive-stay-in-regulatory-doghouse-60666446.

28   'OCC Assesses $400 Million Civil Money Penalty Against Citibank,' Office of the Controller & Currency, News Release 2020-132 | October 7, 2020.

29   Citi CEO Jane Fraser pledges to fix tech mess and appease regulators. Here's what she told analysts: *Business Insider*. Jul 12, 2024. Link: https://www.businessinsider.com/citi-jane-fraser-regulatory-citigroup-transformation-2024-7.

30   'Citi's regulatory nightmare still haunts CEO Jane Fraser,' *Business Insider*, Oct 15 2024, Link: https://www.businessinsider.com/citi-jane-fraser-regulators-occ-frb-consent-orders-asset-cap-2024-10.

31   Traditionally the activities of the business and its big projects were business as usual. But as the everyday becomes more complex and less routine, it can be more helpful to map initiatives on a scale from BAU to BU (rather than seeing BAU as binary 0-1). See: https://shorturl.at/oV2Tu.

32   Organizations report only 67% productivity and efficiency, prompting questions about the remaining 33%. Contrary to popular belief, the productivity gap isn't mainly due to remote work or employee disengagement. Our research suggest that the real productivity killers include bureaucracy, workload, internal processes, and priorities – issues inherent to large organizations. See: https://shorturl.at/JJaM6.

33   Lafley & Martin argue that strategy 'is a set of choices about winning. ...that uniquely positions the firm in its industry so as to create sustainable advantage and superior value relative to the competition.' A.G. Lafley & R.L. Martin, *Playing to Win: How Strategy Really Works*, Harvard Business Review Press (February 5, 2013).

34 In addition to the publicly proclaimed 'why,' stakeholders may have their own self-interested motivations too. For example, suppliers need to grow their revenues and their reputations, while project leaders want to boost their careers and get a bonus.

35 As strategy guru Richard P. Rumelt puts it: 'A strategy is a way through a difficulty. An approach to overcoming a problem. A response to a challenge.' See *Good / Bad Strategy*, Profile Books, 2012.

36 'There are only two ways to influence human behavior: you can manipulate it, or you can inspire it.' Simon Sinek, *Start with Why*, Penguin; 1st edition (October 6, 2011).

37 Aligning intrinsic motivation with corporate goals has the potential to generate up to 3 times the level of commitment and determination. That makes it difficult to see how extraordinary performance can be achieved without it. See: https://shorturl.at/ZyPM3.

38 While 2023 was the Year of Efficiency, 2024 could be seen as the Year of Value Creation. In business conversations normally dominated by issues of consolidation, cuts and efficiency, there was increasing talk of innovation and growth. The result was often a more energizing, customer-focused and forward-looking conversation. See: https://shorturl.at/E4041.

39 As Roger L. Martin puts it: '... putting shareholders first is a bad way to enrich shareholders. Rather, putting customers first is what will lead to the success of the corporation – and the enrichment of shareholders.' *A New Way to Think: Your Guide to Superior Management Effectiveness*, Roger L. Martin, Harvard Business Review Press, 2022.

40 Want to grow revenues by 47% and profits by 81%? Then look beyond this quarter or the next, making strategic investment decisions that will underpin longer-term success. This is the compelling data from McKinsey and others. See: https://shorturl.at/ZtJ3M.

41 To lean into the technology of the moment, we formulated this list of sources of value creation from Chat GPT and thought it was worth sharing with just a few tweaks.

42 It can be argued that unlocking the full potential of a project / organization's people is the ultimate test of a leader. We published our research on performance potential in 2017, with the startling finding that people are on average utilizing just 63% of their full potential. Ray Collis & John O'Gorman, *Pitstop to Perform*, ASG Press, 2017.

43 It is a serious problem that could affect as many as two out of three strategic initiatives and project team meetings. It is called 'nodding dog syndrome,' although it has nothing to do with dogs and everything to do with project success! See: https://shorturl.at/xR1nR.

44 The stereotype of the confident leader is universal. Yet, leadership at a time of accelerating change and uncertainty requires curiosity, experimentation and fast learning too. They also need humility and the ability to engage with doubt and

uncertainty. All this amounts to a new form of super confidence. See: https://shorturl.at/QeKed.

45 In tackling the myth that confidence improves performance or success, Don A. Moore writes: 'Many people think that fooling themselves into being more confident will improve their performance and outcomes. ...I've found little evidence that simply being more confident actually helps you. In fact, deluding yourself into being overconfident actually exposes you to many risks.' See: *Perfectly Confident: How to Calibrate Your Decisions Wisely*, Don A. Moore, HarperBusiness, 2020.

46 Traditionally, it was believed that talking about success was positive, while talking about obstacles, risks, or failure was negative. However, today psychologists tell us that talking about obstacles, setbacks and impediments has an important motivational value. It also builds resilience and ensures preparedness. See, for example, *Re-thinking Positive Thinking* by Gabriele Oettingen, Current Books, 2015.

47 Many senior leaders operate a 'don't ask, don't tell' approach to strategic priorities and projects. Leaders at the top (e.g., the CEO or the board) don't ask, while leaders in the middle (e.g., project leaders) don't tell. This two-way silence has major implications.

48 Much has been written about the vagaries of human decision-making, including best-selling books by Nobel Prize-winning economists. Here we explore just a few of the reasons why you may be prone to over-confidence with respect to your strategic initiatives and critical projects: https://shorturl.at/u5ZVb.

49 Werner De Bondt & Richard Thaler, quoted by Don A. Moore in *Perfectly Confident: How to Calibrate Your Decisions Wisely*, HarperBusiness, 2020.

50 'Wobbly moments' happen when doubt sets in and obstacles loom large. Every strategic initiative, project and team has them! However, if handled the right way, they can boost the likelihood of success. Find out more: https://shorturl.at/xOojF.

51 Most big projects are far removed from the everyday run of business or business as usual. They are business unusual, involving something new – a new process or system, perhaps a new product, channel or business model. Explore the implications here: https://shorturl.at/E3ij2.

52 Big projects that are managed as 'business as usual' will inevitably struggle when it comes to speed and agility, collaboration and innovation. So, a new way of working is required. Also, a new approach to project management. This theme is explored in *Seeing Around Corners: How to Spot Inflection Points in Business Before They Happen* by Rita McGrath & Clayton Christensen, Houghton Mifflin Harcourt, 2019.

53 We add the word 'strategic' to 'strategic curiosity' for two reasons. First, it connects to the well-established concept of 'strategic conversations.' Second, because it might otherwise be mistaken as something that is a 'nice-to-have,' rather than a factor that is associated with success.

54 While much has been written about psychological safety and respectful challenge, a balance is essential. If the conversation is always polite, then things are likely to go unsaid. That means risks will remain hidden, concerns unspoken and alarms silenced. Find out more here: https://shorturl.at/oW1ho.

55 'Being courageous doesn't mean being stupid,' says one of our project coaching partners. Moreover, we are not saying that by not speaking out, people lack courage. Indeed, given the circumstances in which people are working, often they must stop themselves even when they want to speak out. In environments where there is limited trust or psychological safety, it takes personal courage to stay silent.

56 Massive ambition, with some niggling doubts. That sums up the results of the first phase of this super projects research encompassing 371 transformation initiatives, 129 project consolidations and 50 productivity drives. It suggested that this unlikely 'ambition / doubt combo' is critical to success. Find out more: https://shorturl.at/SNwdb.

57 It is a serious problem that could affect as many as two out of three strategic initiatives and project team meetings. It is called 'nodding dog syndrome,' although it has nothing to do with dogs and everything to do with project success! Read the research here: https://shorturl.at/3uPWj.

58 It is not unusual to talk of pharma as a high stakes gamble with substantial investments and uncertain outcomes. See for example: https://www.pharmavoice.com/news/pharma-biotech-pipeline-genmab-jnj-patent-market/718247/.

59 'Unlocking Productivity in Biopharmaceutical R&D. The Key to Outperforming,' by Peter Tollman, Valery Panier, Diana Dosik, Francis Cuss & Paul Biondi of BCG, January 20, 2016.

60 The EU's DORA (Digital Operational Resilience Act) is part of a global trend in financial regulation, aligning with similar efforts such as the Cyber Incident Notification Rules in the US and the Operational Resilience Framework in the UK, all aiming to strengthen the stability and security of financial systems amid increasing digital risks.

61 Explore the implications of re-thinking CYA, including the steps that you can take to 'make it happen' here: https://growthpitstop.com/2025/01/22/c-y-a-the-latest-addition-to-your-work-responsibilities/

62 *Financial Conduct Authority Final Note to TSB Bank PLC*, Dec 22. See: https://www.fca.org.uk/publication/final-notices/tsb-bank-plc-2022.pdf

63 The cost of the TSB debacle is estimated at over GBP400 million (including fines, customer compensation, and so on). The bank lost an estimated 80,000 customers. Source: 'TSB Migration Crisis – Lessons Learned,' review by Beyond Blue – https://www.beyondblue.tech/wp-content/uploads/2024/02/TSB-Lessons-Learned-.pdf

64 In addition to the sectors already covered by NIS 1 (from 2016), such as energy, transport, healthcare, finance, water management and digital infrastructure, these rules apply to providers of public electronic communications services,

more digital services such as social platforms, waste water and waste management, manufacturing of critical products, postal and courier services, public administration, both at central and regional level or space. See: https://digital-strategy.ec.europa.eu/en/policies/nis2-directive.

65 Projects can easily lose sight of the business need they were meant to address. This 'project myopia' is increasingly prevalent in a time of fast-changing business needs and priorities. See: https://shorturl.at/RHPnt.

66 'How Citibank's Culture Allowed Corruption to Thrive,' Insights from Adam Waytz, *Kellogg Insight*, Jan. 2015.

67 This is seen in frameworks like the Senior Managers and Certification Regime (SMCR) in the UK and the Enhanced Prudential Standards in the US, the Capital Requirements Directive V (CRD V) and the European Central Bank's (ECB) Supervisory Expectations, which stress that senior leaders must ensure comprehensive risk oversight and operational resilience.

68 Risk management and operational resilience, in the context of DORA (the EU's Digital Operational Resilience Act) and similar regulations in other territories.

69 The requirement for those in senior management functions to 'act to deliver good outcomes for retail customers' came into effect in the UK in July 2023. See: https://www.bankofengland.co.uk/prudential-regulation/publication/2023/march/review-of-the-senior-managers-and-certification-regime.

70 According to Gartner: 'CIOs who successfully communicate the business value of information technology will maintain 60% higher funding levels than their peers who don't.' Source: https://www.gartner.com/en/information-technology/topics/business-value-of-it.

71 As leaders, how we talk about our organization's big projects is important. So, isn't it time to stop 'trash talking' our biggest projects and initiatives? Explore this issue here: https://growthpitstop.com/2024/12/16/isnt-it-time-to-stop-trash-talking-its-biggest-projects/.

72 The #1 reason for project failure – guess what it is? Well, it is changing business needs or, to be more precise, changing organizational priorities. It tops the list of factors identified by leaders as the primary cause of project failure – accounting for a whopping 41% of all failed projects in 2021. That is according to data from PMI's *Global Pulse Survey* of that year. Read the detail here: https://shorturl.at/NH96E.

73 'I am not paranoid, but my boss may be' – that is the message that we heard from leaders in our research. This puts an interesting twist on the long-running productivity and engagement debate. But, what if it is OK to be paranoid? Maybe, it is even necessary! More here: https://shorturl.at/mr0X7.

74 Is everybody on the same page regarding your initiative, especially the business fundamentals that underpin it? Find out more about the one-page business fundamentals tool here: https://shorturl.at/eJfRt.

75 Complexity is a byword for the modern age. Yet, the full extent of complexity can be difficult to grasp. While leaders are typically well-attuned to external

complexity, many are blind to high levels of internal complexity and its implications. Explore the research: https://shorturl.at/Mq2D6.

76   Too many organizations only do good news when it comes to projects and initiatives. This is a form of 'Project Pollyanna' where people have learned to silence their doubts and concerns. Find out more: https://shorturl.at/Ytkuz.

77   The #1 reason for project failure – guess what it is? Well, it is changing business needs or, to be more precise, changing organizational priorities. It tops the list of factors identified by leaders as the primary cause of project failure – accounting for a whopping 41% of all failed projects in 2021. That is according to data from PMI's *Global Pulse Survey* of that year. Read the detail here: https://shorturl.at/NH96E.

78   Which comes first, the project plan or the business strategy? With few exceptions, most leaders say that the business strategy comes first. After all, the project or initiative is derived from the strategy and aims to bring some aspect of that strategy to life. However, the link between any project and strategy cannot be taken for granted. Find out why here: https://shorturl.at/ZTEvN.

79   The business fundamentals of an initiative are explored in **Chapter 3: Super Alignment**. They are the fundamental business rationale or 'why' behind the big project, including business needs, market reality, business impact and investment. Their importance is in connecting to strategy, aligning cross-functional stakeholders, accessing power and justifying resources.

80   This data was provided by Pitstop Analytics – a solution that provides big project leaders with F1-style performance data.

81   Scott D. Anthony talks of 'the first mile of innovation, where you take those precious early steps to translate an idea on paper into an honest-to-goodness business.' See his book: *The First Mile: A Launch Manual for Getting Great Ideas into the Market*, Harvard Business Review Press, 2014.

82   'Don't fall in love with your plan...' warns Jeff Sutherland, the grandfather of Agile. We say: 'Sure, fall in love with your plan, just don't get married to it!' Find out more: https://shorturl.at/phsDh.

83   When it comes to the successful execution of key strategic initiatives, the first mile matters. Indeed, a more cautious approach in the initial stages is one of the most effective ways of engaging with big project complexity. Find out more: https://shorturl.at/hkNRn.

84   When senior stakeholders are on the sidelines, project success is at risk. Moreover, the people running projects are denied one of the most valuable organizational resources – the experience and foresight of its senior leaders. Find out more: https://shorturl.at/i7C9l.

85   'We are like a deli counter.' That is how one busy leadership team described the challenge of aligning internal stakeholders. Find out more: https://shorturl.at/eFUZP.

86   We describe 'Project Pollyanna' as a culture where only positive outcomes are discussed, often silencing doubts or concerns. Find out more: https://shorturl.at/0Iasg.

[87] It is a serious problem that could affect as many as two out of three strategic initiatives and project team meetings. It is called 'nodding dog syndrome,' although it has nothing to do with dogs and everything to do with project success! Read the research here: https://shorturl.at/3uPWj.

[88] Nodding dog syndrome describes the all-too-common scenario where people attend a meeting, nod in agreement with what is being discussed or decided, but then go away and either do nothing or the opposite to what was agreed. See: https://shorturl.at/i0qyj.

[89] *Financial Conduct Authority Final Note to TSB Bank PLC*, Dec 22. See: https://www.fca.org.uk/publication/final-notices/tsb-bank-plc-2022.pdf.

[90] 'TSB Migration – Lessons Learned' by Beyond Blue. See: https://www.beyondblue.tech/wp-content/uploads/2024/02/TSB-Lessons-Learned.pdf.

[91] The Federal Reserve defines operational resilience as 'the ability to deliver operations, including critical operations and core business lines, through a disruption from any hazard. It is the outcome of effective operational risk management combined with sufficient financial and operational resources to prepare, adapt, withstand, and recover from disruptions.' See: *Sound Practices to Strengthen Operational Resilience*: https://www.federalreserve.gov/newsevents/pressreleases/files/bcreg20201030a1.pdf.

[92] In a complex and fast changing environment, perfect and perpetual alignment, even if it were possible, is probably not desirable. It is an illusion. Find out more: https://shorturl.at/RJ9mx.

[93] Two-thirds of leaders (66%) say they have had projects or initiatives scrapped or stalled, with the average number of projects affected being 3.71. However, most leaders (84%) still believe there are too many projects and initiatives competing for time, attention and resources. Find out more: https://shorturl.at/wCJJr.

[94] If you want to go from thinking like a director to thinking like a VP, President, or CEO, think 'strategic portfolio.' A portfolio mindset is very different from a project mindset. It is as diverse as strategy and project management or as different as being a project manager and a business leader. Find out more: https://shorturl.at/kv436.

[95] This insight emerged from strategic conversations with business leaders on the requirements of delivering today's performance and tomorrow's transformation. Find out more here: https://shorturl.at/h8deu.

[96] Many organizations are playing 'whack-a-mole' with priorities, projects and initiatives. No sooner do they scrap one project, but another appears. Thus, while consolidation has been widespread, its impact has been limited. Find out more: https://shorturl.at/MBSTI.

[97] Our research suggests that 'Disciplined Prioritization' requires adopting different hats – 7 hats in total. For example, one leader will take the principle of 'trade-offs' and 'wearing that hat' will bring up the issue of trade-offs throughout the dialog, making sure that any trade-offs required are made. Another will push for

'simplicity' and another for 'intensity' and so on. Find out more: https://shorturl.at/MFQ2X.

98   In these times of economic uncertainty, the strategic portfolio is a dangerous blind spot that could cost organizations dearly. We argue that a portfolio of strategic projects and initiatives deserves the same level of care and attention that would be given to any million-dollar investment portfolio. In short, it needs to be managed the 'Wall Street way.' Find out more here: https://shorturl.at/aOk8k.

99   'Visibly frustrated, Mark Zuckerberg responds to staff questions about extra vacation days,' by Johanna Chisholm of the UK *Independent* newspaper, July 28, 2022. See: https://www.independent.co.uk/tech/mark-zuckerberg-meeting-vacation-annoyed-b2133661.html.

100   As John Kotter and Holger Rathgeber put it: '...mature organizations have a built-in tendency to kill off or marginalize anything that looks like a more egalitarian, fluid, innovative, and fast entrepreneurial structure.' John Kotter &Holger Rathgeber, *That's Not How We Do It Here! A Story about How Organizations Rise and Fall – and Can Rise Again*, Portfolio 2016.

101   Strategic initiatives have both an accelerator and a brake. The brake is bureaucracy, and the acceleration is innovation. You must take your foot off one in order to press the other. More on this here: https://shorturl.at/ieyHf.

102   Typically, it is seen as the opposite of business as usual – as something exotic and rare. However, that marginalizes strategy and innovation, whereas it should be a part of everyday business. Isn't it time that business unusual became more usual? More here: https://shorturl.at/n5lod.

103   The challenges of competing in an increasingly complex and fast changing world are nicely summed up in one phrase: 'seeing around corners.' That is the title of a best-selling strategy book by Rita Gunther McGrath. The challenge is that our traditional mode of thinking (i.e., business as usual) is based on straight-line acceleration. More here: https://shorturl.at/B5Hgb.

104   'CIOs take note: Platform engineering teams are the future core of IT orgs' by Robert Mitchell in *CIO Magazine* online, June 19, 2024. See: https://shorturl.at/2Z2YI.

105   Read the story of one leadership team for whom 'work about the work' accounted for more than 50% of its working week: https://shorturl.at/5IQzz.

106   What is really draining executive productivity? Leaders point to the challenges of dealing with bureaucracy, juggling multiple priorities and internal meetings. Find out more: https://shorturl.at/IftJW.

107   This is a theme expanded upon by Cal Newport in *Slow Productivity: The Lost Art of Accomplishment without Burnout*, Penguin Business (1st edition, 7 March 2024).

108   Project Management 3.0: Are You Ready to Upgrade? Find out here: https://shorturl.at/B1kkE.

109   Hot or Not? Unfortunately, it is not. Increasingly, people are 'swiping left' on project management. Meanwhile, many are falling in love with Agile. But what

do these fads and trends reveal about the challenges of executing on ambitious strategies in a time of accelerating change and complexity? More on this here: https://shorturl.at/yGarD.

110 A detailed Gantt Chart with grids, lines and colors can be a thing of beauty. But, when it comes to delivering on your strategic priorities it could hinder as much as help. More on this here: https://shorturl.at/5oF6s.

111 In times of market uncertainty and slowing growth, the focus turns to cost-cutting, consolidation and efficiency. But has value creation gone out the window? That is a question being asked by a growing number of leaders. Find out more: https://shorturl.at/Go0t4.

112 'Performance is potential minus interference' according to the famous business coach Timothy Gallwey. See: *The Inner Game of Work*, Random House, 2001.

113 This is a quote from Gary Klein in 'Performing a Project Pre-mortem,' HBR Sept. 2007.

114 Here are some examples of the interdependent nature of the various big project vulnerabilities (*aka* kryptonite) For example: Project Myopia (losing sight of business needs) can be a symptom of functional silos and poor cross-functional collaboration; Project Pollyanna (good news only) can be a symptom of poor psychological safety or a culture of low trust; Project Whack-a-Mole (proliferation) can be the result of functional solos and a lack of focus and alignment on strategy.

115 'Complexity conscious' leaders is a phrase used by Aaron Dignan in *Brave New Work: Are You Ready to Reinvent Your Organization?*, Portfolio, 2019.

116 Explore the rise in the 'messiness' of big projects and transformation initiatives here: https://growthpitstop.com/2025/04/02/surprise-finding-big-project-transformation-messiness-up-11/.

117 Threat rigidity is defined as 'the contraction of authority, reduced experimentation, and focus on existing resources' by Donald Sull in *Upside of Turbulence*, HarperBusiness, 2009.

118 At a time of global market uncertainty, many leaders feel less in control. For some, it is even starting to feel chaotic. But should leaders try to take back control, or embrace complexity and change in a new way? Explore this issue here: https://shorturl.at/BXptX.

119 Ensuring alignment despite changing business needs and priorities requires being able to fluidly move resources (assets, people, etc.) to where they are needed. These 'resource fluid' organizations are primed to profit from change. More on this here: https://shorturl.at/MD1mg.

120 'Individual work' now accounts for just 30% of the working week! The rest is spent on internal meetings and other forms of internal collaboration! See: 'Performance is a Team Sport, So Why Aren't We Managing it that Way?' Link: https://growthpitstop.com/2022/10/01/performance-is-a-team-sport-wouldnt-you-agree/.

121 Data gathered *via* our analytics platform Pitstop Analytics, encompassing a sample of 1,000 executives.

122 Performance Interrupted: The surprising impact of unmanaged interactions is explored here: https://shorturl.at/bEK9c.

123 Are you a super-juggler – effortlessly juggling tasks, emails, meetings and projects? Or are you a victim of run-away multi-tasking? The answer and its implications will surprise you! Find out more: https://shorturl.at/9ICj6.

124 'What gets measured gets managed' is a saying often attributed to Edward Deming. More controversially, Deming also said that '97% of what matters in an organization can't be measured.' Reconcile these two viewpoints here: https://shorturl.at/DPHAk.

125 KPIs – everybody has them, but in an increasingly fast-changing world, indicators of today's (or yesterday's) performance are not enough. The sustainability of performance in a VUCA world requires more future-focused KPIs – indicators that don't just measure 'what is' but also 'what could be.' The next generation of KPIs measure performance and potential or performance potential. That is why we call them KPPIs – Key Performance Potential Indicators. Find out more: https://shorturl.at/RMKFI.

126 Many leaders have a peculiarly hands-off or 'laissez-faire' approach to teams. They assume that their teams will rise to the level of their ability, achieve a high level of productivity and efficiency, and also bring out the best in each other. It is as if bringing talented people together is enough to create a high-performing team. Find out more: https://shorturl.at/Q6am0.

127 When it comes to teams, form matters every bit as much as function. Yet, it is a factor that is all too often overlooked. For example, most people fail to distinguish between 'groups' and 'teams,' expecting both to deliver high levels of performance. The result is frustration and disappointment. See *Teams Don't Work (Unless You Do)*, Ray Collis & John O'Gorman, ASG Press, 2018.

128 It is a powerful realization for any team that its ways of working are largely within its control. It affords executives a level of power greater than they might imagine. Find out more here: https://shorturl.at/aV6IK.

129 Ways of Working can mean different things to different people. Sometimes it can be a little abstract or vague. When this happens, it can lose its power and relevance. To avoid this, we distinguish between the general and the specific – between 'Ways of Working' and the 'Way We Work.' Find out more here: https://shorturl.at/xqiMM.

130 The 9 Rights – also called 'ways of working' or 'performance design' – were first outlined in the book *Pitstop to Perform*, by Ray Collis & John O'Gorman, ASG Press, 2018.

131 The term 'performance paranoia' appears in the countless articles and papers written on the subject. The advice offered includes: 'Get over it – stop being paranoid!' But what if that's wrong? What if the concerns about the way we work post-pandemic are valid and real? Find out more: https://shorturl.at/4ytc9.

132 This is the year of Productivity & Efficiency, or to be more precise of productivity drives! Yet, in spite of it all, levels of productivity and efficiency stand at just 67%. Thus, the cynical would say that productivity drives have not been very

productive. As one of our straight-shooting colleagues puts it: 'While the talk has been plenty, the actual progress made has been scarce'. Find out more: https://shorturl.at/3daoH

133　Report after report is calling for a new model of (a) work (b) the workforce (c) the workplace and (d) ways of working. That sounds scary, but don't worry: the solution may be closer to hand than you think, with the 9 Rights as a model of performance and productivity for the knowledge worker. Find out more: https://shorturl.at/1841c.

134　We talk of the 7 Rs as being the equivalent of a 'Swiss Army knife' – a versatile and easy-to-use tool that can be applied in any work situation. Find out more here: https://shorturl.at/j1xK0.

135　The Zone of Peak Performance is where a team is realizing 75% or more of its potential. See *Pitstop to Perform*, Ray Collis & John O'Gorman, ASG Press, 2018.

136　See: Mihaly Csikszentmihalyi (1990) – *Flow: The Psychology of Optimal Experience*, New York: Harper & Row.

137　Based on detailed research conducted with 10 pharma product development and commercialization teams over 5 years. Full details can be found in the Pharma Industry edition of *Super Projects*.

138　What happens within our teams is more important than what happens in the boardroom with the corporate strategy or the corporate culture. Put another way: 'The team is the sun, the moon, and the stars of your experience at work' say Marcus Buckingham & Ashley Goodall in *Nine Lies About Work: A Freethinking Leader's Guide to the Real World*, Harvard Business Review Press, 2019.

139　We define peak performance as the realization of 75% of an individual or team's full potential. This is a radical definition for a new age, as explored in *Pitstop to Perform*, by Ray Collis & John O'Gorman, ASG Press, 2018.

140　Imagine a project team had 12 members and 20 stakeholders – if all of these were to interact with each other just once a month then that would amount to almost 500 interactions (i.e. emails, calls, IMs and so on). Each interaction is two or more people, so the number here needs to be multiplied by 2 or 3 to get a picture of the busyness of a team and thus our figure of approx. 1,000 interactions. See: https://shorturl.at/N8TtO.

141　The ratio of interactions to interruptions is a key measure of efficiency, as well as collaboration. But, given the number of team members as well as stakeholders we deal with, the possibility for ongoing interruptions is enormous. Find out more: https://shorturl.at/ewKl0.

142　The 8 Dynamics – also called 'the way we interact' or 'performance dynamics' – was first outlined in the book *Pitstop to Perform*, by Ray Collis & John O'Gorman, ASG Press, 2018.

143　'Projects are the new way of working... you must organize around projects not jobs' according to Roger L. Martin, *A New Way to Think: Your Guide to Superior Management Effectiveness*, Harvard Business Review Press (May 3, 2022).

144 Our research suggests that 'Disciplined Prioritization' requires adopting different hats – 7 hats in total. For example, one leader will take the principle of 'trade-offs' and 'wearing that hat' will bring up the issue of trade-offs throughout the dialog, making sure that any trade-offs required are made. Another will push for 'simplicity' and another for 'intensity' and so on. Find out more: https://shorturl.at/MFQ2X.

145 'Culture – you can only change it by alternating how individuals work with one another' according to Roger L. Martin, *A New Way to Think: Your Guide to Superior Management Effectiveness*, Harvard Business Review Press (May 3, 2022).

146 Vision and mission may have gone out of fashion, but purpose is more important than ever. The questions are: How can leaders make purpose meaningful enough to rally teams around key projects and priorities? How do you know if you have a purpose that works – one that motivates? Well, the test is: Will it rally your team for the next few laps? That is for the next 3, 6 or 9 months. If it does, then it is what we call 'FIT for PURPOSE.' Find out more here: https://shorturl.at/GZqLC.

147 Read the full story of how one leadership team tackled the issue of focus and alignment here: https://shorturl.at/Ab2Qc.

148 What is required is a very modern type of alignment – a fluid alignment where people and resources can flow to where they are needed most. That is something that the annual budgeting and multi-year strategy cycle often struggle with. Find out more: https://shorturl.at/klF90.

149 Bottom-up, agile, innovative, iterative and team-centric. This is what we call Project Management V3.0. Contrast this to the traditional linear and more rigid approaches to project management (V1.0) here: https://shorturl.at/LrzUx.

150 Increasingly reports are calling for a new model of (a) work (b) the workforce (c) the workplace and (d) ways of working. The argument is that much of our thinking about work is steeped in the last century. That makes it ill-suited to the knowledge worker, the digital economy and the reality of working in a large organization. Read more: https://shorturl.at/qxawl.

151 If you analyze the annual reports of Big Pharma you will find that talent is a key strategic pillar. Not all use the word 'talent;' some use related concepts like 'people,' 'workforce,' and 'human capital.' Companies like Pfizer and GSK directly link talent to their strategic goals and competitive advantage. Others, like AstraZeneca, Eli Lilly, and Novartis, dedicate substantial sections to human capital management strategies that emphasize attracting, retaining, and developing a skilled and diverse workforce.

152 Find out what can be achieved when a team takes ownership of its big numbers and ways of working: https://shorturl.at/w6C98.

153 Explore the gap in perceptions of complexity between leaders and their teams here: https://shorturl.at/wC3jl.

154 Jeroen De Flander, *Business Strategy Heroes*, Performance Factory (April 2, 2012).

[155] 'The economic potential of generative AI: The next productivity frontier,' McKinsey, June 14, 2023.

[156] 'I've always thought of AI as the most profound technology humanity is working on... more profound than fire or electricity or anything that we've done in the past' – Sundar Pichai, CEO, Alphabet, as quoted in 'AI in the workplace: A report for 2025,' McKinsey, Jan 2025.

[157] 91% of leaders highlight productivity / efficiency and cutting costs as the key benefits of Gen AI, compared to 29% for improving existing products / services and 23% for enhancing customer relationships. Source: Deloitte State of Gen Ai report, 2024

[158] Leaders and sponsors tend to be well versed in the business benefits of their strategies and initiatives. That is 'music to the ears' of senior management and shareholders, but how much does it really mean to most of the people involved in or affected by a project or strategy? Link: https://growthpitstop.com/2022/08/22/what-is-the-people-impact-of-your-strategy-or-initiative/.

[159] 'Generative AI adoption in the enterprise,' *Writer Survey*, 2025.

[160] The stock market values Ai dreams above scientific-medical breakthroughs, with Ai giant NVIDIA's valuation being the equivalent of the Top 6 players in pharma. It takes the top 6 pharmaceutical companies to reach a total valuation of approximately $2.36 trillion (just above NVIDIA's April 2024 valuation).

[161] CoreWeave, an AI-focused cloud infrastructure company backed by Nvidia, completed its IPO in March 2025. See: https://www.investors.com/news/technology/coreweave-stock-ai-stock-crwv-news-ipo-nvidia-openai/.

[162] F. Scott Fitzgerald is quoted as saying: 'The test of a first-rate intelligence is the ability to hold two opposed ideas in mind at the same time...'

[163] *The B2B Revolution*, published by ASG Press, ISBN 9781907725005, 2010.

www.ingramcontent.com/pod-product-compliance
Lightning Source LLC
Chambersburg PA
CBHW061136220326
41599CB00025B/4248